adoption not an option

adoption not an option

a métis woman torn from her family
and her 40 year battle to find them again

Eugenea Couture

Eugenea Couture
Kendall
May 14/2017

Book Cover Design: Marla Thompson
Typeset: Greg Salisbury
Author Photographer: Neil Edwardson

DISCLAIMER: This book is a work of non-fiction. Readers of this publication agree that neither Eugenea Couture, nor her publisher, will be held responsible or liable for damages that may be alleged as resulting directly or indirectly from the use of this publication. Neither the publisher nor the author can be held accountable for the information provided by, or actions resulting from, this book. This is a work of non-fiction and real people inspired all the cases reported in this book, but most names have been changed to protect their identity. Any stories shared are recounted from the best recollection possible.

To my generous husband and family for supporting my search
and for helping me identify and find my inner self.

Testimonials

"Eugenea reveals her childhood journey in foster care. During her crusade, she moves from home to home but is determined to find her long-lost family members. As a mother of four, Eugenea has an enormous will to safeguard her children and find her roots. Her story provides a window into the emotional odyssey to reunite with the family that she loved so long ago. She looks back at her family's tumultuous path through the generations, and shows how to move through the mistakes of the past towards a positive future."
Don Kendall, Group Publisher, Black Press

"The longing to belong and find a sense of family, is touchingly and powerfully articulated in this book. Eugenea shines a light on the challenges faced by children in the foster care system through her own experiences."
Rob and Tammy McCormick, Supporters of AFA

Acknowledgements

There are many people I wish to thank for the help they have given me during the writing of this memoir.

I want to thank Mark Handley and Liz Hall from the United Native Nations for their devotion, counsel, and encouragement to me, and for all the compassionate work they do to support foster care and adoption reunification. Many, many thanks to Alice from Canadian Adoptees for all her timeless work reconnecting families.

I am sincerely grateful for the wonderful support from Sue Olsen and Linda Sloan, MLAs for the Legislative Assembly of Alberta. For sharing my story, I thank Suzanne Fournier of the Vancouver Province and Tom Barrett of the Edmonton Journal. I would like to acknowledge Sorcha McGinnis, a reporter from the Calgary Herald; and CTV News - Calgary for their coverage.

Special thanks to Sally Tisiga for being a part of my journey and inviting me to be a part of hers in the documentary, *One Of Many*. I would also like to thank Jo Béranger and Doris Buttignol from Lardux Films: Doriane Films, for their voices of encouragement to begin my memoirs.

It has been most rewarding to work with the publisher, editors, and staff of Influence Publishing: Julie Salisbury, Nina Shoroplova, Alina Wilson, Gulnar Patel, Amy O'Hara and Lyda McLallen.

I am forever indebted to Ella Louise Zobell Garbraith, and Hugh and Geraldine Court for your timeless and unconditional love.

I am truly grateful for my husband's selfless devotion and my family's loving support, including Nadine Gott, April Wallach, and Christy Dunsmore.
I want to thank all those who have shared similar journeys: you are an inspiration for our future generations.

"In the midst of a land without silence, you have to make a place for yourself. Those who have worn out their shoes many times know where to step. It is not their shoes you can wear; only their footsteps you may follow– if you let it happen." Kwanlin Dän Ch'a (Chief Dan George), July 2007

Contents

Foreword

Eugenea and I met back in 1981. As we learnt more about each other through the years it became clear that our friendship would last a lifetime. Unlike Eugenea, I never grew up in foster care, never suffered through sexual abuse or a loss of identity, yet I was able to relate to her story in a powerful way and have always felt connected to her. Today, we still call each other "twins"—souls united by a special bond.

After thirty-three years of friendship, what I know about Eugenea is that the driving force in her life has always been a desire to help others. This is what has fueled her to break her silence and share her experiences. This is what has motivated her to write this book. There are thousands of books about adoption and the foster care system, but Eugenea's is a very unique story narrated through the lens of her deeply personal experiences and inspired by three generations of women in her family.

As a writer, mother, and advocate, Eugenea has always been passionate about sharing her life story. Having experienced what it feels like to be a child lost in the world, to be without a family, to feel uprooted and unwanted, she is now a strong advocate for the empowerment of youth in the foster care system and encourages young people to stand up for their rights, especially when they are at the mercy of strangers. This book is meant to provide hope and help to children, teens and young moms searching for direction in their lives. It is meant to show all readers that in facing the challenges of their lives they are not alone.

Eugenea's road towards healing and reuniting her family has been a long one and traveling it has not always been easy. Along her path to self-discovery I have often been at her side. Together we have shared many moments of happiness, pain and love. It has been incredible to be connected to her, both physically and emotionally, as the scenes of her life have unfolded, as she journeyed to find her family and in doing so also found herself.

Nadine Gott
(Special Support Assistant in Education)

Part One: Elaine

1: Elaine and Lloyd

Elaine was already dead to her husband. It would take a lot of guts, but she was willing to take the consequences and put up with her husband's brutality, just as she had done in the past. In those days, there was no calling the police for domestic violence. Right after Lloyd's early dismissal and homecoming from World War I, he learned about his wife's betrayal. Elaine's steamy affair was public knowledge and Lloyd could not look at her face anymore.

Lloyd planned his departure to begin a new life, but first he had to square things up with his wife. The impact of his vendetta against Elaine would torture her emotionally for years to come.

He called two men from his church and asked for their help. They would be his co-conspirators to make Elaine pay for her adultery. The men came immediately and found Lloyd outside the house screaming at his wife; they waited in the car.

"You filthy woman," he shouted for everyone to hear. His eyes were chilling as ice. He looked more like a stranger than a husband.

"You couldn't wait for me to return, could you? I go to war and you find a lover and become his whore," Lloyd persecuted. The words from his mouth pierced Elaine's soul as though she were naked to the world. When Lloyd saw his supporters had arrived, he reeled away from his wife and stormed into the house, kicking the door in his path. He yelled in search of his five kids and demanded that they come at once.

The children huddled in fear, but they didn't dare disobey. Their father told the oldest ones to get in the back of the truck. His impatience moved his rough hands swiftly as he pulled them together and made them sit in the box.

"No, Daddy. Please don't make us go!" They screamed for Lloyd to stop, but that only aggravated him. The two men from his church got out of the car and rushed to help Lloyd get the kids. Geo—the toddler—was wailing as the men interjected and put him in the pick-up. Elaine was flabbergasted as Lloyd went for Eddie, the baby.

"What are you doing?" Elaine shrieked in hysteria. Her eyes had suddenly grown larger than a quarter. Lloyd's intentions had become clear as glass, so

Elaine quickly reached down and snatched her baby. Lloyd cut in front of her.

"Let go of me. You can't take my children away." Elaine clutched Eddie so tight that he was crying too.

"Please, I'll do anything you…" Elaine's eyes turned into a watery well.

"They are not your babies anymore," Lloyd shouted, and tore the baby from her arms.

"Give me back my babies." Elaine clawed at his sleeve. The rough denim of his shirt chafed her fingers as he yanked his arm away. The two men cut in and grabbed the baby as if they were playing a game of keep-away. Elaine pounded her flailing fists against Lloyd, but she was no match for her husband's strength. Lloyd pushed Elaine and she tumbled to the ground.

"Please! I'm sorry…" Her voice was squeaky as she pleaded with Lloyd and scurried onto her feet. "I gave birth to these babies; they're mine."

"You are never going to see them again," he said, tight-lipped. He made no time for her apologies and empty promises. By then, all the children were bawling and reaching out for their mother.

"Get out of the way, Elaine! The kids don't need a whore for a mother."

"You can't do this to our children."

"You did this. Not me! I don't want to see your face again and I don't want you near my kids. If you try to contact or see them, I'll beat you so hard you'll wish you were dead… and then I'll have you arrested and thrown in jail as an unfit parent," he roared. With that, he shoved Elaine again and walked briskly to the truck.

"Sit down now!" Lloyd ordered his five children. Then he swung the door wide and hopped in. Elaine got up and ran to the truck. The kids cried louder as the wheels began to roll.

"Take my hand." Elaine shouted to them as tears poured from her eyes. Lloyd practically shoved his foot through the floorboards. In the rearview mirror, he could see his wife running like a dog with a broken heart.

Within seconds, the only thing left was a choking cloud of dust. Empty-handed and rocking on her knees, Elaine mourned as though her children had died beneath her feet. The two men followed the truck in their car, driving right past Elaine without looking.

Elaine's mother Opal was collecting the eggs from the chicken coop when she heard strange sounds. Apart from the usual noise of clucking hens, she knew something was wrong. She gathered up her skirt, grabbed the basket of eggs, and quickened her pace to the door of the hen house. She saw and heard the last of her grandchildren as the truck sped over the horizon. She was old and heavyset, but she could move fast if there was trouble. She dropped the eggs and ran toward the gate.

"He took my babies. My babies are gone." Elaine shook her head as she rocked back and forth like a crazy woman. Opal pulled her daughter up and took her into the house. There was nothing they could do. The world was a big place and Lloyd could hide them anywhere.

Lloyd held the steering wheel so tightly that his knuckles went white. Maybe he would hate himself tomorrow, but for now he had enforced his rights and he didn't have to vindicate his actions. Elaine deserved what she got. Her affair would be a personal memory that Lloyd would use to portray the kind of mother she was. The children would know their mother as a whore and Elaine would carry the title to her grave.

He couldn't care for his children alone, but there was no way on earth that he would allow their mother Elaine to see them again.

2: Elaine and Gordon

Back home, reality set in for Elaine. She got through the first night and then the second, but it was the most insufferable year of her life. She had made zero progress in knowing her children's whereabouts. Day and night, she reminisced about her babies and wondered what was happening to them.

Neighbours sneered and called her a squaw, but she held her head high. Inside, she was heartbroken, but she refused to wallow in self-pity. She had the constant reminders of her children's belongings to give her hope.

It helped that her lover Gordon was good to her. But after a while, she just hurt too much. The pain made her feel like she was swimming around in a fishbowl and going nowhere. Birthdays passed and Christmas became a blur of self-medicating cocktails. But the facts don't lie! Elaine would never find her kids.

On the weekends, she would hit the bars and drink until she had the courage to ask strangers if they had seen her kids. She opened her purse and displayed a wrinkled and frayed picture of five cute little children.

"These are my kids. Aren't they beautiful? Do you know where they are?" She hoped someone would recognize a toothless grin or a head full of curls. Either they didn't know or didn't care, but it was always the same answer. Gordon drank right along with her and didn't care if she could out-swig him. He didn't make it his job to keep her in line.

Every Christmas was darker and gloomier than the last. She had racked her brains trying to get the kids back. It hurt to think that her two smallest babies would have no memory of her. In the past, she had bought gifts that were never opened, so it was pointless to put up a tree.

Gordon came home on the eve and set up a wiry little pine. The skeletal tree drooped with the weight of each ornament. But it didn't matter; no one came to see it anyway.

Grandma Opal had died early that year from cancer. To make matters worse, Elaine's father was stricken with cancer too and it was only a matter of time before he would join his wife in paradise.

Part Two: Karina

3: Don and Karina, Uncle Rollin and Aunt Beth

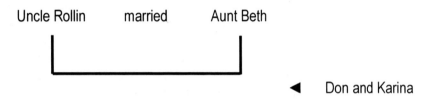

Uncle Rollin   married   Aunt Beth

◄   Don and Karina

In one day, Karina—Lloyd and Elaine's middle child—lost both her parents.

Her father, Lloyd, split the children into different homes. Karina and her brother Don would live with their Uncle Rollin and Aunt Beth. As a little four-year-old, Karina was very sad. She had no idea where her father was going or if he would return. There was no contact with her big sister Latisha or with Geo and Eddie, so she had no clue if she would ever see her siblings again.

Karina and Don shared a big bed in the attic with their cousins. At night, the children snuggled under a colourful patchwork quilt and picked the sticky pitch off the ceiling rafters and chewed it like gum. Karina was happy to be with her cousins until one of the kids stole matches and lit them in the outhouse. Uncle Rollin found out and tried to force the kids to confess. Since no one knew who was at fault or would own up to it, Rollin gave every child a whipping.

At the back of Rollin's property was an abandoned shed that stood on a hill not far from the river. The kids wanted to use it for a playhouse, but their Uncle Rollin gave strict rules that they were not allowed in there.

When the kids finished playing and went into the house, Uncle Rollin was on the prowl. He took Karina to the shed. He locked her inside and put his nasty hands on her tiny body as he had done since the first week she had arrived. Karina pulled away so he pinned her down to the floor and pushed himself on top of her. Rollin was moaning in her ear as she was screaming. The smell of his sweat and the dust from the floor was suffocating. Then she felt a searing pain and the tears were unstoppable.

Her Uncle Rollin told her to shut up, but she was hysterical. That caused him to roll away and Karina flipped on all fours and went on a wild goose chase for the door. As Karina scurried along the floorboards, her uncle caught her around the waist. He swung her tiny legs in the air as he covered her mouth.

He unlatched the door and opened it just enough to see out. Daylight flooded Karina's eyes as Uncle Rollin stole away with her. He crept through the bushes and headed down to the side of the river. After what seemed a long distance to a child, he dropped her to the ground. He found a place where no one would see or hear them.

A breeze lifted off the water as Karina screamed unceasingly. It pierced Rollin's ears and in that moment, Karina had crossed the line. He slammed Karina's head against the rocky ground. The base of her skull split open. She was staring at him as he pulled a stone out of the earth, raised it in the air, and smashed her head.

Red fluid spewed like a fountain, spattering Rollin's face and smudging his disarrayed shirt. He dropped the rock and finished what he had started. He wanted her to be quiet, but when he realized that she hadn't stirred against him, he stopped. He froze for a moment.

Panic lurched inside his gut. He fumbled with the zipper of his grimy pants as he scrambled to his feet and climbed the embankment. He hid in the underbrush of thorny weeds until he could escape unseen. The heat of the sun scorched Karina's cheeks as the trees swirled and danced above her head.

Karina had passed out. When she woke up, she could feel the soft blouse of the woman who was carrying her back to the house. The woman was calling for help, as Karina tried to focus on who had come for her, but she couldn't keep her big brown eyes from rolling back.

She awakened to find herself in bed. A cool damp cloth washed over her and chilled her burning flesh. In those days, doctors made house calls and it was not out of the ordinary to have regular visits at home. The family doctor stood beside the bed and carefully examined Karina. He stitched up her head. He confirmed that Karina had suffered a concussion and she would need to stay in bed for several days.

Much later, when the doctor had gone, she was startled awake by an awful noise. Still groggy, she heard voices exploding in the house. Outside the room, her father boomed with anger. He was hollering all kinds of allegations about rape and Rollin was denying it. Karina wanted to stay in the warm bed where it felt safe. Maybe Lloyd was coming to take her home. Oh, how she wanted to go home. She had suffered too long. All she ever wanted was her family.

She closed her eyelids again. Her daddy was back with the promise that he would take her, but she had to get better first. No more tears! He told her that big girls don't cry.

For the sake of the family's name, the matter was closed and Karina was sworn to secrecy. Lloyd saw it as a personal travesty and all he wanted was to put that miserable business behind him. After all, he was the crown head and disciplinarian, and he didn't want people talking. If he could carry on as though nothing had happened, it could be covered up and he hoped Karina would have no memory of it.

Besides Rollin, Lloyd had a lot of things on his mind. Five to be exact: he needed to shuffle his children around until he was able to handle them himself. He made plans for Karina and Don to stay with Uncle Tom and Aunt Jessie. They would take the two kids until Lloyd was able to come for them.

4: Don and Karina, Aunt Jessie and Uncle Tom

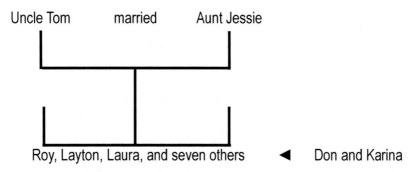

A very disgruntled Aunt Jessie with ten kids of her own was already overloaded with work and resented the extra responsibility. She was disgusted that Lloyd burdened her with two more mouths to feed. But they were family, so she didn't turn the children away.

Once Lloyd was gone, Aunt Jessie spared no time for any heartfelt charity, as she slapped them around and ordered extra chores for their keep. She openly showed her outrage with her abusive display. Don was spared from Aunt Jessie's wrath, because he stayed outside and worked the farm before and after school.

As the weeks passed, it got much worse: Jessie's two oldest boys had a temporary stopover from the army. She hadn't seen her sons Roy and Layton for many months. The homecoming was a great celebration and there were a lot of fancy side dishes to go with the roast dinner.

Everyone gathered around the table and it was a wonderful night until Karina asked her cousin, Laura, to pass the potatoes. Laura scooped a big spoonful and slung it at Karina's plate, causing the mash to hit the edge and splotch on her brother's uniform. Roy angrily grabbed his fork and stabbed Laura in the back of the hand. She screamed, flinging her hand in the air as blood trickled out of the puncture wounds. Laura cried as she glared at Karina with revenge. From that minute on, Laura held a grudge and openly treated Karina like a punching bag, and she got away with it! Aunt Jessie turned the other cheek and it became a family affair with each member's involvement, except for the two oldest who were away most of the time. Consequently, it got worse.

After that day, dinner was set up for Aunt Jessie's family only; Don and Karina were not included. Instead, they had to wait until supper was over. When the plates were scraped, they got whatever was meant for the garbage. If there was nothing left to throw out, then Don and Karina went to bed hungry.

Karina was starving and couldn't concentrate in school, so she scavenged out of garbage cans or stole food from other students' lunch boxes. She would hide in the bathroom to eat, but she got caught and was sent to the principal for a strapping. Later, when she got home from school, she got another strapping from Aunt Jessie because stealing was a sin!

Karina was not alone. There were other children who wandered through the streets begging for food, so Karina tried that too. She went to a neighbour's house and asked for a piece of bread with butter. She said it was for her Aunt. Then, she went down the alley and hid inside a folded mattress where she ate and fell asleep. Her Aunt Jessie found her and dragged her back to the house. With all the screaming and crying that went on, it was shocking that no one called the police.

Bedtime was not much of an escape for Karina. In the winter nights, she shivered from the damp mattress that she shared with her bed-wetting cousins. The old mattress had a hole right in the middle and it was peppered with an infestation of tiny bugs, so Karina slept as close to the wall as possible.

In the morning, the children smelled of urine, but there was no tub or shower. Bathing was done on Saturday night. The kids lined up in the kitchen and one by one they washed in a large galvanized tub that stood in the middle of the floor. Karina hated to be last, because Aunt Jessie was always in a snit after dealing with heating the kettle and refilling the tub. Why did Aunt Jessie take her terrible mood out on Karina?

Bath time was burn time and Karina shuddered at the thought. She screeched in pain when Jessie poured the kettle of hot water into her bath. The throbbing and searing was excruciating. Karina squirmed but Aunt Jessie held her by the hair until her skin turned raw. She cried incessantly as Jessie dressed her into a nightie and pushed her off to bed. It took several days before the blisters drained and the healing began externally, but the healing would never happen internally.

Karina was always trying to find ways to get food. She snuck out of her aunt's house and plucked the corn stalks from the field out back. She ran to an old pigpen overgrown with weeds, climbed inside, and ate the raw corn. It wasn't tasty, but she was full and didn't have to lie or steal anymore. Then she would be in Aunt Jessie's good books. She would stay close by and be helpful so Aunt Jessie would be more tolerant.

Aunt Jessie was busy in the kitchen preparing a chicken for dinner. She cut the intestines out and threw the guts in a pan. Then, she wrapped the good meat and stored it in the freezer box. After she finished cleaning, she took the pan and placed it out back of the house for the dogs. Karina went out the back door and took the pan to the shed and ate all the cooked guts.

"You are a pig."

Aunt Jessie was going to teach that child a lesson. She took three big text-books and slammed them down on Karina's head. The books were so heavy that Karina couldn't balance them properly. The burden was unbearable and she was in a fret of tears. Jessie went to the closet and took out her husband's shotgun.

"Stop being such a big cry baby!" Jessie shouted and pointed the gun at her. It went off and a bullet fired into the bathroom door, blasting an enormous hole through it. For a moment, Karina was completely deafened by the sound. All she heard was a loud ringing in her ears. She stood frozen as a puddle of her own urine soaked her feet.

Nothing held Aunt Jessie back from doing the most unthinkable acts of malice. So Karina did her best not to fidget, wriggle, or move in a way that might cause Jessie to go off the deep end. But it was hopeless to try and please her aunt, because Karina wasn't helpful; she was just in the way. She was always in the wrong place at the wrong time, like the time Karina was squeezing through the tiny kitchen and stopped to give the baby a toy. Aunt Jessie was busy peeling potatoes and turned to see Karina.

"How many times have I told you to stay out of my kitchen?"

Karina backed away and tried to squeeze between the table and the baby pen, but she wasn't quick enough. Aunt Jessie flung the paring knife and stabbed Karina in the top of her left shoulder. Karina stood paralyzed with shock. A hot flash of pain sent a message to her brain. Her aunt was the enemy who would kill her niece. Karina was too numb to put up a fight as Jessie held her down on the floor like a doll and pulled the blade out.

Aunt Jessie soaked up the blood with rags and applied pressure until the bleeding stopped. She stripped off Karina's dress and threw it in the trash before anyone could see it. Then she covered the wound with a large piece of gauze and sent Karina to bed.

For the rest of her life, Karina would see that scar the size of a quarter and be forever reminded. There was not a moment that Karina didn't live in fear that Aunt Jessie would torture her again and again. She had to run away and find her mother Elaine. The tears came as she remembered her mother's tear-stained face and outstretched arms. It was terrible to feel so much hate and be in an environment that was out of her control. All she ever wanted was to feel safe and be loved again.

Karina's cousins were constantly plotting ways to rough her up. Whenever they were being nice, it was just a ploy to trick her and toy with her mind. She had learned to keep her distance but one day the cousins invited her to go swimming in the river and like any normal child, she thought that would be fun.

As soon as Karina entered the water, the fight was on. It happened so fast that she didn't have time to turn back. Her arms flapped wildly but she couldn't escape the hands that pulled her head under the water. She thrashed about and gasped for air. She fought hard for every breath but her body became exhausted.

She gulped and gasped mouthfuls as she frantically struggled to get her head above the surface until it all went black. When there was no fight left in Karina, the kids laughed as they pulled her up and threw her onto the grass. Don was so scared that he hid in a grassy shrub and watched in paralyzing horror as the cousins passed by, leaving his little sister choking on the bank.

Don ducked down as low as he could and waited until the kids were out of range. He prayed that Karina would get up. The lack of oxygen had taken away her strength, but after some time she pulled herself together and walked alone to the house. Aunt Jessie didn't want to hear what had happened at the river; she was busy cleaning out the fireplace. When Karina tried to explain, Aunt Jessie cut her off.

"I don't want to hear about it," Jessie warned as she stoked the ashes.

"But the kids tried to drown me," Karina blurted out. She wanted Aunt Jessie to know the truth. Maybe then her aunt would see that her kids were abusive too.

"But, Aunt Jessie, they are mean."

"What did I just tell you?" Aunt Jessie reacted so swiftly that Karina regretted her choice to not back off. Before Karina could dodge out of the way, the poker came down on top of her. She toppled to the floor and withered in agony. It was double the pain of the curling iron that Aunt Jessie had often used.

Karina wanted no part of Aunt Jessie anymore. Nothing she did or said would ever change her aunt from being a monster. It was obvious that if there were no intervention for protection, sooner or later, Karina would be dead.

Don suffered abuse as well, but the worst of it fell on Karina. It terrified him to see his sister scrubbing the floor on her knees, as multiple hands dragged her back and forth by her hair. He wanted to rescue his little sister from the hard shoes that kicked her when she was down, but he was a little boy too and his punishment would have been unbearable.

10

During the Christmas season, Karina was forbidden to go to any of the public functions or festivities that Aunt Jessie's family attended. Even Christmas morning was not a day of joy for her. Karina was excited to open the one little gift with her name on it. She untied the ribbon and peeled away the paper to find a small handmade doll with big green beaded eyes, wearing a blue woolen dress. She was so happy that she wanted to hug the doll, but in a blink of an eye it was ripped out of her hands and the head was torn off as the other girls fought over it. Again, she cried, not only for the doll, but for the lack of love that made her feel so shameful.

The Cinderella nightmare that Karina was living would soon be at an end. She had taken her last beating from Aunt Jessie. She would rather die trying to escape than live with the regrets. Before it was time to leave for school she looked for some food to pack into her pockets, but there was nothing to sustain her. If she were caught going through the cupboards, Aunt Jessie would be on to her. Karina left the house with only the coat on her back and the canvas shoes on her feet. Her coat had a thick old fox collar, but the matted pile was full of lice that had laid eggs into the fur. Karina's bald shaved head had some new growth, but already the new lice infested her scalp and without a hat she was freezing.

It was the middle of winter and girls were not allowed to wear pants to school. Karina didn't own any socks or underwear, so by the time she crossed the schoolyard her legs were numb: she could barely feel her toes. She was already having doubts about the idea of running away, but her life hung in the balance. It was life or death. She needed love and a safe environment, but no one seemed to care what happened to Karina so it was up to her to find what she needed.

5: Grant and Abby

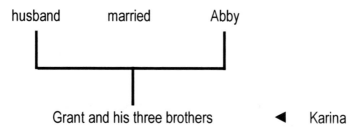

On her way to school, Karina met up with a pupil named Grant. Unlike many of the students, he didn't pick on her or make fun of the clothes she wore. He wasn't close to Karina, but he was the only friend that she had. She shared her secret with Grant, telling him that she was not going home after school. She wanted to say goodbye and leave forever.

"Where will you go?" Grant asked. His face was sad.

"I don't know, but I can't go home," Karina said quietly as they entered the school.

For most of the day, Grant was distracted with Karina's disturbing news. He sat at his desk and knew he could help, but he wasn't sure how. Somehow, he had to find a way to get Karina to meet his mother. He trusted his mother; she was kind and loving all the time.

Grant didn't get to talk to Karina until the end of the day when school was over. Before Karina stepped outside to face the frigid air and disappear, Grant coaxed her to come over to his house and eat some food. It was the first time that Karina had ever gone to visit a classmate's home; she was already late and Aunt Jessie would be waiting to do some serious damage. Grant was a smart and caring little six-year-old; he didn't have the answer, but his mother would know what to do.

Karina sat on a high stool next to Grant while they both ate hot soup and crackers. It was the only meal Karina had eaten all day, so she had been very happy when Grant's Mom, Abby, suggested she stay for supper. But it would be all-out war if Karina went home late, so she told Abby that she was running away. With the climate so deathly cold at night, there was no way that Abby would send Karina away—especially when it was shockingly obvious Karina had suffered greatly from the hands of others.

Karina was dressed in poverty and showing signs of pneumonia. Her weakened and frail appearance wore signs of malnutrition. Abby was careful not to stare, but she couldn't help noticing that Karina's limbs revealed many darkened and bruised areas, and the child had no socks or underwear. Although Karina fearfully protested, Abby talked her into staying for the night. After dinner Abby gave Karina a bath and picked all the lice eggs out from her scalp.

Karina had never seen a white porcelain bathtub. It was amazingly beautiful and she was even more surprised to see it in a room that came with a toilet and a sink. That night, she wore a pair of Grant's pyjamas and for the first time, she slept in a bed alone and in a room that was not full of other kids. Abby took all the clothes that Karina had been wearing and burned them in the fireplace. Later that evening, Karina's Uncle Tom learned of her whereabouts and banged on Abby's front door, demanding to have his niece returned to him at once.

Abby barred the entrance and refused to let Karina's Uncle take her home. In no uncertain terms, Abby told the so-called Uncle he was not allowed to encroach on her property. When he staked his claim she threatened to have social services visit his family.

Abby would do whatever it took to keep this child under her roof.

For Karina, it was as if the angels had come and granted her a wish. She was out of her Aunt Jessie's house and no longer living in fear. Abby had so much empathy and loved Karina with all her heart. From that day on, it was as if Karina had been reborn. Her life transformed from the calamity of an ugly past to a beautiful future that offered the most devoted love, nurturing, and understanding.

There was no trouble with Aunt Jessie; she didn't even show up to claim Karina, but Abby didn't take any risks. Every day, Abby walked Karina to school and, at the end of the day, she waited outside to walk her home. At school, the kids were shocked, especially Aunt Jessie's children. They had all behaved like Cinderella's evil stepsisters and treated Karina lower than the trash she'd been fed.

What a blow it must have been for Aunt Jessie to see her niece Karina. The child had never owned anything pretty. She had gone from dirty rags to a closet full of cute little pinafore dresses in various prints of little yellow field flowers and pink polka dots. She wore puffed sleeves and dainty frocks tied with a big bow. Lace-edged socks and black patent shoes completed every outfit.

Grant had three brothers and they loved having a girl in the house. It was different from what they were accustomed to, but Karina happily engaged in learning how to play with trucks, and they in turn played with dolls. Once Karina was cured of her pneumonia, Abby had her family doctor schedule her for a tonsillectomy. After the surgery date was set, Abby went to the department store to do some shopping. She brought home a big box and hid it in the top of the front hallway closet.

Karina started eyeing that box for some time and, when no one was around, she got a chair and climbed up to reach the package. Pulling it down, her eyes widened with excitement as she opened the lid and stared at a beautiful, big doll. She closed her bedroom door and carefully lifted the doll out of the box.

Karina had never come across any doll so large and colourful. The doll had an uncanny resemblance to Karina as she noticed the big, soft brown eyes and small pink lips. The ebony hair was tied in ribbons with straight little bangs cropped over the hand-painted eyebrows. The cheeks dimpled with only a hint of blush.

Karina placed the doll on the bed and smiled down at the treasure. She was instantly in love with it, but when she heard Abby coming in the front door, she hid the box and the doll under the blankets.

"Did you take the big box that was up in the top of the closet?" Abby asked as she entered the room. Karina was afraid that Abby would take the doll away and punish her so she lied. "You don't have to lie. I'm not mad at you," said

Abby, as she pulled the blanket up and exposed the evidence.

"I'm sorry. I was afraid that you would get very angry," Karina said, wishing she could undo her lie. She was sure that Abby wouldn't love her anymore.

"The doll is a present for you to take to the hospital and it is yours to keep," Abby replied. "You need to give her a name."

"Oh, thank you, thank you." Karina said and she leaped up for a big hug. She no longer worried herself with doubts, because Abby loved her as if she were her own daughter. Karina looked at her guardian as a martyr who gallantly fought to protect her; Abby led an exemplary yet simple life that could sustain Karina with all the happiness a child deserves. Karina proudly showed her doll to every visitor who came to the hospital. Having to go through an operation was scary, but her bravery was rewarded with plenty of popsicles and ice cream.

Karina was allowed to attend birthday parties, church socials, and all the Christmas events. She loved her new family and wanted to stay there forever.

6: Lloyd and Lorraine

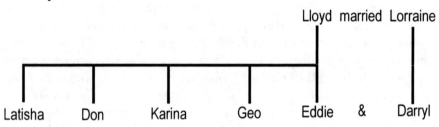

In the meantime, Lloyd was very happy. He had gotten back on his feet and was doing well. He finalized his divorce, remarried, and bought a house on Canada's West Coast. His new bride, Lorraine, had a son Daniel and the three of them were ready to start a life with the rest of the family. It was already two years since Lloyd had seen his children. He could hardly wait to introduce them to his new wife.

When Abby and her husband took the kids camping in the summer, Karina's father showed up. He was driving a big fancy station wagon with shiny wooden paneling on the sides.

At first, Karina didn't recognize her father; somehow, he was different. The man was in good spirits and it was noticeable that he was ready to make a fresh start.

"Hello, Karina," Lloyd addressed her, catching her off-guard. His new bride stood next to him and smiled down at her. The second Karina recognized her father, her heart skipped a beat and all her dreams came to a screeching halt.

Recently, she had been living an enchanted life. Her memories raced back to her and she saw Lloyd as a threat. Biologically, he was her father, but he didn't cut it as a Dad. Instead, he had ripped her from her roots and turned her world upside down.

"I want you to meet Lorraine. She is my wife and your new Mom," he added. "She has a boy close to your age, and you will have a new brother to play with." All his enthusiasm couldn't compensate for the revulsion and disappointment. Karina didn't want a new mother. She had Abby!

Lloyd had come to take his daughter away from everything she loved and she began bawling beyond her ability to control. In the midst of tears, she begged to stay with Abby, but Lloyd would have no part of that. Abby had always known the day would come when Karina would leave, but she never anticipated the pain. Abby had no say in the matter. She clung tightly as Karina whimpered and cuddled against her for the last time. Grant tried to negotiate with his mother and offered to give up his toys if he could keep Karina.

"Mom, please don't let them take my sister," he cut in front of her.

"It's alright. That's her Dad and he misses her." Abby pulled her son into a hug and tried to ease his sadness.

Karina cried like a baby as she walked to the car and waved. She wanted to turn around and run back, but it was hopeless; she had no choice but to surrender and go with her father.

Lloyd drove straight to Banff National Park and got a suite at the famous hotel. It looked like a castle out of a fairy tale. The backdrop of snow-capped trees glittered like a winter wonderland. The kids had never stayed in a hotel, so it was quite a surprise to see a real shower and tub all in one unit.

Her little brothers Geo and Eddie had grown so much. They both had learned to talk, but they didn't know their Daddy or their siblings. They cried and cried and everyone was upset. The night grew harder for Lloyd when Karina talked about what happened between her and Aunt Jessie.

The look on her father's face was beyond rage. Karina was sure that he would pack up right then and drive for the next four hours. Karina was scared of what he might do, but to her shock, he did nothing. Karina expected at the very least that Lloyd would confront his sister-in-law and be a stickler for the truth. Especially after the way he had treated Elaine.

7: Karina and Her Family

Lloyd bought a big house in the town of Fort Langley. A new home with a mother to give the children the proper care seemed like the ideal life. It was

15

quite an adjustment for all, but it was a happy time. Lorraine and her son Daniel had the most difficult task, because she had married into a family of six.

The siblings had to learn how to live together, as they barely knew each other. It wasn't long before they got into the normal scrapes and fun adventures that kids do.

Fort Langley was a laid back town where kids had to rely on their imagination and creativity to stay amused. They often walked the railway tracks and hung out at the train station. When the steam engine rumbled into town, they cheered and screamed with excitement as the engineer waved and blew his whistle.

On hot summer days, the siblings met up with neighbours and friends. They walked to the outskirts of town to go for a swim in the creek. On the way back, they stopped for a two-bit cone. If they didn't have a quarter, then they went to the corner store. In those days, a nickel could buy a bag full of penny candy. There was enough red licorice that everyone got three or four pieces.

Main Street was completely covered in cobblestone. On both sides of the road, the chestnut trees arched over the unpaved sidewalks making a long narrow cove for pedestrians. In the spring, the trees foliated with lush blooms and leaves that lasted right through till late fall. They hung over like willow trees and it was a breath-taking view. The old Victorian-style homes spread across velvety green lawns. Flower boxes decorated the window ledges and wooden trestles flourished with creeping vines. Most of the lots were squared off with white picket fences. Some of the properties were closed in with wrought iron gates covered over by hydrangeas, roses, and lilacs.

Karina dressed a lot like other girls. On school days, she wore a sundress. She had short-cut bangs and hair braided neatly, tied with ribbons. Her brothers, like most boys, ran around barefoot in bib overalls and no shirt.

It was a wonderful place to grow up. Weekends were filled with activities. Musicians and stage performers played at the town hall. Everyone came and later there was dancing for all ages. The elderly sat on the side benches, tapping their feet to the rhythm, while bouncing the grandbabies on their knees.

It wasn't like the big city of Vancouver; it was a small community with a lot of fellowship. During the winter, parents went out on the ice-covered lake and skated with their children. The winter months were occupied with family hayrides and homemade hot chocolate.

On Christmas Eve, groups of friends got together to sing carols. The teenagers hung out at the malt shop and cruised up and down the main street. Fort Langley was still small enough to hold a tight embrace as families stayed together and neighbours watched out for one another. Karina bonded to the treasured memories of this sleepy little town. It was perfect.

8: Principal Walker

Two years later, Lloyd sold the house and they moved to the outskirts of the town of Langley, closer to Vancouver, but still in the Fraser Valley.

After the move, the kids could no longer walk to school; they had to bus back and forth.

Moving was hard on Karina. After she had settled into a new elementary school, the principal, Mr. Walker, called Karina to his office. He gave her the responsibility to run errands three or four times a week during school. She had to drop off papers, books, or materials to some of the classes. The principal always praised her for helping and each time he would give her a big hug. He treated Karina differently from the other students, and her confidence grew.

At first, it was wonderful; he was like the loving father she didn't have. Sometimes, he pulled Karina over to sit on his lap, where he would stroke her head, caress her arm, and tell her that she was beautiful. He rubbed her back and shoulders as he convinced her that she deserved this affection. He used every plausible way to gain Karina's loyalty. In the mornings, Karina always made her rounds and finished her duties as expected.

Next, Principal Walker needled his way further into her affections. Candy was the bait to reel her in. It worked. He checked the hallway to make sure no one was around and then he locked the office door with Karina inside. He sat the child on his lap and kissed her cheek. He would not let her out until she was willing to accept "his gift." It was a lie. He had no gift; he was luring this child into a web of deceit and doing what came naturally to him.

He cleared a space on top of his desk and drew graphic pictures with step-by-step instructions as though it was a part of her studies and no amount of crying would change anything.

After a time he grew careless and he almost got caught when a teacher knocked hard on his door. He pushed Karina into the closet and threw her clothes in after her. As she was trying to dress, the principal told her not to move or she would get into big trouble. Karina was terrified, not knowing which was worse: the teacher finding her naked in a cloakroom or the perpetrator waiting to finish his filthy deeds.

Karina was allowed to come out when the teacher had gone; Principal Walker was in a rush to get rid of her. No more risks. He sent Karina back to class. Karina was so young, so naïve, and living in a world of adults with no protection.

During class, she made copies of Principal Walker's diagrams and gave one to a little boy in her class. The kid took the picture and showed it to his older brother who gave it to his parents. When the parents found out who had drawn the picture, they went to see Lloyd. Karina's Dad flipped out, just like always.

"You dirty little tramp! You are just like your mother," Lloyd said as soon as they were alone. He had always spoken ill of Karina's mother, but this was the first time he had compared Karina to Elaine. Before Karina had a second to explain, he began to unbuckle his belt.

"No Daddy! I didn't mean to…" she screamed as Lloyd dragged her into the bathroom and closed the door behind them.

"How dare you shame your family with your filthy drawings." Karina stood rigid with fear as Lloyd slid the belt out of the loops on his pants. He raised his hand and swung the belt. The first lash cut into her skin and tore a line across her bottom. She saw his determination to cast out the demons from inside her.

Later, Karina suffered from hearing many lectures of her mother's iniquity. Lloyd ranted on and on, but Karina was nearly senseless when he banished Karina to her knees where he demanded she pray to be forgiven. Outside the bathroom, Lloyd was relentless. He told the kids that Karina was like their mother Elaine.

Karina understood she had been conned by Mr. Walker, a cunning snake. From that day on, she tried to avoid him and deliberately failed to show up for the morning routine. The despicable man got the teacher to bring her in. She had skipped school three or four times a week and hid from her principal and her father, the two people who had the most power over her.

Sly Mr. Walker listed all Karina's absentees on her report card and she got a disciplinarian strapping in the office. She got another whipping when she got home.

She returned to school and begged Mr. Walker to leave her alone, but she had become his toy and he would never give her up. Nearly every school day, she was forced to be his playmate until the end of her last elementary year when she moved up to middle school. She would never have to submit herself to this man again. She thought that she was finally free, but it wasn't over.

9: Lorraine's Brother-in-Law Bob

In the summer, most families did their own fruit picking so Lloyd took the boys away to pick in the valley. Karina stayed at the house to help her stepmother Lorraine with the chores and the little ones.

She was happy to be home and not have to worry about her father's temper. Her stepmother, Lorraine, had her two sisters come to visit from out of town. Bob, a husband to one of the sisters, drove out two days later. He slept upstairs in the empty boys' room.

In the middle of the night, Karina awoke to a hand creeping under her nightgown. Bob had waited until the house was dark, and then he had tiptoed into Karina's room and crept into her bed. He was already underneath the covers and groping her when she tried to scream. He slapped his hand over her mouth and held her down with the weight of his body.

With a new baby, Lorraine woke at the slightest creak in the house. Aroused by the distant noise, she got up and walked toward the muffled sounds that came from Karina's bedroom. She opened the door and switched on the light.

"What the hell is going on?" Lorraine screamed.

Without any explanation, Bob released his grip that barred Karina's cries and scrambled out of bed. Without stopping, he grabbed whatever he could get of his belongings and raced for the stairs. Lorraine tore after him, but he jumped the bottom steps as he leaped down to the floor and bounded across to the entrance.

He bolted out the front door and left it wide open. He sprinted headlong over the grassy yard, got in the car, and peeled down the road. The sisters woke up to Lorraine shrieking at the top of her lungs that Bob had raped Karina. All three women stood face to face, screaming at each other with all kinds of misleading accusations; soon all the children were awake and crying.

Karina was standing in the doorway of her bedroom. She was weeping so loudly that Lorraine ran upstairs to comfort her. Lorraine pulled her over to the bed and Karina sat on the edge with her head in her hands, sobbing. Lorraine explained that it was possible she could be pregnant and tried to explain what had just happened, relating it to the birds and the bees.

"You can't tell your father about this," Lorraine begged her.

"Why not?" Karina was confused. She knew that keeping secrets from her father could lead to a severe punishment if he found out.

"You have to promise not to tell him. He will kill both of us," Lorraine begged.

Karina couldn't believe what she was hearing. Even Lorraine was terrified of him.

"What if I'm...?" Karina couldn't say the word, because she was feeling the panic rise and she was struggling.

"Let's hope it doesn't come to that." Lorraine clasped her fingers over her own mouth and shrugged her shoulders as though she didn't want any part of it. Karina already decided that if she was pregnant, her only option was to leave. As a girl just shy of her eleventh birthday, she had nowhere to go, except maybe to Alberta. Back to Abby.

10: Lloyd

In the days that followed, Karina's Dad came home with the boys. He was completely unaware of what had happened. He teased Karina by telling her that she looked like she was getting fat. Her worst nightmare had come true and in her mind she was sure that a baby was growing inside her. That beast had impregnated her and now she was left to tell the truth. She knew her father would blame her and never understand. How was she to tell him without serious repercussions? She had to talk to someone and decided to confide in her sister Latisha, who was a little older and wiser, and would know what to do. Latisha tried to comfort her and explained that she would tell their father because he needed to know.

Lloyd came flying up the stairs and straight to the bedroom where Karina sat on the bed. Grabbing his daughter, he shook and slapped her several times. He demanded to know who had done this to her. He wanted every detail and repeated the same questions over and over. Crying and pleading, she told it all. He stared straight into her face and wanted to know why he hadn't been told right away. Karina cried as she told him how Lorraine was afraid of what he would do to both of them, so Lorraine had sworn her to secrecy. He stood up from the bed and stormed to the stairwell.

"Lorraine! Lorraine! Where are you?" Lloyd's voice barreled over the side of the railing. He took a step down and waited in silence. He was gone in a flash. Karina got up; her gut feelings told her to run like mad. She ran down the steps and came to a sudden halt as if she was held under a strange power not visible to the naked eye. She heard Lorraine's pleading voice from the kitchen.

Lloyd was holding Lorraine by the hair and she was crouched down to the floor. He was screaming that he was going to kill her and he had a butcher knife in his hand.

Lorraine was screaming for help. Don was the hero. He leaped through the air and grabbed his dad from behind. Latisha stood in the doorway with her hands covering her mouth as though she was struck dumb.

"Get the knife! Latisha, get the knife!" Don screamed as Lloyd thrashed back and forth to shake him off.

Latisha snapped out of her trance and went for the knife. Lloyd dropped his arms to his side and surrendered. Everyone fell silent except Lorraine, who cried out in her own defence.

"I couldn't tell you because I knew that you would react this way."

Lorraine was shaking as she sprang away from her husband. Karina watched her Dad back away from everyone's shocked eyes. Without another word, Lloyd turned and walked out of the house. He got in the car and floored the pedal. The tires squealed as bits of gravel shot out from behind.

Lorraine didn't run after him; she knew where he was going. Lloyd had gone after Bob and no one would dare to intervene.

It was nearly light out. Lloyd spent the entirety of his night driving aimlessly as he searched for Bob. Lloyd came back, but he never did find Bob because the guy had disappeared. He had left his wife and children.

Karina wasn't pregnant after all, but there was so much misery in the house that she felt responsible and put most of the blame on herself. She believed that her father didn't love her anymore. He looked at her differently. His eyes showed objections, marking her as a bad seed, because she had been spawned out of Elaine's bad blood. Lloyd was on to his daughter; she was a harlot for attention and he could prove it.

Shortly after that day, Latisha packed up her belongings and moved to Vancouver. Karina wanted to go with her sister, but she knew that was impossible. She was too young.

She missed Latisha so much. It was hard not to have a big sister around. To add to Karina's pain, Lorraine also went away, so Karina had to stay behind to take care of her father and the boys.

Long after the boys had gone to bed one evening, Karina passed through the hallway and heard Lloyd call out to her.

She thought there was trouble, that maybe she was too loud and had woken him. She entered the bedroom and saw her father was in bed totally nude. She was so embarrassed and turned away.

"Come here, Karina," Lloyd ordered and patted the edge of the bed.

She walked slowly in his direction and stopped within inches of him. Her legs were trembling and she was sure that she would fall to her knees right there in front of him. She believed that her father was the same as all the others; no different.

She had endured a whole life of sexual monsters and now the only person she trusted to protect her was waiting to hunt her down for his pleasure.

"Please don't make me do this. I can't do it," she pleaded and cried. "Please let me go."

She whimpered so much that Lloyd told her to leave. Karina stepped back and ran to her room. She quietly closed the door and braced herself against it. Why would he do this?

In her heart, Karina wanted to forgive her father, but she felt that men had all the authority so that they could get sexual control of others.

11: Karina and Louis, Josh, Sheila, and Me

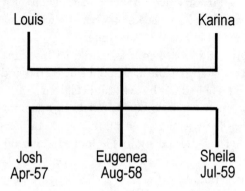

Karina did not feel valued or loved until she met Louis, a teenage boy at school. Having a boyfriend was a way of getting out of the house. On weekends, the two teens went to sock hops and drive-in movies.

Afterwards, they would cruise to the drive-in for burgers and shakes or hung out in the parking lot with their friends. Louis drove a fancy roadster that looked great, but he spent hours fixing it up. He fused motorcycle fenders on it. Every time he hit a bump in the road, the fenders would come unglued and fly off into the ditch. He sure got mad when he had to wade through the dikes in search of his fenders.

After two years of dating Louis, Karina became pregnant and decided not to go back to school in the fall. She knew better than to tell her father. Lloyd had no idea and sent her to camp for the summer holidays. She ran away while she was there and went to live in the city with Latisha.

The two girls worked in a drugstore and soon Karina was six-months pregnant, so it was impossible to hide it. She told Latisha and then she moved to a doctor's house and became a live-in maid.

Later, when Karina was eight-months pregnant she moved into a home for unwed mothers and stayed until she went into labour. A few hours later, she went to the hospital and gave birth. She could hardly believe this darling baby boy belonged to her.

During Karina's hospital stay, the staff and caregivers at the unwed mothers' home came to visit. They tried to talk Karina into giving up her baby for adoption. She told them clearly that she hadn't gone through nine months of pregnancy just so she could hand her baby over to someone else. She had to go through life without her mother and she would never do that to her baby. Karina kept her baby right beside her and named him Josh.

News spread fast. Lloyd went to visit Karina and his new grandchild. Karina was scared as a rabbit when he showed up, but Lloyd couldn't lay a hand on her; Karina didn't live under his roof anymore. Lloyd held his temper but, contrary to what it looked like, there would be no mistake. Karina knew where she stood.

Lloyd paced the hospital room. His smug approach was much worse than Karina anticipated. She turned her face away, making sure her father wouldn't see her uneasiness. He didn't hide the disgust he felt about his daughter having a baby out of wedlock.

"Guess you had a good time. What are you going to do now?" He smirked coldly, but she didn't answer him.

"What do you have to say for yourself?" he smiled, but it wasn't a good smile—more like, "Look what kind of daughter you turned out to be and I told you so."

"Who's the father?" he asked, as he pretended not to know.

"You know who the father is! I have been dating Louis for two years now," she replied. Bitterly, she fought back tears. She wouldn't give her father the satisfaction of knowing that his cutting remarks caused her so much pain.

"You will have to come home. You can't just live out on the street or in a shelter and you can't expect your sister to take care of you and your kid. You have to come home where the baby can be taken care of."

"I don't want to live at home."

"Look at yourself. No husband and you've got a baby. Who's gonna marry a girl like you?" Lloyd said.

Karina didn't want go home, but she had no other choice. She and her baby left the hospital and went home to live under her father's watchful eye. Lloyd continued to badger Karina and compare her actions to her mother's. It didn't matter what others believed: Karina would never accept that Elaine was as bad as Lloyd claimed. From that day on, she would defend her mother and be on her side.

Karina didn't love Louis, her roadster-loving boyfriend, but Lloyd wanted her to be married right away, so he met with Louis and made the arrangements. Karina tried to get her father to understand that she was not prepared to spend her life with Louis. Once the baby was down for a nap, Karina walked out to the yard to find Lloyd working under the hood of the car.

"I need to talk to you." She hoped that he would listen.

"I'm busy. Can't you see that?" He was already irked.

"Dad, I can't marry Louis. I don't love him." Karina knew her timing was bad, but she was desperate to put her father's ideals into reality.

"You are stupider than I thought. I give you a chance to make things right and you want to blow it. What is wrong with your head? Don't you have a brain in there? If you didn't want to marry Louis, you should have thought of that before you got yourself knocked up. Like it or not, you are getting married. I have had enough of you shaming our family."

His face turned hard and ugly as he pointed his finger so close to her face that Karina could smell the engine fuel.

Maybe a shotgun wedding wasn't such a bad idea. If Karina got married, she could get away from her father. She could learn to love Louis; it was the only way to make her life tolerable. To make sure the wedding happened, Karina's father paid for everything.

Louis's mother Norina didn't attend the wedding. Like Karina, she was the only other person who didn't want the wedding to happen.

On the night of the honeymoon, Louis moved into Lloyd's house and slept in Karina's room with her and the baby. Even though Louis and Karina were officially married, Lloyd wasn't comfortable with the arrangements. As a wedding gift, Lloyd cleaned out the chicken coop and gave it up as a home for the newlyweds.

Karina wanted to be grateful, but she knew it was not healthy to raise a family in such a dirty environment with no running water, electricity, or floors. No matter how hard she cleaned, it still smelled of chicken poop. Lloyd installed water, but the rats kept getting into the pipes and contaminating it, so the couple moved to a little apartment.

When baby Josh turned six months old, Karina was pregnant again, so they moved to a quiet place in Langley. Karina went into labour and I was born in the hall between the labour room and the delivery room. My arrival came on an early morning August of 1958. When I was only two months old, Karina was pregnant again. My sister Sheila was born and we were eleven months apart. Our parents had three babies in diapers.

Louis struggled with finding work. He spent much of his time fixing his vehicles. Mom didn't know how to deal with a husband she felt was so immature, and raise three kids at the same time. After three years, she pulled the plug and separated with her children.

12: Karina and Elaine's Reunion

Karina told her father that she wanted to find her mother. Lloyd was adamant that she should stay away from Elaine. He refused to help in any way. To the amazement of everyone, Latisha had already found Elaine. She told Karina that Elaine was living on a small farm in southern Alberta.

Karina remembered every second when she had dialed the numbers, clenching the phone tightly, waiting for the other end to be picked up, waiting for the beautiful voice of her mother.

"Hello?" It was a woman talking.

"Hello. Is this Elaine?" Karina swallowed hard and tried to talk without shaking.

"Yes. Who's calling?" The voice came again, followed by another long pause.

"Hello, Elaine, this is your daughter, Karina." Then she was silent and she waited.

For a while, nothing happened and the stillness made her feel ill, like she needed air. What if her mother didn't want to see or hear from her? What if everything Lloyd had said was true? Now, she was trapped on the other end of the line.

"I don't know what to say." Elaine seemed reluctant to answer. "I mean it has been a long time and I haven't seen you since you were small."

Elaine was soft and comforting, but Karina was still not convinced that she had done the right thing.

"I have waited many years for this moment to arrive, but I must admit I'm really terrified that I might say something wrong. I barely know you." Elaine answered. That was quite a jolt for Karina; she hadn't thought about how difficult the call would be for Elaine.

"You can't imagine how much I've missed you. My little girl and all my kids." Elaine lost herself and began to cry. In one incredible moment, her child had lifted years of waiting. There was something purely magical—almost dreamy—as Karina listened to the first words from her mother's lips.

They talked about the past, present, future, and everything in life that mattered to them. Karina no longer thought of her mother as a woman who had forgotten about her children. She knew that her mother loved her as she heard the longing words of devotion that cut through all the years of emptiness.

Karina learned that her mother Elaine was still with Gordon. Things had gotten much better once Elaine faced the truth that her kids were gone forever. She had sobered up, but occasionally she drank and it would go on for two or three days. They had made a life together working on the farm. They didn't have much, but they had each other. Elaine told her daughter about her rodeo awards in the barrel racing at the Calgary Stampede and how she had got the title of rodeo queen. The minutes seemed like sand pouring through an hourglass, until Karina finally had to say goodbye and hang up.

It wasn't long before Karina made the decision to leave British Columbia and move out to Alberta. She couldn't wait. We moved to Calgary, only three hours away from Elaine. Without telling our Dad Louis or her family, Karina bought four train tickets and helped us up the steps to a new threshold of life.

When we got on the Canadian Pacific train, Josh and I ran upstairs to look out of the panorama dome car windows. At the tender ages of four and three, we were entranced by the magnificent views of waterfalls, lakes, and animals that wandered through the foliage. During the night, Mom slept in a berth with Sheila while Josh and I enjoyed the top bunk and its viewing window.

Each berth had a curtain that closed around the bed for privacy, but Josh and I would poke our heads out every time someone made a noise or passed by. We would wave to the conductor when he made his rounds, as we made sure not to miss out on anything. In the morning, we got up and had breakfast in the diner. When we returned, we were surprised to discover the conductor had folded up the sleeping berth.

We arrived late afternoon and stepped off the train to find it already dark with freezing cold winds and bitter gusts of snow. Mom grabbed the luggage. She reminded us to stay close beside her and hold onto her coat. Fortunately, the train station extended to the hotel so it was only a few steps to the door.

"Look, Josh. You see that building in front of us?" she asked him. Josh looked upwards at the hotel that overpowered the sky.

"That's where we will be sleeping tonight," she smiled.

The grand chateau was adorned in white lights; it carried an ambience of elegance. It could have complemented any part of Europe, but for us it was just a cozy place to sleep. The regal-sized mansion seemed far too stately for a single mother of three. We stood waiting impatiently and fidgeted while Mom stopped at the front desk to sign in. The Palliser Hotel was beautiful but, after such a long ride, we were more excited to be tucked in for a bedtime story.

In the morning, Mom put up the money for a cheap motel and began to search for a place to rent. A few days later, we were living in a basement suite near Bowness Park.

Over the months, our new home seemed perfect. It came with everything, including two overstuffed chairs that Mom sometimes pushed together to make into a couch for Josh and me. The two of us would sit cuddled in front of the television and watch the Ed Sullivan show until we fell asleep. Mom would stay on the sofa next to us and in the morning we woke up to find ourselves huddled under a quilt.

In the summer, Mom took us on the bus to see her mother Elaine. The farm was hot and fun for three little ones who spent every day in the old metal wash-tub splashing around in the front yard. Mom and Elaine sat on an old Indian blanket and watched us. Mom was dying to talk; she wanted facts. She was full of questions and wanted to know everything about her mother. It took more than a day for Mom to find the courage to ask. As she stared at Elaine, who was lovingly splashing water at us, she tossed the questions around in her mind.

"What happened between you and my Dad? Why did you split up?" Mom cut in.

Elaine turned to Karina in alarm, her eyes widened as her mouth fell open.

"That is none of your business," Elaine said, point blank.

"Sorry, I just thought that you might want to tell your side of the story. That's all." Mom was stinging from hurt. Instantly, she could feel her eyes water as she bit down on her lip, refusing to let it tremble.

"Karina, I am your mother. I don't have to explain myself. I'm not ashamed of who I am. I'm not going to shake my dirty laundry out for anyone to smell. Whatever happened in the past is over," Elaine finished. Her memories with Lloyd were very unsettling for her, but it was better left behind. Elaine didn't mean to be hard and defensive, but she had done her years of penance. Occasionally, she still had bleak days that brought her back to her old melancholy friend, the bottle, and she would drink for days.

Karina didn't realize how deeply the shame was buried inside her mother. How could she know? Deep into her own thoughts, Karina struggled with the uncomfortable silence. Not being able to find words only made the barrier seem so much bigger. They both wanted so much to have a mother-daughter relationship, but it was all too new and feelings were tender. They simply didn't know each other and time just couldn't seem to fix that.

That night, Mom took Josh, Sheila, and me camping. We stayed in a trailer down by the campsite. I will never forget Mom tucking us into bed. There were two big red plaid curtains on each side of the bunk. She drew them shut around us so that they closed in the middle. She sat on the bed and gave each of us a big hug.

To this day, I can still picture her. Her face was warm with a mother's loving pride and I loved her so much. We promised to be very quiet if she told us a story.

"Once upon a time, there was a Mommy with three kids who were very tired. So she kissed them and tucked them into bed. The end." She raised her eyebrows and made a funny face. Sheila and I laughed as we tried to copy her.

"That's not a story," said Josh as he crossed his arms over his chest and snorted with his bottom lip pouting. "That's not funny." He frowned at us for being so silly.

"No, but tomorrow you get two stories if you go to sleep right away tonight," Mom promised and tickled Josh in the ribs. His sour face lit up. She was back in his good graces. She reached inside the covers, and tickled Sheila and me.

"Okay. Go to sleep now," she warned and rained us with kisses. I could hear a guitar being played outside the trailer. A man was sitting near the fire and strumming a beat and it flowed with a lull that made us drift off to sleep.

13: Karina and Andrew

Looking back, I can make some sense, now, of what might have happened during that time. Mom had a boyfriend. I don't remember much about him, except the fact that he was there and he was blond. Sometimes we treated him like he was our dad. Mom told me how she really had a big thing for Andrew; she didn't want to get serious, but it happened anyway. It wasn't love, but it was definitely a deep crush. In the beginning, she was content to see Andrew once or twice a week, but the long nights were miserable without him.

Andrew was good to Mom. He had a car and offered to drive her kids to the doctor or anywhere she needed to go. Many times, she saw Andrew behaving weirdly, but she couldn't figure out what was wrong. One moment, he was full of life, but then he would take a strange twist, sleeping for days or not showing up at all. His moods changed from romantic and sultry to uncaring and rude. On a good day, it lasted long enough to give her faith in him.

Then, it came: it was a horrible shock to find out he wasn't what she believed.

We had gone out for groceries. When we returned, Mom brought us in the house while Andrew unloaded the trunk of the car. It wasn't until all the food was put away that Mom realized she had left her purse on the floor of the passenger side of the car.

She swung the car door open wide and there was the purse. At the same moment as she reached in, something caught her attention from the corner of her eye. A silvery thin piece of sharp steel reflected in the light. Curious, she bent down, trying to see what was underneath, and stuck her hand in to pull out a bundled-up towel. Carefully, she pulled out the towel and unwrapped it. Inside, she found a syringe had caught in the fabric.

A strange, caustic odour hit her nostrils, causing a little flutter in her tummy. She had never smelled anything like that before. Inside were more needles, an old rusted copper spoon, and two small bags of heroin. Panic raced over her as she stared in disbelief. Then she realized that Andrew was inside the house with her babies and her hands trembled erratically. She tried to remember exactly how she had unfolded the towel so she could put it back exactly the same way she had found it. She quickly wrapped it up and slipped it under the seat, then turned and came face to face with Andrew.

"Why are you snooping around in my car?" he asked, as he put emphasis on the words "my car." At first, her heart was pounding rapidly from the shock of his unexpected appearance, but as soon as she was over that she let him have it.

"How could you do this?" She was shaking her head and stepping backwards, still afraid of what he might do.

"It's not what you think, Karina. Don't overreact." He reached for her hand, but she was still trembling and pulled away.

"How dare you act like it's nothing? I'm not some stupid little girl. I know what that is." She stiffened as Andrew grabbed for her hand again and dragged her to the house.

"Let's take this inside. There are lots of nosey neighbours."

She didn't want to be alone with him, but they went inside and closed the door.

"That's just it. You know the situation with my kids. When did you plan to tell me?" Karina's voice was still escalating.

"I only do it once in a while to keep me calm. That's all—nothing more." He wiped away his expression of anger and changed it to a no-big-deal reaction.

"That explains why you act so strangely. Don't lie to me. You think I am so naïve because I have never seen drugs, but I know more than you think. My Dad has always told me that heroin is the devil's advocate. It makes people go crazy in the head and that terrifies me. I don't want you here. You have to go." She was infuriated and didn't plan to back down.

"Where's your Daddy now, Karina?" Andrew had already heard stories about Lloyd and knew how sensitive Karina was about her father. Then he took a step closer and leaned toward her without breaking his glance from hers. "You need me. Your family isn't here and you have no one. If I go, you will be all alone again. You'll be begging for me to come back, because that's all you have to keep your bed warm at night." She knew it was true, but she couldn't stand to hear him gloat.

Andrew had no place to go himself, but he didn't want Mom to know how much his addiction had taken up his share of the rent and most of his possessions. He didn't tell Mom that his landlord had recently served him with an eviction notice. He only had another two weeks left before he was faced with sleeping in his car.

"I guess it's what you call a no-win situation," Mom broke the silence. "No matter what you say, Andrew, it's not enough to make me change my mind." Mom's emotions leaped between anger and rage as they haggled back and forth all afternoon.

At the end of the day, Andrew felt battered from the long, drawn-out fight.

"It's not a habit and I can stop right now," Andrew lied, and then he gathered up his stuff as he closed the door behind him.

More than anything, Mom wanted to believe the words that fell from Andrew's lips. Andrew was barely inches from his car when the truth hit Mom: Andrew was a good actor, but he couldn't fool her. He was a junkie.

In the weeks ahead, Mom had to admit that Andrew was right. She missed him and hated being alone. She had no one. She couldn't afford to take her kids and visit her mother whenever she felt the urge. Getting away from her father and husband was great, but she hadn't anticipated that she would miss her siblings so much. Especially Latisha and Don who made her so mad at times she could spit, but she loved them no matter what.

Call it intuition or a sixth sense, but even at the tender young age of three, I sensed something was wrong with Mom. There was this particular time, I recall, that she took me out on a dark rainy night. We had left our suite to go across the busy street from our house. Mom was holding my hand as we hurried to a gas station. A huge neon sign lit up the entire corner. The darkness scared me, so I stayed close to her, but I still didn't feel safe. We stood inside a phone booth while she dropped her change into the slot of the coin box.

She was crying but I didn't understand what was bothering her because I was so little. Her period hadn't come and she knew why. She was pregnant. She called Andrew, but the operator said that his line was out of service. She called the manager of his apartment and was told that he had evicted Andrew.

"Evicted?" Mom could have hurled something right there on the spot. She was having his baby and if she didn't find Andrew, he would never be part of the picture. She called all his friends and asked them to find Andrew.

Andrew was shocked but grateful for the message from his friend. He sat at the bar, feeling anxious to get out of there. The relationship had been a lot more important than he had wanted to believe. He missed Karina and it was seventh heaven knowing he had a second chance. He had never figured that she would reconsider. He was ready to run back into her arms but there was no need to rush it. Better to give it a few days and make her really sweat. He swallowed his beer and pushed the glass toward the bartender.

14: Karina and Andrew and the Four of Us

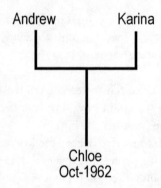

Andrew   Karina

Chloe
Oct-1962

Mom was physically exhausted. Her kids came with built-in alarm clocks that went off no later than 6:00 a.m. I can recall having done something to make her mad only once during one of those early mornings. It's not one of my favourite memories; I can still see my mother's angry face.

Josh and I had got up early and snooped through the cupboards until we found the peanut butter. We must have been quiet as mice, because Mom was sleeping on the couch while we raided the fridge for jam. We climbed on top of the counter and I held the jar while Josh twisted it open. We used our fingers as a scoop. Large blobs of jelly dropped onto our pyjamas, but that wasn't a problem; we just took them off.

The jar slipped out of our grip and smashed on the floor. Mom leaped to her feet and almost stepped on the glass. We both got a scolding and a smack before she scrubbed our hands and faces.

In the heat of the moment came a knocking on the door. Before Mom could stop me from turning the handle, there was Andrew looking in the doorway. Andrew looked around in the middle of all our chaos. It must have been quite a sight: Josh and me running around in underpants, and Sheila's feet stained a purplish-red. Mom was still on her knees in her soiled nightie with her long messy hair hanging down to the floor. The walls, counters, and flooring were smudged everywhere with brown and red sticky goo.

"Hi, I heard that you were looking for me."

"Please sit down." Mom motioned him to a chair where he was safe from any splinters of glass.

"I need to talk, but first I have to clean this up before one of the kids get hurt. Make some coffee or tea." She said and continued until the kitchen was clean.

"There's no easy way to say this so I am going to be straight on the level. I'm pregnant." She held her breath and let it out slowly. Andrew's eyes came alive but he remained silent.

"Say something, please." Mom was allowing the silence to eat her up. What was going on in his head?

"Wow! That's why you wanted to see me? Because you're pregnant?" Andrew's happy smile vanished. "What do you want me to do?" he asked.

"You have to ask?"

"You want me to marry you?" Andrew was clueless to what was next.

"No. Damn it. I want you to be a father. Do whatever fathers are supposed to do. Okay?" she asked, feeling more upset that he had to ask.

"I'm not clean, but if you give me some time I will change. Honestly, babe. I will." Andrew's confession was weakening Mom's sympathies.

"I need to make this clear that you can't be a part of the baby's life unless you get help." She dreaded giving the ultimatum; she was afraid he wouldn't pass the test.

Andrew pulled out every trick up his sleeve to convince her that he would be on the level with her.

In Mom's ninth month of pregnancy, we had our first visit from social services. The woman came early in the morning and knocked relentlessly.

"Do you have any idea why I'm here?" she asked.

Before Mom could speak, the woman made her way into the kitchen. She looked around without consideration to my mother's discomfort.

"One of your neighbours has phoned in a nasty complaint."

"Against me?" Mom had no idea why anyone would want to give her trouble. By now, Josh and I were full of questions and telling the woman all kinds of stories.

"Kids, go in the bedroom and play." Mom gave us "the look," but we ignored her and continued to be a distraction. The woman was pretty and it was fun to have a visitor.

"I will make some pancakes if you go in your room." Mom was searching Josh's face.

"Pancakes!" we screamed and ran into the bedroom, slamming the door behind us. In our young years, we considered Mom's pancakes to be the best in the world, because she made them for us.

"You were seen drinking beer in your backyard with a man." Miss Renault waited for a confession.

"I don't see what the problem is. Why can't we have a cold beer outside? It's hot out and we aren't out in public disturbing anyone," Mom said. Her mind trailed off as she had a flashback of Andrew holding a big paper bag and two beers. They had both gone out to the patio and sat on chairs to sip a cold beer. Now, her belly protruded past her chest, but the social worker wasn't there to condone her for drinking a beer during her pregnancy. In those days, no one knew anything about alcohol affecting infants.

"It's illegal to drink in public unless you go to a tavern."

The woman left, but not without reminding Mom that she had the power to intervene and take her kids at any time. Mom was very upset. She couldn't believe this woman would dare to threaten her.

"Who does this woman think she is and what does this have to do with my kids?" Mom asked.

The woman next door always stared at Mom like she was a dirty piece of trash, so Mom wanted to move to the other side of town and get us away from there. Her gut reaction was to get rid of Andrew, but she didn't want to punish him for her mistakes. The relationship was on and off. She knew Andrew had stayed clean and he was trying to do better.

At the end of October, Mom had a baby girl and named her Chloe. The baby fascinated Josh and me. She was so small that she couldn't do anything for herself. Mom was breastfeeding her. Josh stood so close to Mom that she sprayed him with breast milk. He giggled and asked her to do it again and that made her laugh too. Josh bragged about being the oldest. When we were out, he loved to tell people that he was the big brother.

In December, Mom decorated our suite for the holidays. She warned us that we had to be good if we wanted Santa to visit with his reindeer. On Christmas Eve, we were so excited and we didn't want to go to bed, but Santa wouldn't come until we were all sleeping.

The next morning, we could hardly believe our eyes. We circled around the tree, staring at the packages. We didn't even have a chimney, but somehow Santa came and he brought dolls, trucks, and building blocks.

On New Year's Day, Mom and Andrew were going to a party. It was Mom's first outing since Chloe was born. All the sitters were already hired, except for this one boy who lived a couple of doors over. He was fifteen and he hadn't taken a sitting job, so Mom offered to pay him well if he was interested in watching us three kids overnight. The party was only an hour's drive out of town, but Mom wasn't comfortable with leaving Chloe, because she was only two months old. She bundled up the baby and took her along.

During the night, there was a whiteout; the highways were closed because of snow. There was no possible way that Mom could get back that day before the roads were plowed. She called her landlord who lived upstairs and gave him a message for the babysitter that she would be back the following morning on January 3. That day, the buses were back on the roads. Mom couldn't wait another day. She got up early and stood at the bus stop waiting in the freezing cold with baby Chloe.

The bus was slow and turned down many side roads, causing Mom to feel more anxiety about her children. When the wheels rolled onto her street, she pulled down on the cord for the bus to stop and got off.

It was a long walk uphill and her arms ached. Her face stung from the cold air as it pricked her cheeks. By the time Mom reached the door, her fingers were numb to the bone.

"Hello, it's Mommy. Josh? Eugenea? Sheila? Where are you kids?" she called out, but there was no sound. She waited for the patter of little feet to come running; there was nothing but dead air. Mom put Chloe down on the couch and ran from room to room, calling our names. A little shiver ran up her spine. Something was wrong, terribly wrong. Then she ran back to Chloe, picked her up, and went upstairs to the landlord's door. She heard his footsteps approaching the foyer. Her eyes focused on the knob as it turned as slowly as the hands on a clock.

"Have you seen my kids?" she asked the landlord.

"Yes. Your babysitter took them to his mother's house," the landlord told Mom as he stood in the doorway trying to shield himself from the bitter cold.

"Did you tell him that I couldn't get back because of the storm?" Karina asked, feeling there was more to this.

"Yes. There was a lot of crying and then I saw him leave with the kids. I'm really sorry to tell you, but I think the babysitter's mother called social services and told them to come and take the kids away. I saw a big car come to her house. There was a woman and a sheriff. I'm really sorry," he said. He crossed his arms over his chest to keep his body heat in.

Mom stared with disbelief. She nearly squeezed the life out of Chloe as she turned and ran in panic. The landlord called after her but she didn't stop. Mom headed straight to the home of the sitter and repeatedly bashed her fist against the door.

Both the babysitter and his mother hid inside, refusing to open the door. Mom ran around to the back door and banged harder. Still, they didn't answer, so she went to the window, but the drapes were suddenly closed. So Mom screamed and begged for them to answer… but nothing.

She went back to her place and laid Chloe in the crib. Then she lay on the couch and bawled hysterically. So many questions raced through her head. She could not believe this was happening and she was full of sadness, anger, and remorse.

Andrew returned home. He had no idea what was going on. He had come in the doorway to find Mom throwing her things and screaming. Something had cut into her hand, but she didn't feel it. All she could feel was grief and anger.

"Karina, my God, what's wrong with you? Why are you doing this?" Andrew rushed to her and grabbed her hands. He carefully wrapped her hand in a dish-towel. Andrew hadn't crossed her mind since she had left the party.

"It's your fault this happened. How could I let you back into my life?" she cried. Her fists banged against him. Andrew pulled her close and held her tightly until she slid down and dropped on her knees.

"What happened? Tell me, what happened?"

Mom knew that Andrew had never seen her this way and it was frightening him. She had begged him to take her home, but he had refused to drive on the highway. He claimed it was unsafe. She had insisted on travelling in the snow and had left without him.

"They took my kids," she sobbed.

"Who took your kids? What are you talking about?" Andrew looked around. He was so caught up in Karina's hysterics that he hadn't noticed that she was alone. He heard the baby crying, yet he felt the panic rise in his chest. His eyes scanned the room until he spotted the infant lying in the crib. His baby was safe and sound, but the other three were missing.

"Where are they?" Andrew asked.

Mom spilled her guts and sobbed until her eyes had swollen into a blistery red.

Andrew wanted so badly to help, but there was nothing he could do. He felt terrible, but there was no way that Mom could deal with him or anything else. Andrew knelt down and put his arms around Mom and promised to help her get the kids back. But what could he do? Especially when he was part of the problem in the first place. Mom was afraid that Andrew would make things worse, so she told him to leave her alone. She couldn't bear another second of him.

Andrew didn't leave. He stood waiting as Mom and Chloe cried from different ends of the room. Finally, he slipped his hands under Chloe and held her like a china plate. He wasn't very good at holding a baby, but he had to try and get one of them to stop crying.

"I think she's hungry. What should I do?" he asked.

"I just want to be alone. Can you understand that?" Mom cried out, ignoring the question. Andrew got Chloe settled and put her back in the crib.

The next morning, Mom was exhausted, weak, and loaded down with the conclusion that she had failed her children. Nevertheless, she forced herself out of bed. She had never imagined that the silence of her children would be such torture. Although she was overcome with her loss and didn't know what to do, she had to work fast in order to find her kids.

Mom stood outside her neighbour's home, waiting in the cold with her baby. The door creaked open and a short little woman stared out.

"Could I please use your phone? My landlord is out and I don't have a phone in my place," Mom asked.

"I heard the rumours about you losing your kids." The woman's face was peering out from behind the door as though Mom had some sort of illness. "I can't help you," she added and shut the door.

Mom believed that all the neighbours would give her the same rejection. Regaining her composure was not going to be easy but she had to find strength within herself. When the landlord returned, he let Mom in to his place and she called the local orphanages and children's emergency shelters. After much searching, she didn't find her kids, but she was told by social services that she would have to wait until February 12 before she was allowed to know of our whereabouts and be given permission for any visitation. Six weeks to wait.

Mom woke up every day to find the box of toys still waiting for our return. Everything was left in its place. The empty beds were still cold. At night, she woke up in sweats and went into fits of crying. She had terrible nightmares of her children screaming as they were being abducted and tossed into a big black car. She could see crying faces looking out of the back window as she ran behind. She saw herself as a baby and her own mother reaching out to her.

How could she go on living without her children? She had walked the same path as her mother Elaine and shared the unbearable grief that her mother had also suffered. But this was much worse, because she would live through it twice: first separated from her mother and second separated from her children.

Would they take her youngest baby away as well if she brought Chloe to see her other children? Mom was so afraid to hire another sitter and decided that hiding the baby was the only way to protect Chloe.

She took her baby to her mother, then rode the three-hour bus trip back to Calgary and visit her other three children. Only her mother Elaine could be trusted, because she was the only person who understood since it had also happened to her. Forty-three days passed before Mom was granted approval to visit us. The big day came and she was excited—so blissfully happy—to see us, yet terrified at the same time. She dressed up as neat as a pin. As she entered the doors of the shelter, she prayed for a second chance to prove she was a good mother.

15: Karina and Social Services

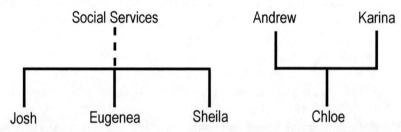

The social worker wore a heavily starched white uniform that buttoned up the front. It barely showed any form except where the narrow belt cinched in her waist. The white stockings and shoes made her look more like a nurse than a guardian. Her stiff hair was pulled back into a high bun and she looked like all the other women there.

"I am the head matron here. Follow me and I'll take you to see the children." The matron spoke as if the children were alien to our mother, no longer connected. Was she making a negative observation? Mom sensed the woman had drawn her own conclusions long before they met.

She led Karina into a room with a small window and closed the door. There was nothing friendly about the place. It looked like a hospital. The walls had no pictures or anything to give a warm lived-in look. Mom felt so sorry for her children.

"When the children come through the door, you must be very calm. Please do not upset the children; they have been though a lot and are still adjusting. So far we haven't had any behavioural problems and we need to keep it that way."

Mom's first reaction was defensive. What is she talking about? My children don't have behavioural problems. What kind of place is this? Maybe it's not an orphanage; maybe it's an institution. It certainly looks like an institution. This woman thinks that she is better than me. She is looking over me like I'm something dirty on the bottom of her shoe. It doesn't matter—I'll do whatever it takes as long as I get to see my babies, Mom thought to herself.

She looked down at her feet feeling ashamed and nervous. She thought about Chloe and the long bus ride to her mother's farm and she remembered her mother's last words as Elaine waved goodbye from the gate.

"Karina, keep your chin up. Be strong and don't let them get you down. Remember who you are and be proud."

The door opened and Mom stood up to greet us. Her heart was melting as we came into the office and began running to her for affection. To us, she was the most wonderful woman we had ever known.

"Mommy! Mommy!" All three of us called out with excitement. We threw ourselves against her body, each of us trying to get a piece of her.

"Look at all of you. You're so big." She stared into our faces as she smiled, fighting back the desire to cry.

"My babies have grown so big," she said, turning to the matron, who was looking down in disgust. Mom turned back and lovingly gathered us into her fold, wanting to shield us from the hostile eyes.

"Please, Mommy, take us home. We don't want to be here," Josh begged.

"I bet you have made some new friends here," she said, changing the subject.

Josh stayed on the topic. "Mom, we want to go home."

"So what do you do all day? Do you get to colour, paint, or play any games?" Mom asked, hoping to stir him away from leading us all into an emotional turmoil.

"Me, too. I want to go home too, Mommy," I began pleading as I clung to her.

The social worker sat quietly watching and taking notes. She never left the room because Mom was not allowed to be alone with us.

"I can't take you home today, but I will soon," Mom said with motherly calmness, but her hands were shaking.

"Why can't we go home? We don't like it here. We don't like this place." Josh protested as he defended his siblings' rights.

"I want to go home with you. I want to see Chloe," he said softly, his big brown eyes fixed on hers. "Eugenea needs you. She's always crying for you, Mommy. I heard her screaming for you and it made me cry, too," he admitted but his little voice trembled. He was working so hard to protect his little sisters. He had taken the responsibility upon himself to hold up the fort. Mom's heart was breaking as she thought about how important it was to her little boy.

Luckily, not one of us asked where Chloe was, and Mom didn't dare to talk about her. She wrestled with thoughts of storming out with all three of us. Could she make a run for it? How far would she get with three small kids and no getaway car? The whole idea was stupid. She would never see her kids again if she were caught.

"We'll be good. I promise we'll be good." Josh was speaking for all of us.

"You are such good kids. You didn't do anything wrong, Honey." Mom's guilt surfaced and she choked on the words as tears laced her eyelids. No matter what kind of explanation she gave, nothing worked. We became more agitated and the crying turned to wailing.

"Excuse me, I am going to have to shorten your visit. The children are not handling it well. It is not good for them to see you right now," the matron interrupted.

"But I am allowed to have my hour with them. I've only been here a few minutes," Mom argued.

"I'm sorry, but these are the rules. You will have to make another appointment with the front desk. It is time for you to say goodbye to the children." The matron stood like a jail guard still holding her steno pad.

"Just give me ten more minutes. I haven't been allowed to see them for weeks. Please… that's all I'm asking."

"You're upsetting the children. Can't you see that?" The matron stood her ground.

"Mommy, you can't leave us here," Josh interrupted as he swallowed hard to keep his composure.

"I can't. I'm not allowed," Mom said as she turned back to Josh. She didn't know any other way to tell us. She looked at the matron again. "Please, let me take them. I'm sorry. Let me prove to you that I can be the perfect…"

"You have to leave now." The matron cut her off. Her voice soured with rejection as she dismissed Karina's pleas.

"No, Mommy. Don't listen to her," Josh was yelling.

"Josh, Honey, I have to go and I need you to be brave. Your little sisters need you. I'll be back soon." She swiped at the tears that rolled down her cheeks out of control.

Josh was always the bravest, but this time he didn't want to be courageous; he only wanted to go home with his Mommy and sisters. Tears burned the corners of our eyes.

"Madam, you have to go this minute. Don't make me call for security," the matron snapped.

"They won't let you go with me." Mom had to come out with the truth. There was no option. She had no choice but to turn her back on us and leave. She pulled away and stood up.

"Mommy, don't go. Please don't go." Josh and I were now screaming the same chant. Mom bent down to kiss us, but Josh and I saw the aggravated social worker coming for us and we clawed at our mother. Her hair hung over and I could smell her sweet scent as it draped over me.

"Let go of them," the social worker barked. "If you don't let go, I will call security." She began tugging at us.

"I can't. Please don't make me leave them," Mom cried out and pulled us closer.

"Security! I need security now!" the woman bellowed at the top of her lungs. Within a matter of a second, the door flew open and a flood of women entered.

"Get out," they ordered.

Tears spilled and rolled out of control as Mom tried to move forward, but we wrapped ourselves tightly around her legs. With each step, we weighed her down, as though she were in a pool and trying to run. Slowly she dragged her feet across the floor with three little bodies clinging to her legs.

We screamed, kicked, and pleaded hysterically as we slid across the linoleum floor. It took an army of social workers to wrench us apart and hold us down. Mom looked back to see us fighting to break free from our captors. She was escorted by security and the doors closed, leaving her babies to go on without her.

Mom had barely made it down the concrete steps when she heard the doors lock behind her. She turned and ran back. The knob didn't budge. She planted herself on the stairs and heard her own screaming and the screams that came from inside the walls. Her hands washed in her own tears. She pried herself away from the ugly view of the building that held her children like animals. She ran into the street and crossed to the sidewalk.

Night came. Mom was still walking. Her arms around her middle as she tried to shield out the cold. Her lips were frozen and cracked, but she couldn't go home. She wanted to give up and die, but she had a baby to look after. Could she go on living with only Chloe?

16: Karina and Lloyd

She was dog-tired, but sleep was not a priority. There was still hope. Mom wanted to hold her pride, but she couldn't afford to be stubborn. She had to ask her father for money so she could hire a lawyer and get her kids back. Lloyd was only one province away. All she had to do was ask.

Her children's lives were at stake and no amount of humbling was too much. Lloyd would shame and guilt her with quite a tongue-lashing. It would make her feel worse, but she would suck it up and take the punches. She went to a pay phone and called him collect.

"Sir, you have an emergency collect call from Karina. Do you accept the charges?" The operator asked Lloyd.

"Yes." Lloyd waited. His breathing deepened and he huffed in annoyance.

Mom knew they were off to a bad start.

"Hello, Daddy," she spoke up. Her mind was whirling, unsure of what to hope for.

"Where have you been hiding for the past year and a half, or has it been longer?" He wasn't wasting any time on small talk. "You must be in trouble, Karina. Why else would you be calling? What is it this time? Divorce? Another pregnancy? A quickie marriage?"

There was a long silence.

"Well, what is it? I know you had another kid and it's not your husband's baby," he barked at her.

Mom was so shocked she nearly dropped the phone. How did he know? The conversation was going much worse than she anticipated. She would never be able to ask him for money. She couldn't back out; she would have to go with the plan.

"Dad, please, I need your help. I made a big mistake. Social services took my kids away and I have to go to court. I won't get them back unless I have a lawyer." Mom waited for him to answer, avoiding the word "money."

"You're expecting me to bail you out of your problems? Is that it? Shame on you, sleeping around, acting like a slut, and now your kids have been picked up by social services," he hammered away at her.

"It's not my fault, I tried so…" Mom cried, but Lloyd cut in.

"It is your fault. You had a man living in your house while the kids were there. It's against the law. Don't you know that? Are you so stupid that you have to be told everything?"

Mom cried.

"Well, you made your bed. Now you can sleep in it. You are going to figure out how to solve this yourself."

He dropped the phone into the cradle.

She was convinced that Lloyd had hated her from the moment she was born. For the most part her life had been a living hell with or without him, and it was obvious that Lloyd wasn't about to make up for it now or any time soon, if ever. She could accept the fact that he didn't want to show any love or support to her, but how could he reject his grandchildren? Didn't he realize that he would lose them too? How could he turn his grandchildren away?

17: Karina and Chloe

Over the next days, Mom was aware that Andrew had fallen in love with her. She wasn't sure if it was out of sympathy or what, but she would never be happy with him again. A big part of her hated Andrew. Because of him, she had lost her children. It wasn't his fault, but his face was still an agonizing reminder.

Andrew couldn't handle Karina's rejection and in no time he was shooting up. It was only once, but Mom knew better and she cut Andrew out of her life.

The pressure was too much. Mom packed up Chloe and disappeared. She went into hiding so that social services would not find Chloe and take her too. Hiding the baby and dealing with the depressing supervised visits, Mom was losing faith. Every time she came to the emergency shelter, the visit was cut short and the ending was the same. She was forced to leave with three children screaming as though the end of time was coming to take us away. And, in some way, it was.

Social services told Mom that if she found a place to live, they would keep us until she was settled in, but she would have to sign some papers giving her consent. Folding the forms, they pointed to the line indicating where her signature would go.

In her eagerness to be united eventually with her babies, she grabbed the pen and happily signed the agreement. At last, the social worker was on her side and willing to give Mom a chance to prove herself. Mom got a cute little apartment, and filled it with clothes, furniture, food, and toys. Then she called social services to plead for our return.

"Your children won't be coming back. Don't you remember? You signed them over to us." The woman from the government office informed her.

"Yes, I know, but you said that was only temporary until I got a place and could prove that I can take care of them."

"No. You misunderstood. Didn't you read the contract? You signed papers consenting to give up your parental rights, so that makes your children Wards of the State. That means they are legally adoptable. You signed your kids up for adoption," the voice finished.

"No. No, I didn't. It wasn't an adoption consent form. I would never agree to give up my kids." Mom was starting to panic.

"I have the adoption paper right in front of me and it is a signed document in your handwriting, giving legal permission to the Province of Alberta to release these children from your care permanently. We need your address, so we can send you a copy," the woman said curtly.

Mom wasn't sure if she was trying to provoke her or just weeding out an address to scoop Chloe as well.

"I need to come for my visitation," Mom said, feeling disoriented. How could I have been so stupid to trust that woman? Or anyone? The government had the ultimate power to take control, to manipulate if needed, Mom thought to herself.

"We have to inform you that all visitation rights are now terminated," the matron added.

There was another long silence as Mom tried to absorb the information that was drawing her closer to the brink of insanity.

"When do I get to say goodbye?" Mom was sobbing.

"You don't. The children are no longer with us. They have already been placed into foster care," the social worker said.

Mom was thinking back to that day when she was given directions where to sign and remembered how the matron was rushing her, by implying that the children were anxious to see her. Now, Mom could recall that her kids had no idea she was there and that was confusing at the time, but it all made sense now. The social workers would do whatever necessary to remove the children permanently, even if it meant deception.

"You already sent them away? Foster homes! You mean they're not together?" Mom didn't understand.

"Josh and Eugenea are in one home and Sheila is in another," the woman explained.

"Oh, my God, you separated them? How could you?" Mom was crying hysterically.

"If you wish to appeal, you need to attain a lawyer and take up your matters in court. Until then, we will see you in court for the finalization."

"I don't believe it… you tricked me into giving up my kids? It was you who folded the paper in half. You did that on purpose so I would believe you. I trusted you when you deliberately tricked me into signing."

Now it was becoming clear to Mom that social services had no intention of ever giving her back her kids.

She felt numb. The blood rushed to her head and suddenly the room circled around her. The phone slipped from her fingers and banged against the wall.

The woman on the other end of the line was calling, but Mom couldn't answer. She couldn't move. The shock hit her so hard that she couldn't find the strength to mutter a sound.

She could no longer hold a thought as her knees gave out and a blanket of darkness silenced her. Each day moved into the next as Mom slid into a well of depression. With every passing reminder of her missing children, the pain grew like a creeping vine that squeezed around her heart with every twist. If it weren't for Chloe, she might have given up.

On court day, Mom arrived unprepared. She could not afford an attorney. All sorts of accusations and lies went around the room. She couldn't believe what was happening. She kept saying, "It's not true" and "I didn't do that." No one would help her, except Elaine, who wrote to the government asking to see and care for her grandchildren. But she was poor, old, and not what they considered a good provider.

Given the way Mom's life had been going, it was not surprising that she turned to drinking. However hard she tried, alcohol was the only way to mask her feelings; it was temporary, but it sure felt good.

Mom had no confidence in the justice system. She believed that her children had become part of the big dollar market of adoption. However painful and bitter, she had to move on with her life. Mom eventually met her future husband Bart.

"Karina, you are the most beautiful girl in the world," Bart would tell her over and over. He loved Karina and he didn't care about her past mistakes. They got married and moved to Toronto, taking Chloe with them. It was a sad experience for Mom to move away from Calgary with only one child.

18: Louis

By this time, Louis had gotten his divorce papers finalized, and he was able to move on and get past the pain Karina had put him through. She had deserted him and his children. How could he forgive her for that? The government was punishing him for Karina's actions despite the fact that he had had nothing to do with her decisions.

He didn't even know that Karina was out of the province until he got the call from Child Services. They told him that his kids were in custody and the only way he would ever see or get his kids back would be if he went to Calgary, Alberta. They also implied that he would have to be there a long time, fighting for custody, and it would take so much time he would lose his job. Without a job, they reminded him that there was no way he would get us back. They were letting him know that it was a damned-if-he-does and damned-if-he-doesn't situation, and not to mess with them.

The ministry wanted Louis to sign an adoption release for his children to become permanent wards of the government, and give allowance for adoption if possible. They needed signatures from both parents. Louis took a lot of harassing from the government, but he never signed a single paper.

Part Three: Eugenea

19: Me

Mom told me later about that particular January 3. I did not remember going to the babysitter's house or the car ride to the orphanage. My social worker made notes though, which I now have to fall back on.

Before I arrived at the emergency shelter, I was stripped down and physically examined by a physician and a social worker. There were black and blue bruises over my back that went all the way to my feet. The complete inner sides of my legs and forearms to the wrists were covered in bruises, with dried blood in my left ear. The doctor and my social worker asked me what had happened to me. Why was I covered in bruises?

"The babysitter was mad and he hurt me." I told them. I had tried to get away from the babysitter by hiding under the bed.

20: Josh and Me, Mr. and Mrs. Ross

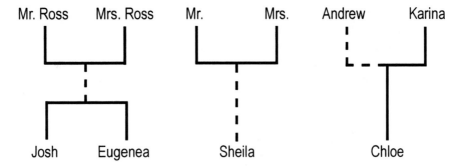

The first foster home started us off on the wrong foot. Josh and I arrived unaware that Sheila would not be with us. We had no idea what had happened to our sister; she was simply gone and that was it. It was almost as if we imagined that she even existed. I missed my little sister so much, even though no one spoke of her. We didn't understand why the parents were telling us what to do.

During our stay, we played and fought like regular siblings. Josh was older and naturally a bit tougher; he knew how to get what he wanted. I didn't fight back or if I did I usually lost. We shared most of our toys, except for the red slide projector. That was a big market toy; every kid wanted one and we had to share it. When Josh wasn't around, I would take my chances and run off into the bedroom with it. Then, I would hold it up and look at the colourful slides.

"Hey, it's my turn. Give it to me," Josh tried to snatch it and I would quickly hide it behind my back.

I backed away, not willing to part with it, and we ended up in the hallway scrabbling in a tug of war that sent me sailing down the three stairs that led to the living room. The sibling fighting was more than Mrs. Ross could handle. She lied to my social worker that I was wetting the bed, but it was dry. We never had this issue. To add to the problem, if she scolded me, I would freeze, then stare at her and not respond because she was not my mother. It was weird to have a stranger filling my mother's role. She disciplined by shutting me into a room and I would get scared. I didn't like to be alone, so I would hide under the bed. The social worker tried to make Mrs. Ross understand that she was working with a child who, in her terms, had had a deprived and poor life.

"Please try to accept this child. If you are willing to be a loving and affectionate person toward her, eventually her problems will work themselves out," the worker said.

"Well I don't believe that Eugenea's problems are emotional. I'm quite certain that she is retarded." Mrs. Ross didn't have the compassion or time to deal with children who were suffering emotionally from losing their family. In less than two months, she split Josh and me apart. Mrs. Ross was booked for surgery, so she asked a family who lived across the street to take me in. Although she knew nothing about the family, she went ahead with her plan.

It was total confusion. Josh and I were no longer allowed any contact, even though we could see each other across the street from our respective front windows.

21: Mr. and Mrs. Brockton

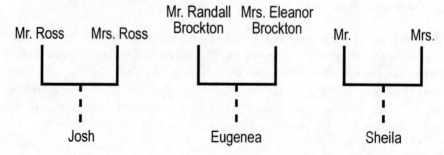

My new "mother," Eleanor Brockton, was a serious clout of a woman who never smiled. When she was in a tolerable mood, I was allowed to colour and watch *The Friendly Giant* on TV. I still remember how my legs extended to the front of the couch cushion. The colouring book lay out like a newspaper with my feet peeking out at the edge. Eleanor and I didn't exchange any love. It was a house of rules and authority.

If I talked, played, or laughed too loudly, Eleanor would burst into a rage. She didn't spank; she grabbed whatever was closest, like my arm or hair. Then she would take me down with one agonizing blow after another. When it was over, I hid from her and refused to call her "Mommy." That showed little progress. She told the social worker that I had so much hatred for my own mother. She added that I hated anyone who reminded me of Karina, but she was mistaken. It was Eleanor whom I hated, not my mother. Although I shared a room with Eleanor's two girls, I was lonely. I slept in an old army-style hospital bed that looked exactly like the ones in the orphanage. After the move, I had nightmares, and sometimes I did wet the bed, and my so-called mother went ballistic.

When she found the wet sheets, I was yanked out of bed and hauled into the bathroom where I was stripped down. I cried, but she was hell-bent on revenge. With all her force, she plunged my head into the toilet and held me under as I struggled. While Eleanor was over top of me, my tears mixed with the water. All a while, she berated me, but I couldn't make out her words. All I heard was the roar of the toilet flushing.

Alone in my room, I stared out at the house across the street. There he was— my brother Josh. I could see him making a snowman with his "family." It was near Christmas; they had decorated with coloured lights and there was a sparkly tree in their window. Eleanor had no tree or lights, so I knew there wasn't going to be any celebrating. As Josh played in the snow, he looked so happy. In the middle of all his excitement, he saw me and stood there looking for a long time.

When the snow had nearly melted away, I knew well about the danger inside the house, but I didn't know about the dangers outside. Running away from Eleanor meant survival, so I got on my three-wheeler tricycle and left. That day had been particularly awful, so I didn't care where I went as long as I could get away from her. Within a few blocks, I looked back and, to my horror, Eleanor was there. She was only a few feet behind me.

She called for me to stop, but I pedaled faster. She overcame the bike while I was on it. She pinched my arm so tightly that I screamed. She hammered down the street with me on one side and the bike on the other. The second we got home, she tore down the steps to the basement and I was forced to go with her. My feet banged and scraped along the wooden steps to the floor below.

Eleanor grabbed my wrist and swung me around like a rag doll. I swung back and forth in her grip, which whipped me from side to side like a dog on a leash. It was terrifying as I tried to grab onto anything, but there was nothing to grab on to. Then she let go and I flew into an open space and crashed to the concrete floor. At first, I was frozen with shock. In the next second, I wanted to get away quickly, but there was pain racing through my body.

When I saw her coming for me, I ignored the ache and scurried to a corner. I tried to inch away, but I had nowhere to go. I huddled into a ball and tried to become invisible. Eleanor reached for my leg and I felt the pierce of her nails dig into my ankle. She dragged me across the floor, toward the middle of the room. The brunt of her anger and hate continued into a second round. The span of the room whirled around me with Eleanor in the centre. Again, she let go and I was sent airborne.

I couldn't help but scream louder as I hit the floor. My crying made it worse. She shook me so hard that my teeth rattled. She wanted me to shut up. When she let go, I shrank away. I didn't struggle as her shadow passed by. It was done and she went upstairs.

I stayed there trying to understand why this woman had never touched me with kindness. From that day on, the basement became Eleanor's little dungeon of discipline. Nothing could stop her and no one could directly see what was going on.

During the months of February and March, Eleanor and Randall Brockton had decided to give me up, but twice they changed their minds. They didn't want to keep me, but something was holding them back from letting me go. Years later, I often wondered if it was something to do with the monthly payments that made it easier to keep me around. Eleanor told the social worker that I started chanting words of hate and hit myself a great deal when I was in bed.

The worker looked at my face and asked what had happened. Eleanor told her that I was gouging my face with my nails. She complained that I ate almost nothing and was losing weight. She stated that she had stopped using the cold-water treatment.

Her husband was aware that there were critical problems between Eleanor and me. He booked off work early on a Friday and went alone to see the social worker.

He explained to the worker that his wife was dunking my head under water and it frightened the entire family. He felt I was in danger and he was afraid that something drastic would happen if his wife were left to care for me. The social worker offered to come immediately to either remove me or see if she could calm things down. Randall said he was going to be home on the weekend, so he could handle the situation until Monday.

The social worker arrived as promised. Mrs. Brockton handed me over along with all my clothes, including a bag of new socks. I wondered if she was trying to show some sort of remorse or affection. She clearly could not show it physically; she didn't even fake it for the social worker. From the day I met Eleanor until the moment of departure, I never saw her smile; she was a miserable woman. The social worker took my hand and I willingly went along, knowing I was finally free from her.

22: Me

As for me, things weren't going to get better for some time. Thankfully, I had been spared from a childhood of more abuse from Eleanor, but I had nowhere to go, except the shelter. My social worker let me sit on the passenger side of her car. As we drove along, it never occurred to me that I was leaving Josh forever.

"Will I ever go back to the Brocktons?" I asked, still not aware of what was happening.

"No, I don't think so. Did you like living with the Brocktons?" she asked and glanced in my direction.

"Yes, I think so, but not the mother." I frowned.

"What are your feelings about the Mom and Dad?" she asked.

"I like the Dad. I don't like Eleanor, the mother."

"Why?"

"I don't like her; I just don't," I added. "Sometimes I sit and stare at the mother when I hate her. I like to hate her."

"What does the mother do when you are hating her?" the worker asked in curiosity.

"Oh, she gets mad," I spoke up, but I never told her about Eleanor's abuse. "I hate the mother. She is mean," I said, sensing I was out of harm's way but feeling uneasy at the thought of Eleanor.

"How do you feel when you hate Eleanor?" she asked.

"I'm not sure. I forget." I didn't want to talk about it anymore. My social worker kept a note of our conversation and added to my file that I was a most interesting child. We stopped in front of a large building that I didn't recognize until I was inside. After thirteen months, I was going back to the children's orphanage.

The shelter was very clean, orderly, and smelled heavily of disinfectant and ivory soap, just the way I remembered. Everyone knew this was a home for long-term kids, and I wanted out of that place. All the joy of my departure from Eleanor had been squelched. It was different, this time, because I came alone. Mom couldn't visit, because I was supposed to be adopted, and she didn't know that I was there.

"Please don't leave me here," I begged the social worker. "I don't want to stay here alone."

"You'll be okay. I will come back and get you as soon as I can." The social worker's face was soft and convincing, but I had seen that poker face before.

"No, take me with you."

"Eugenea, there are a lot of little children who would like to get a chance to play with you. You will make new friends here," she promised, like it was some kind of reward.

"I don't want friends; I want to go home," I said, though I wasn't sure where "home" was, or if there was such a place anymore. My social worker smiled and promised to be back soon, but that didn't win me over. I was scared it would be light years before I saw her again. How could she leave an abandoned child with nothing but a doll, a suitcase, and a bag of socks?

The matron took my hand and we went into a big foyer where she explained what was expected. All my belongings were stored away, so I had to wear the clothes provided. She picked a bunch of stuff out of a wall of cubbies that had everything from shirts to shoes.

I didn't fight her when she took away my baby doll. She promised I would get it back when I moved to another home. Just then, an alarm went off and dozens of children herded in from all directions. They went into a dining room that looked like a mess hall. Inside there were long rows of tables covered in linen.

The food arrived just as I was taken to a chair, but I didn't eat, so the attendant came and we left. We passed through a nursery with babies in iron cribs. At first, I thought that I would be sleeping there, but my room was next door and I felt badly, because I didn't want to sleep alone.

I had a private room with a square window in the door that was too high for me to see out. The attendant put me to bed and closed the door, and I cried in the dark as the sound of her shoes marched away. What a cheerless place. I shut down. I stopped talking as though I had turned into a mute. The social workers would try to get me to communicate, but I disconnected. The women in white were cleaning, dressing, changing beds, feeding babies, and I was there in the shadows. Bedtime was lonely and I always cried myself to sleep.

There, I lived a pipe dream that one day I would wake up to see my Mom in her pretty yellow dress sitting beside my bed. My Dad would be there as well and he would hold me in his big arms and then we would go home. Night after night, I had the same fantasy and I couldn't wait to wake up in the morning to the love of my parents.

But eventually, I realized they weren't coming, not ever. True or not, my childhood dreams swept me away to a wonderful place. My attendant could take my doll away, but not my memories. Like the time I remembered when Mom had taken us to the park. Sheila, Josh, and I had rolled and laughed on a grassy hill as Mom sat on a blanket watching. For some reason, that memory stuck and it gave me a fight-back attitude.

During the day, the attendants supervised the outdoor play area, but I had no interest in playing on the swings or slides because I was trying to get away. Every morning, I waited for the delivery truck to pull into the lane. As soon as the gate was open, I tried to slip through. The deliveryman balanced his groceries without letting me escape. No matter how hard I tried, I could not get out. It seemed hopeless and I thought I would be there forever, but then one day my social worker returned and I was so happy that I started talking right away.

"Are we going to see Josh?" I asked, growing more excited.

"Not today, but we are going for a drive. I have a family who wants to meet you and they have a little boy. His name is Rickie and he's the same age as you. Would you like to meet him?"

I agreed even though I felt disappointed, but anything was an improvement over where I was at the moment.

23: The Schafers

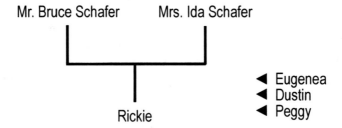

Ida, a friendly young mother, opened the door and invited us into her home. Her son Rickie was five years old, so we were the same age. We got along right away. However, I was not quite sure how this pertained to me. I didn't realize that I was moving to a new home. I was completely confused. Although I don't have much of a memory of my first night there, my reaction was quite miserable. When it was time for bed, I cried with great feeling. The more the family tried to comfort me, the worse it got. Eventually, Ida and her husband gave up and left the bedroom.

Rickie sat on the bed beside me and I opened up. I told him that I was scared his parents would shackle my hands and feet to the bed. Rickie's life changed forever when I cried about the pain of having been raped and beaten. He told me that I did not have to be scared anymore because his parents never harmed him.

It was a rocky start for everyone, especially when I refused to call my new parents "Mommy and Daddy." However, Ida did everything possible to make me feel safe and secure.

I had no toys, so Ida got a few second-hand dolls and sewed them a wardrobe of outfits. A few days later, she got a stroller and a crib for my new babies. She also signed me up for the last two months of kindergarten, so I could catch up with other kids.

On a sunny day in mid-May, Mrs. Schafer took me to a special clinic where blood was drawn to check for syphilis using the Wasserman. I didn't like the idea of getting a needle and I had never been to the clinic before, so I remember it very well. The nurses were in one room and the doctor waited in another room. I had to sit on a high stool. After a brief exam, I had a needle injected in my arm to take blood. The doctor was impressed that I didn't cry. He told me I was a good girl and very brave. The test came back negative.

I also had many IQ tests and there were big improvements every time.

Then Christmas came and it was very special. After dinner, Rickie and I were told that Santa was on his way. We ran to the bedroom and pretended to be asleep. We climbed under the covers and giggled with anticipation. Then, we heard Santa's boots stomping on the roof.

"Ho, ho, ho! Merry Christmas!" a loud jolly voice shouted out. We could hear Santa moving about the house, but the minute he was gone, we were out of bed. Rickie ran to the living room window to get a glimpse of the flying reindeer. He saw Rudolf's nose blinking, so I strained my eyes in search of a big red sleigh, but it was already gone.

My heart was bursting with excitement. I opened my gifts to find a little red suitcase for my doll clothes and a cute little muff warmer. Life couldn't be better.

Later that year, Ida fostered two more children. Dustin was a nine-year-old boy with brown eyes and olive skin. His seven-year-old sister Peggy would be my new big sister. I didn't want older siblings to boss me around, but Peggy was a good sister and we became very close.

My first year in school was hard and it wasn't long before I got into trouble. The teacher, Miss Gill, was out of the room when I had a problem with a student in front of me. Cathy was bossy and huffy, and her long ponytail was on my desk.

"Get your hair off my desk," I demanded as I swiped her tail away.

"I can put my hair wherever I want." She turned to me and stuck out her tongue. She flipped her head and her braid fell on my desk.

I took out my blunt scissors and pretended to chop her hair off. She swung around in her desk and screamed at the top of her lungs. Miss Gill came running and asked what was going on.

"Eugenea cut my hair with the scissors," Cathy cried.

I tried to explain that it was only a joke, but Miss Gill saw the scissors in my hand and she snapped. She threatened that she was taking me to the principal's office and then she yanked me out of my seat. I was so scared that I started screaming. We were about to pass through the doorway when I tore myself out of her grasp. With both hands and feet, I clamped onto the sides of the doorframe like a giant X.

"Let go."

Miss Gill tugged at me as tears streamed down my face. In the middle of all this raucousness, another classroom of students entered the hallway. Peggy's class was lining out of its homeroom. I knew my new foster sister was somewhere in the line and if she saw me, she would tell our parents. I quickly composed myself and took my teacher's hand. I pretended we were just going for a stroll. As we passed the group of kids, I waved to my big sister. After we rounded the corner, I remembered the dreaded place that we were fast approaching. Before I had a chance to act up, a huge door opened and I was shoved in.

Behind a large wooden desk sat the Principal; he was staring at me.

"What seems to be the trouble?" he asked.

"I don't know."

I was amazed how calm he seemed; he certainly didn't look like the monster that I thought he would be. My runny nose and swollen eyes must have softened him. He looked at me and waited patiently for an answer.

"I wasn't really going to cut that girl's hair. I was only pretending, but she started screaming and I got in trouble."

"Do you think you can go back to your class and behave?"

"Yes," I answered, feeling ashamed as I looked down at the new scuffmarks on my shoes.

"Go back to class and do your work," he ended and I quickly went on my way.

Peggy was not fooled by my act though. As soon as I arrived home from school, I was sent to bed with no supper.

Every now and then, I would test the waters to see what I could get away with. One day after school, I decided to go to a classmate's house without permission. I knew it was wrong, but I went anyway. We played dress-up in her basement until her mother came downstairs and told me to go home.

It was very dark when I crossed the schoolyard. It was night and no one was around, so I knew I was in big trouble. As I came in the back door, I heard the TV. The smell of dinner still lingered in the air, but the dishes had already been cleared to the sink.

"Where have you been?" Ida stood in the light of the kitchen. She looked relieved to know that I was safe, but she was very mad at the same time. I had disobeyed the rules.

"I went to play at Joanne's house." I choked on the words.

"You had no permission to go there, so why did you?" She was glaring now.

"I thought it would be okay," I lied.

With bowed head, I walked away quietly. I would have gladly taken a spanking rather than have to go in my room. Poor Bruce and Ida, they must have been out of their minds with worry.

Ida was a big fan of the outdoors, so every weekend we went skiing or hiking. I hated it, because I was the smallest and struggled to keep up with everyone. My idea of relaxation was spending two days in front of the television, watching cartoons all morning the way our friends did. Afternoons could be a lot more fun playing with the kids in the neighbourhood.

I was always pessimistic, but I grunted my way up every mountainside until one Saturday came and we did something different. Ida had a gala to attend, so Bruce thought it might be fun to take us to the forest and pick mushrooms. It was late afternoon when we hopped into the Volkswagen Beetle and headed out of Calgary.

"Pick as many as you can fit in your bag, but don't wander off so I can't see where you are," Bruce warned.

The mushrooms looked like upside-down saucer bowls. I picked the oyster-coloured ones with the cute little spots and filled my bag to the top.

"Okay, kids. It's getting dark. We need to go back to the car," Bruce advised.

We followed him through the woodland, passing huge timbers that never seemed to end. We hurried along the path, but the sun went behind the trees and darkness came so fast that soon we were lost. Bruce studied his compass, but we still couldn't find the car. No matter which way we turned, our path took us farther away from civilization. We were hungry and tired, so Bruce built a fire and cooked the mushrooms like hot dogs on sticks. I had always hated mushrooms, but I was too hungry to starve for another second. Afterwards, Bruce made us a bed of soft pine branches and, within minutes, we were sleeping.

The fire died out and we woke up to snow. Bruce was sitting with his back against a tree and I knew he had stayed awake to watch over us. We set out once more to find the car. Our light sweaters did nothing to keep in the heat and, no matter which way we went, we seemed to be going in circles. We reached a rocky cliff side and stared down into the dark pit. Bruce hesitated for a moment, then braced himself carefully, stepping down the rocky slope until he reached the bottom.

"Boys, give me your hands so I can help you," Bruce called out. One by one, the boys tirelessly steadied each step until they safely reached the flat ground.

"Come on, girls," Bruce called up to Peggy and me, but we were too scared and refused to go another step.

"C'mon. It's safe," Bruce pleaded as he climbed halfway up to meet us, his hand extended.

In that brief moment, I reflected back to the many times when my trust had been betrayed, and now we were lost and I was blaming him. I pulled away; his outreached hand was of no assurance to me. He sighed and gave in and the three of them climbed back up to the top with Peggy and me.

To this day, I can still hear the rangers calling out to us from across the thicket. It was hard to see, but in the snowy mist our rescue team was coming to us. They took us to the ranger station and I could see smoke coming out of the chimney.

I knew we were safe when I saw the lights in the windows. It wasn't home, but it sure was a wonderful sight. Once we were inside, they gave us blankets and hot chocolate. After checking us for hypothermia, the rangers escorted us to our car.

When Ida had come home the night before, she entered the house to find a thick haze of smoke. It reeked with the burning smell of charred chicken so she ran to the stove and pulled the oven door open. We had not come home to eat the meal she'd left cooking. Ida knew her family was in some sort of trouble, so she called the police. There were no accident reports but, even so, she could do nothing but wait; the weather was too unpredictable.

We huddled inside the Beetle as Bruce turned the key in the ignition. The little car was frozen and showed no signs of life. It took a few tries to get her little ticker going, but she finally sputtered down the road. I sat in the back seat, feeling cold, damp, dirty, hungry, and exhausted. Soon I would be in the comforts of a warm house. For the first time since I had lost my birth mother, I connected Ida's house as my safety net. I was going home.

We could see Ida in the window as the Beetle stopped in front of the house. We got out, ran inside, and threw our arms around her. Ida looked so worried that we knew she had stayed up all night until we came through the door.

"Mommy, Mommy," I yelled, as I squeezed in with the others. I cuddled in to absorb some of her body heat. It was the first time I had ever called her Mommy. From that day on, she was Mom, but Bruce didn't get the same honour. He had messed up with my safekeeping and would remain indefinitely "Mr. Schafer."

The following weekend, we drove back to the forest. This time, Ida came too and we really had some fun. We designed and built a refuge using two slanted pine trees that met at the top. We covered the trees with thick moss until our refuge looked like a fort. When we had finished, everyone stood back to view our masterpiece.

We had constructed the cutest little A-line hut with a two-seated log bench inside. The little fort was so simple that a child could make it and we knew how to protect ourselves if we were ever lost again. That winter, we all learned how to ski. Rickie was very good, but he fell and broke his leg. He cried as the paramedics lifted him onto a stretcher and carried him away.

Our weekend trips ended for a few months. Part of me was happy. I didn't miss the yodeling off the mountains, but it was hard to see Rickie in so much pain. He couldn't go outside and play or ride his bike. He had to miss school and didn't see his friends. After several days of Rickie lying around on the sofa, Ida said he had to get up and use crutches. He cried so much that I thought she was cruel, but she didn't give in and soon he was up and about.

Then I understood why she insisted on Rickie getting back on his feet. Within a couple of months, he was out of his cast. But Rickie never seemed to be as happy. At that age I didn't know anything about death or suicide until one day when I was in the backyard with Rickie. He told me he wanted to die. His eyes were sad, but he didn't tell me why. I doubt he had any idea what that really meant.

From my first day in his house, he had learned a lot of sad things about my life and maybe it reflected on him in ways that no one could see. However, he told me to help him, so I followed him to the playhouse. I thought he was going to get his Tommy gun.

I could shoot him and he would play dead like the way we played cowboys and Indians. He got the skipping rope, made a noose, put it around his neck, and told me to take the other end of the rope to the top of our backyard fort. Once I was at the top, I looked over the side to see Rickie staring up as he waited. He told me to pull it as hard as I could, and that's exactly what I did. I was supposed to wrangle that cowboy's neck and hang him, so I pulled with all the strength I could muster. It was all part of catching the bad guy, except I wasn't supposed to... but I didn't know any better.

That was the stupidest thing I had ever done in my six years of life. He screamed so loudly that I almost fell over. What had I done? I panicked beyond all sense. I'm guessing I didn't actually have any sense at the time. The first instinct that came to my mind was to run, so I took off and hid around the side of the house. I leaned up against the wall, trying to become so flat that I was invisible.

Ida shouted my name and demanded I come at once. I wished I could vanish into the plaster. I walked slowly out of hiding and came into view on the front lawn. Ida was standing beside Rickie and he was bawling out of control.

"Did you choke him with the skipping rope?" she asked. She was furious and I wanted to explain in self-defense.

"Yes, but…"

"Go in the house," she ordered and I had to go to bed with no supper again. I lay in bed like a mummy in a coffin, while everyone else was having a great time, especially Rickie. The kids played in the street until dinnertime. I heard all the talking around the table during supper and then the noise of chairs moving away as everyone cleared the room.

The screen door opened and slammed, and the sound of feet ran off to play. I was miserable as I waited for the sun to creep out of my room. Later, Peggy crept into the room and slipped under the covers of her bed. The sheets rustled as she tossed around until sleep overtook her. I wasn't alone anymore, but that gave little comfort as I stared out in the dark. I guess from Ida's view, she was figuring that I was more messed up than she had calculated.

She got ahold of the social worker and they decided to send me for evaluation. It was a day in the not-so-distant future that I began sessions with the guidance clinic. On my first visit the social worker laid out several flash cards and asked me to describe what they were.

"I don't want to play this game; I want to play dress up," I told her defiantly, knowing fully that she was trying to analyze me.

She agreed, and from that day on, I wouldn't give her any time to take notes or size me up mentally. Every appointment was the same: we would go to the hall closet to get the dress-up clothes and take them back to her office. She was so busy digging through the costumes that I was sure she had no time to open any doors in my mind to see what made me tick.

At home, most of my frustrations were taken out on Suzie, my doll. After long periods of brushing her knotted hair and getting nowhere, I would clench my fists. Then, I would grit my teeth and throw the hairbrush against the wall. I was sure Ida would come and punish me. I waited for the doom of punishment. After some time had gone by, it was obvious that no one even noticed.

In the second year of elementary school, Rickie moved up to the next grade without me. I was tiny for my age, so I fit right in, but it was humiliating. I felt like a failure and I didn't understand that moving around in foster homes would obviously have delayed my ability to learn. I took it very hard and, later that year, it was my turn to say that I wished I was dead. I didn't know what purpose there was in living nor did I understand the real concept of death.

We were in the basement when I blabbed to Rickie about my wishes. The look on his face was more than I had anticipated. He ran off and told his dad. Bruce stopped whatever he was doing and came for me. He was mad and he looked like a wild-eyed crazy person as he came into the laundry room where I stood. I was scared and wanted to take back the words, but it was too late.

"Rickie tells me that you want to die. Is that true? Did you say that?" He was flummoxed and I wouldn't answer.

"Come here, I'll kill you!" He grabbed a small penknife from the workbench. I was terrified. The knife was so close that I could see its ridge. "Is that what you want? I can do it right now!"

"No," I said, feeling ashamed and scared.

I wondered if he would really kill me. I noticed the knife was mere inches from my heart. I bent away, not wanting to find out.

"Don't you ever talk like that again. Understand?"

"I won't," I promised. I had never been as disappointed in Rickie as I was at that moment. Yet later, I sensed he understood my feelings and he was afraid. After all, he had been there too.

At the end of my second year of Grade One, everything seemed to be going well. But the ministry was not willing to let me stay with the Schafers unless they were able to adopt me.

The regional social worker drove from Lethbridge to Calgary and made a special visit with Ida and Bruce. This social worker was not from the Calgary district, but she had found a family in the Lethbridge district who wanted to adopt me. During her visit, she dropped the bomb on Ida and Bruce. The topic of adoption was immediately raised to the forefront because she wanted a commitment.

"We can't adopt Eugenea because we would have to adopt Peggy and Dustin too. We have to be fair to all three children, but we don't have that kind of money." Ida wasn't sure where the subject would lead.

"Well, if you will not adopt her, then I have to put Eugenea in a home that will."

"This is Eugenea's home and we have no plans to send her away. It shouldn't matter that we can't adopt her and she isn't concerned about whether we adopt her or not," Ida spoke up.

"Yes, but Eugenea has a chance that most kids her age will never have." The worker was good at pointing out what she believed was best for everyone.

"I'm not sure that is what's best for Eugenea. She finally has stability. If you take her away from the only family she knows, it will be bad for her. We are her family now. She fits in and loves her siblings. They love her too. That is not fair to Eugenea if you uproot her life again. She'll be alone and won't know her surroundings. I can't bear to do that to her."

"It will be a shock to Eugenea, but she will adjust. She won't have to share the attention with so many and that will be a big help." The social worker smiled.

"That didn't matter when we were accepted as foster parents for Peggy and Dustin. No one cared if Eugenea had to share the attention. Why is it a problem now?" Ida was confused.

"I found a family that is able to adopt and give Eugenea a permanent home." The social worker went on to say that the new family promised to adopt if the government could find a blonde female ranging in the six-to-seven-year bracket. The family was seeking a girl who could be a playmate for their nine-year-old daughter, Charlene, whom they had adopted at birth.

"This is going to be very hard on the kids. Especially on Peggy. They share a room together."

Ida and Bruce had no way to stop the ministry and so the decision went ahead without their approval. I was released to social services.

24: The Osters

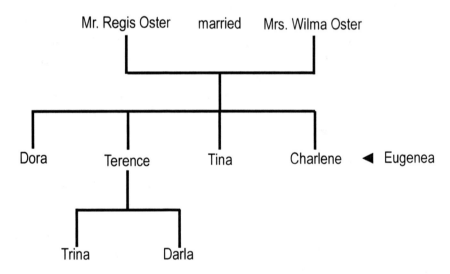

A high-profile family had met all the criteria for adoption and was anxiously waiting for an answer. They had viewed my picture and chosen me from the placement adoption file, so the regional social worker went ahead and scheduled a meeting for a family introduction with Mrs. Oster and her daughter Charlene.

Wilma Oster drove from her hometown to meet up with the regional worker and my social worker. Wilma carried years of experience in foster care and social services. My social worker and Ida didn't think the sudden move was a fair way to treat a child who had been through so many upheavals. That led to some controversy, but Wilma and the regional worker had a lot of influence.

The new regional worker joined us for lunch and I was confused about which woman was the mother. I kept hoping it was the social worker, but later found out I was wrong. Wilma was in her late forties and when she smiled, I could see she was no longer young. Her eyes shone, but there was a darkness there that made me uncomfortable. I didn't want to be alone with her.

Wilma's daughter Charlene and I sat in the car. It was an awkward moment as we fidgeted in the back seat. We studied each other as children do. She tossed her bob of dark curls and shyly pressed a gift into my palm.

"I hope you like it. I made it for you."

I looked down to see a blue hand-sewn hair band.

"Thank you."

In that moment, I connected with her loneliness. It was so much deeper than my own. I had siblings my age, but she was an only child. I knew that we would become sisters and I would have to leave everything behind. My old social worker tried to ease my worries, but I didn't like the thought of moving again.

During lunch, Wilma discussed the possibility of taking me on holidays with them for two weeks during the summer. She promised a holiday with lots of fun and soon I was dazzled by her enthusiasm. The thought of being adopted by a loving family was great but my foster sister Peggy at Ida and Bruce's was very sad when I came home and told them the news. I promised to come back at the end of the holidays, but I had no say in the matter. I never returned, not even to get my belongings or say goodbye.

I couldn't understand why I was the only foster child who moved away from Ida and Bruce. Whenever I asked about them, Wilma was defensive. She told me that they didn't want me because I had wet the bed once. I remembered that day. Ida had made me wear a diaper to school and I was terrified that the other school kids would hear the squeak of the rubber pants when I walked. It was a windy cold day and girls had to wear dresses even in the winter. Wilma also told me that Ida had told the social worker so many lies that my foster file records were ruined.

"I don't believe any of it, since we have never had any problems with you. We are going to adopt you and change your name, and then you will be our little girl. We can change your last name to our name too. Then you really will be ours," she promised and I was tingling with excitement.

"Can I change my first name?" I stared at her hopefully.

"Why? Don't you like your name?" She looked concerned.

"It sounds like a boy's name." There, it was out, but I couldn't look at her because I felt ashamed to say that.

"What name do you want?"

"Can we change my name to Suzie?"

"Not Suzie; that's the dog's name. Remember?" she said. "How about Jeanie? That's pretty. You could be our little Jeanie Oster."

I felt like I had been reborn. Wilma continually talked of her big plan to adopt me, but her constant scrutiny was hard to please. Sure, there were a few bugs to work out, but I worshipped my new mom and wanted to do whatever made her happy. Wilma was always on top of keeping up appearances and having good manners. In public, Charlene and I were exhibited like twins. Although we didn't look alike, we had matching clothes and shoes.

Charlene was so playful and good that she captured the hearts of everyone. I loved it, because on occasion some of the attention fell my way. She ruled over me, but I liked having a big sister. Whenever we got into trouble, my new mother was quick to blame me. Because of that, I realized I couldn't hold a candle to Charlene's perfection.

In school, she was athletic, popular, and she aced every subject with minimal study. In my case, it was the opposite and that upset Wilma. It wasn't long before the novelty of her "two peas in a pod" wore off. As I blundered along, Wilma's impatience festered into mental abuse.

She took me to doctors and specialists who were not compassionate or understanding to my situation from the past. One doctor told Wilma that I might have some kind of growth in the brain.

After I had been in my new home for five months, Wilma told the social worker that she was not going through with the adoption. The social worker was shocked and baffled, and wanted to know why Wilma had had a change of heart, especially since the ministry had gone up in arms against Ida to win custody for Wilma. What could have possibly gone so wrong in such a short time?

"Well, I can't really think of anything. I mean Jeanie has never been a problem whatsoever. But there was this one time… you see… I gave her a big tray with a large silver urn of coffee on it. I told her to carry it to the table. It tipped over and spilled onto my mother's lap. Although it was an accident… I just hate to think it, but maybe she did it on purpose," she stated. "I just feel that someday she might need psychological help and I wouldn't be able to give her what she needs."

I was appalled that the social worker didn't come to my defence. Her job was to speak on behalf of children who are wards of the government, and I often wonder whether she was really protecting the children she put into care. Is it not dangerous to give an eight-year-old child boiling hot coffee to serve?

If I had been the victim instead, she would have to do some explaining. It could have been worse; both her mother and I could have been burned. It was notably obvious that Wilma was merely using this as a scheme to get out of the adoption. Because of the sensitivity involved with uprooting children, the ministry didn't intervene and force a removal. I would continue to stay. They hoped it would work into an adoption.

A few months later, Wilma's mother dumped the same coffee urn over and it spilled onto me. As I screamed with pain, Wilma and her mother quickly tore off my clothes and dowsed me with cold wet towels. It was an accident and not once did I or anyone assume it was intentional. Luckily, Wilma's fast action prevented a trip to the hospital and the social worker never had to know.

At times, I was deathly afraid of Wilma. She had a temper like Eleanor's. I always kept one eye on her just in case she got in one of her hitting moods.

25: Trailer Trash

During my second summer with the Osters, we drove from Lethbridge to Ontario. For five days, we travelled over the prairies dragging a trailer behind the station wagon. After many miles of roadside diners and gas station refills, we passed the "Welcome to Ontario" sign. My foster dad Regis never complained. He drove the entire way until we arrived at his sister's house in Barrie, Ontario. His sister Edna stood under her porch light as our vehicle pulled up. Regis was all smiles and I saw his child side—the side that promised an evening of humorous tales. Edna gleamed with sibling pride as they hugged.

"And who is this little girl?" Edna asked, after she finished her round of hugs and came to me. She smiled with curiosity.

"This is Jeanie, our little foster child." Wilma pulled me in front. In the awkward silence, I saw the curious stares and wished she would stop introducing me to everyone as "our little foster child."

"Well, let's go inside. You must be thirsty after such a long trip," Edna insisted and I was grateful.

Almost immediately, the adults began their grown-up conversation that didn't include Charlene and me, so we stayed in the kitchen. Edna's husband Bryce walked into the kitchen and plopped into a chair. His red puffy eyes were fixed on us. A grin spread across his face as he raised his arm and poked Charlene in the ribs. She laughed and pretended to jab back at him.

"Ahh… you wanna have some fun, don't ya, little lady?" He laughed and pulled himself upright. The stench of tobacco and alcohol filled the air.

"Na na na na… you can't get us." Charlene chanted and we laughed when he leaned over to try and poke us again. Teasingly, he pulled Charlene toward his chair and tickled her. Charlene jumped on and off his knee, playing hard to get. He always managed to kiss her cheek before she got loose. I stood there, giggling. Bryce didn't leave me out, as he grabbed my hand and pulled me into the game. I was glad it was my turn; I wanted to be a part of the fun too. He tickled me and I squealed with laughter.

Just then, I saw Wilma in the doorway of the living room and she wasn't laughing.

"Girls, I want you to come with me to the trailer, now!"

We walked out to the back in silence; I was oblivious of everything.

"What were you doing in there?" She asked after she shut the trailer door and clicked the lock. As the three of us stood in the dark, it was strange how the space suddenly felt small and cramped. The light from the house shone through the window of our roomy trailer and yet I felt so confined.

"Nothing. We were just playing," I said, wondering how fun had suddenly become bad. Was I too loud? What had I done? A rush of anxiety urged me to get out as I recognized the onset of a one-sided battle ahead. The doorknob was so close I could almost touch it.

"Playing? Is that what you call it?" Her voice switched to a scowl of anger. Her eyes looked fierce and I felt uneasy to answer.

"Yes."

"Don't give me that! You wanted that dirty old man to kiss you, didn't you?"

"No." My brain panicked for the right answer.

"Don't play stupid. Uncle Bryce likes little girls like you, because he sees you're desperate for attention," she fired back, and I knew I was on dangerous ground. "You like all his touching and stuff, don't you?"

I wasn't sure what she was getting at, but it made me feel dirty in a very unpleasant way.

"No." I shook my head in disagreement.

"All he wants is to put his hands on your privates. Would you like that?" Her question was filled with sarcasm. I wished that I could be anywhere else but standing there.

"No, we were just…" It's not quite the answer I meant. My defence came out gutless and I felt so inferior because she was miles from the truth.

"You are so stupid. Maybe I should let him have his way with you and leave you here. We'll just pack up tomorrow and go home without you. Then, you would be paying a high price for your stupidity. Maybe that would teach you a lesson. Then you would see what you did and what a bad girl you really are."

"I'm sorry, Mom. Please don't do that," I shook my head, whimpering with sadness. Possibly she was bluffing, but the threat that she might leave me there was frightful.

Without a doubt, I knew Wilma had seen Charlene sitting on Bryce's lap too. But for some unknown reason, her actions weren't considered part of the scene. At the beginning of the conversation, Charlene was standing next to me, but she slid away and glided over to Wilma's side. I didn't want to believe it, but there was my sister standing with the same repugnant look as Wilma. The space felt cramped and I desperately wished they would step back a bit and give me some breathing room.

"Do you want everyone to think that you're a tramp and call you a slut behind your back?" Again, Wilma didn't wait for my reply. "If you carry on like this, everyone one will think, 'What a whore.'"

"What do you mean?" Carry on like what? I had no idea.

"That man wants to put his hand in your pants." Her voice lowered as she looked back to the house and I thought maybe she didn't want Bryce to hear. She glared back at me and I was afraid she would start slapping me if I moved.

I must have been standing there for ten seconds before my mouth made any sound. I didn't know what a "whore" was, but I thought it had something to do with my gender. I felt shameful and hideous.

"For the rest of the trip, you keep your filthy eyes down. Don't be talking to that man for attention, and I don't want to see so much as a glance his way."

I felt sickened by the accusations, but I didn't break down. Wilma told me to get into bed and pray, and then she was gone. I could hear her loud talking and laughter from the house. It seemed unimaginable that she could leave and go back into the house and party after what had happened. Her words hurt so much.

Charlene slept on the top bunk and never said a word to me.

The next day, the relatives gathered together for a big reunion in the park. It was such fun, because there were lots of cousins, food, and games. Whenever Uncle Bryce came around, I avoided him. I never made eye contact with him or with any other males in that family.

During that month, we travelled through parts of Ontario with short stops in Kitchener and Formosa, but my favourite place was Niagara Falls. Even though I had to tiptoe around Wilma, the weather was too beautiful to be so cautious. It was hot enough to melt butter and I loved it. To this day, I can see the great magnitude of the Falls in my mind. At the top was a sheet of mirrored water that seemed as still as glass. As the river glided along, it gained speed and streamed right over the edge. The rushing waters struck the bottom with such great force that they clouded into a mass of bubbly froth. The waters were deafening as Charlene and I stood at the highest elevation and screamed with excitement. Wilma laughed as we ran along the rail with carefree spirits.

The trip was memorable, but there were times when it was hard to digest the mixed messages and feelings.

26: Jesus and Chrissie

There were other holidays that I really loved, but Christmas was my favourite. It was amazing how each home had a different way of celebrating. Traditions and culture changed every time I moved. The similarities such as a tree, lights, and music were consistent with the other homes, but each was still a change and I had to be adaptable.

Lethbridge received a lot of snow that winter. Our backyard was packed so high that we could jump off the roof without getting hurt. On Christmas Eve, the family met at our house. All the grownups came in their fur-collared coats and Sunday best. Charlene and I got dressed for Midnight Mass. We looked like Christmas dolls in red velveteen dresses, white stockings, and black velvet shoes. On the way to church, Charlene and I playfully scissor skated over the icy ground. As soft flakes of snow drifted from the midnight sky, I had visions of Santa's sleigh.

The church bells rang in the night air and we heard the beautiful organ music as we entered the steps of the chapel. In the foyer was a large stable filled with statues of Mary, Joseph, and the baby Jesus. I hadn't really understood the spirit of Christmas until I saw the podium lit with candles and heard the carolers singing. It meant love—an unconditional pure feeling that many people never receive or get. I hadn't really felt or understood it until that magical night. The priest stood inside the doorway and greeted the traffic of people as they entered. Our family and extended relatives took up two rows of pews. We sang with our hearts and I thought I would bust from happiness.

There was, of course, one tiny problem—nothing harmful, but rather both-ersome. Underneath our pretty dresses, we had worn the scratchiest crinolines ever designed. Charlene managed to contain herself like the perfect little lady that she was. Unlike my sister, I wouldn't stop fiddling with the tulle. Standing wasn't too bad, but for sitting for any length of time, I might as well have put pot scrubbers in my tights. I was so distracted that I forgot about Wilma sitting in the row behind me. I looked over my shoulder and received a warning glare and realized I had touched a nerve.

My heart melted when the priest stood in the pulpit and told the beautiful story about baby Jesus. To add to the beauty, our neighbour's daughter topped the evening with a musical solo. She wore a stunning china-blue gown and sang "O Holy Night," and I was mesmerized.

Christmas was magical in our house! The biggest box under the tree had my name on it. I tore at the shiny paper and found a pretty walking doll. She was like a real baby and I loved to dress her up and comb her hair. I named her

Chrissie, in memory of Christmas. She was the toy that I cherished above all others.

On the first day back to school in Lethbridge from the Christmas break, I wore my matching scarf and mittens. I also wore my new tights, but I was such a klutz because I was barely a block away from home when I slipped on the ice. I went airborne and did a knee plant. My new school bag sailed across the ice and veered off the edge of the sidewalk.

My kneecap bulged through a gap in the stocking. It looked like a bloody eye peering out a fence hole. There was no way that I could tell Wilma that her gawky kid had had another accident. I was allowed to wear them only on the condition that I would be careful, since they were meant for Sunday best. There were no reasonable theories for accidents. I could be up to my elbows with excuses but that would just make the situation worse.

I went to school but I was lost in thought as to what to do. The day wasn't long enough and, sooner or later, I had to face my fear. When the bell rang for dismissal, I took the longer route home. I crossed the busy street to the shopping mall behind our house. I entered the department store and walked up the children's aisle, searching for stockings. There were all kinds of leotard-type tights, but there weren't any that were an exact match to mine.

I had no money and even if I had, I couldn't have afforded to buy them. I found a pair of tights that were almost a match; the pattern was different, but it was close enough. I took a good look around to make sure that no one saw me and stuffed the package inside my coat. It was the first time I had ever stolen from a store. My heart was pounding like a jackhammer. I went straight to the washroom and pulled off my tights and quickly made the switch.

Spurred by my overwhelming guilt, I thought that Wilma would instantly detect the hallmarks of a thief. Out of fear, I dared not look her in the eye when I got home. She was so much smarter than I wanted her to be. Wilma didn't say a word, so I went straight to my room. I stripped off the tights and hid them in the wash. She was a tough cookie, yet I managed to slip past her radar and I was not about to come clean. I hated to be on the fence. I knew I should do the right thing. However, I believed the risk was not worth the consequences. I was so fearful of what she might do that I just couldn't cope with it.

Wilma frequently expressed how much better my life would be if I were baptized. I agreed I wanted to be included. There was a pressing urgency in me to be freed from my ever-growing sins of the past. It seemed pointless to sit in church and not be allowed to participate. Wilma threatened that if I didn't get baptized, I would be banished to purgatory or hell. The government expected Wilma to put her money where her mouth was. They wouldn't budge on a baptismal consent unless she kept her end of the bargain to adopt me.

"Jeanie, why don't you write a nice letter to your social worker and ask for permission to be baptized? After the baptism is done, I will get the adoption in order and then you will be our daughter. Wouldn't that be wonderful?"

It was so simple; I could hardly believe my ears. That's all it was going to take to make her become my Mommy. It was a bit devious, but I was ecstatic that she was going to bat for me.

My hand-written plea didn't soften any hearts. Again, it was denied until Wilma committed to the original adoption agreement. Otherwise, I would have to wait until my twelfth birthday. At the time, I didn't know that Wilma was not willing to consent. I believed her when she had verbalized her desire to make us a family.

27: Charlene and Tina's Persuasion

Things were moving in a different direction than I had anticipated. I liked being the youngest in our household. It was nice to be the baby in the family, but at my age, it wasn't cute. Wilma chipped away at my childish behaviour, but I was a late bloomer. My sister Charlene was growing up and she had many friends. I wanted to be with her, but she whined when I tried to tag along. I was cool with it but Wilma pushed her to drag me around and we both resented that. In some ways, the split was better, because Charlene often squealed and I didn't want a troublemaker. With Charlene being nearly two years older, we no longer shared the same interests.

It was very difficult to make Wilma happy when she repeatedly asked me why I couldn't be more like Charlene. My sister had a significant impact on me, but I wanted to be me—my original self. She was the figurehead that I felt encouraged to follow, be it good or bad. We made choices that were not always smart. At times, we couldn't be trusted alone and not even with our babysitter.

I remember Wilma going out and leaving us with Tina. She was Wilma's daughter who was in college and didn't live at home.

After Wilma had left, Tina called me from out of my bed. I went to the kitchen and saw Tina and Charlene smoking. They offered me a cigarette, but I didn't want any part of it. I was afraid that Wilma would have our heads on a chopping block if she caught us.

"No way," I barred the offer with my hands, but that seemed to encourage them more.

"Try it."

"No. I'll burn my fingers." I feared the red-hot end.

"Don't be such a scaredy-cat. It's easy. All you have to do is suck in," Tina pressed.

"Mom will be home soon," I stalled.

"We won't tell," Charlene promised, but I wasn't convinced. She was tricky and knew how to get me into trouble without getting caught for the same wrong doings. "Don't be such a baby." Charlene glanced at Tina and they shared a grin.

"I will even hold it for you," Tina assured me and I began to think that I was a chicken and maybe they were right. It definitely looked grown up and smart so I took a big drag.

As soon as the smoke hit my lungs, I went into a wild watery-eyed coughing fit. The smell took me off-guard and whacked me like a sucker punch in the gut. While I was doubled over and wheezing, the two jokers erupted into peals of laughter. As the girls flushed the evidence and opened the window, I vowed never to do that again. It seemed like an easy resolution but then later I saw Charlene collecting street butts after school and I collaborated with her.

28: Wilma and Regis

During my growing-up phase, Wilma's foster skills anchored her a job with the children's shelter. She worked long hours and I was ecstatic to come home from school and see her car was gone from the driveway. In the evenings, I would race to bed before she got home.

On school mornings, I would dash about trying to scramble for a ride with my foster father Regis. I acted that way because I didn't want a simple morning to feel like a life sentence. I grabbed my lunch and books, but Wilma knew my intent and kyboshed my exit. She waved to Regis and told him to go without me and I was scared when he drove off.

"You are not going to school looking like a dirty little Indian." She pinched my arm and forced me to sit on a kitchen stool. She raked a hairbrush along my scalp and down my hair. I could feel the burning and tingling. Wilma plucked her scissors from the drawer and in one big snip, she hacked off my bangs. I looked like Mr. Potato with a Mohawk.

She took two hairpins and pressed any loose ends against my head. So absurd! I couldn't see how she expected the pins to stay in with my hair so short. But she warned me not to take them out or there would be a hefty consequence. I got to school and the kids stared at me like I was a freak. I lost a hairpin and it scared me so badly that I was in a panic. On the way home, I found another hairpin just like the one I had lost and I was so relieved.

At the time, I did not realize that Wilma was a terrible mother; I assumed it was my inability to change into what she classified as the perfect daughter.

My social worker made her rounds every four months for an evaluation of my progress, and to an outsider everything was picture perfect, but it was all staged. Before the social worker's arrival, Wilma prepped me on what to say and how to act; everything was in order. Her mood was jovial and sweet, so I was very pleased to play along. I entertained as the hostess and served coffee with cookies. The social worker would take a look at my spotless bedroom and then I was dismissed. As I stayed out of earshot, my progress was discussed and noted on my files.

I liked Regis. He was gentle and dutiful as a husband and father, but he was not the cuddly daddy type. I could count on one hand how many times I had seen him interfere with Wilma's way of discipline. Often he wasn't home to see what was going on. Only once did he ever spank Charlene and me; we were fighting over a toy. What happened next was total pandemonium in the house. Charlene was so upset with her Daddy that she ran to her mother's arms for protection. Wilma was furious with Regis, so the blame became one-sided and fell on my shoulders.

Regis disagreed and claimed that Charlene was making too much of it. As Charlene wailed incessantly, I saw Regis's defensive side. He was not going to let Wilma have her way with the last word. From downstairs, I heard them upstairs. They were shouting at each other and then the front door slammed so hard that the walls shook. It was terrifying to know he had left and Wilma would be after me any second.

"Where are you?" Her voice boomed as she stormed down the stairwell. Where could I possibly hide? She practically owned and controlled the air that I breathed. "You stupid girl." She caught me hiding in the corner. "You're a home wrecker. I don't know what I was thinking when I took you in." She screamed from so close I could feel the heat of her breath.

"I'm taking you back to the Orphanage. Tomorrow, I am going to call your social worker and have her pick you up. I never want to see you in my house again." Her face raged like a storm and I was petrified.

"Please don't say that, Mom. I'm sorry. I didn't mean to make you and Dad fight."

She was screaming at me to shut up as she raised her fist. I thought she would slam me for sure, but right then, Regis returned. What luck!

"This is not over," she scowled and dropped her arm. Whew! She was gone almost as quickly as she had appeared. Despite how scary that was, tempers gradually died down. It didn't matter, because I felt so unsettled and sad that I was getting the boot in the morning. The next day, there was no mention of the night before and life went on as usual.

However, I was not out of the woods, because there was no way a night of sleep would cool Wilma's heels. After school I came home unsuspecting and walked right into her trap. I went to hang my coat on the hook on the wall beside the stairway. There was a large black braided whip in the way.

"Do you know what that is for?" Wilma asked, as she sat at the kitchen table with a smirk on her face.

"Yes." I could hardly look at it.

Wilma said that she used it on the kids in the shelter where she worked.

"Touch it," she ordered, but her words didn't register.

"Go on. Touch it," she screamed and I jumped. The smell of rawhide hit my senses and I felt like I might be sick. I looked down the stairwell to the darkened basement and calculated that's where it would happen. Wilma had been cruel before, but never to this level and I feared the worst. Surprisingly, the whip was never used, but it was a constant insidious reminder because I had to move it every time I hung up or put on my coat. A few weeks later, the whip was gone and everything ran smoothly for me.

29: Wilma and Charlene

Given the state of Wilma's relationship with my sister, I had concluded that Charlene was beyond mistakes of any magnitude. She never clashed with her mother on anything.

Unfortunately, the tables flipped on Charlene during her last year of elementary school. It all started because she had a crush on a boy. She was only twelve at the time. I was ten so I did not see it as a bad thing. It was kind of cute to see them holding hands. Charlene was hanging out after school and habitually came home late. By the third day, Wilma wanted to know why Charlene was not home.

"Where's your sister?" She directed the question to me.

"I don't know." I shrugged my shoulders with pure ignorance. It was getting late and Charlene had not made it home for dinner. I noticed Wilma's plate was untouched; she didn't say a word. Regis took his dish to the sink and left the house. He was gone for quite a while, but when he came back, Charlene was with him.

My sister barely entered when Wilma approached her with a line of questions that demanded quick answers. The heat was up and Charlene's excuses didn't fly with Wilma. She slapped Charlene and an explosive altercation broke out. What a nasty tussle. I heard every name in the book, including "whore." Wilma chased and clobbered her in the hallway, and it turned into a one-sided boxing match. Charlene tried to escape, but Wilma got her in a headlock and pummeled her.

I knew it was game over for Charlene as Wilma slammed her face in the carpet. It was so terrifying that I wanted to plead with our Mom to stop. Regis tried to intervene, but the beating prevailed. Tears welled up in my eyes as the words caught on the tip of my tongue. I realized nothing could survive such rage, not even Charlene herself.

My sister desperately tried to crawl away, but Wilma overpowered her with kicks and punches. Tinker, our tiny miniature poodle, went hysterical when Charlene rolled into the fetal position and screamed. He barked and tore at the edge of Wilma's housecoat as he tried to force her back.

By the time it ended, my sister was unconscious. No one spoke a word, but Regis stared at Wilma as though he had never seen such brutality. He carefully lifted Charlene and put her on the bed. From across the hall, I heard the whimpers and moans, and it broke me down.

Suddenly that big open house seemed so much smaller. It was terrifying, not knowing where to go or what to do. I hid between the screen door and the front door trying to look inconspicuous. If I went outside without permission, I would have been in hot water for sure. Yet I was so scared to stay in the house, because I didn't want to be the next victim. Wilma came into the entrance and I was sure that I was done for. Instead, I was sent to my room, from where I heard more cries through the walls. I was so glad to hide out in my room until I knew it was safe to come out.

From that day forward, Charlene was a different girl. She was a lot kinder to me, she stopped being a blabbermouth and a tattletale, and she no longer took sides. Whenever Wilma behaved like a bully, my sister would cut in and carefully defend me. Nevertheless, my slip-ups were many.

Whenever I unintentionally broke something, Wilma flipped out and it went into a personal attack and she would call me "retard" or "stupid." If I borrowed a pen and forgot to return it, she would allege that I was stealing and called me "Satan's child." Such persecution! Whenever she called out my name, I shuddered to think what I had done. I was trying so hard to understand what the boundaries were, but the rules were always changing according to her mood.

30: Trina, Darla, and Great Granny Cecilia

I hated my home. I wasn't allowed to have guests in the house, because Wilma was sleeping or still in her nightie. It was rare to see her dressed. She drank codeine syrup twice a day as though it was coffee. She gave me the drink when she wanted me to sleep. It tasted awful. When I think back to those days, I remember her mood was vile and my friends were uncomfortable around her, so they did not come around. So when I was bored or lonely, I went to visit Wilma's two little granddaughters, Trina and Darla, who lived with their dad. Terence was the second oldest of Wilma's kids. As a single parent, he appreciated when

I helped to keep the girls entertained. I had known Trina and Darla since they were babies so I was like a big sister. As I grew older, I didn't always want them hanging around. But Wilma was the boss, so I made the best of it and had fun while staying out of the way. Since their Mom was not in the picture and their Dad worked, their Great Granny Cecilia took care of them during the day. On Sundays, I would hang out and stay for dinner. It was great, but then one day, I really messed up. Kids do dumb things, but this was by far my stupidest.

I was over for supper when I saw a pile of mole-coloured mushrooms on my plate. As a guest, I knew it was impolite to snub my nose, but it was kind of like entrapment. Wilma never made me eat mushrooms and Great Granny Cecilia lived with us, so I thought she knew that. I tried to toss them in the garbage, but there were too many eyes around.

Darla was sitting right beside me, so when no one was looking I quickly scraped the mushrooms onto her plate. It was a childish act, but I just figured that her Dad would throw out whatever wasn't eaten. When Trina and I finished, we had to leave the table and go outside. To my shock, Darla had to stay until she ate every bite on her plate. I could not believe how this had backfired and I felt so bad.

I wanted to sneak back in to grab the mushrooms, but Darla's Dad was in the kitchen with Great Granny Cecilia. When Darla couldn't eat all the mushrooms, she was punished. She wasn't allowed out and she had to put on her pyjamas. From the window, I saw her crying, but I was too much of a coward to fess up.

In the morning when I woke up, I heard Wilma talking on her bedroom phone. Although I heard muffles, I was oblivious to the conversation. When she hung up, she called me to her room. As I opened the door, I could see her sitting upright on the bed with the phone on her lap. The cord trailed over the comforter and down to the floor. She was still wearing her nightie and powder-blue robe. Her legs were crossed, but her foot on top was twitching wildly. I always knew that wasn't a good sign. Before I could wipe the sleep from my eyes, she confronted me about Darla.

"What's wrong with your brain?" She just sat there staring at me, waiting for an explanation. I had completely forgotten about the night before. How had I deluded myself into thinking I had somehow escaped this? Obviously, Great Granny Cecilia knew what I had done.

"Come with me," Wilma said as she wiggled off the bed and shoved her feet into slippers. My stomach went all jittery as I followed her into the bathroom.

"Take your pyjamas off."

Was she kidding? I was in for a harrowing experience. As my pyjamas dropped in a heap I felt so humiliated. Wilma's eyes poured over me as I tried to keep myself from being exposed.

"Get in the tub," she ordered as she kicked my pyjamas out of the way.

"What are you going to do?" I asked, but she didn't answer, and that made me twice as scared. After I climbed into the tub, Wilma plugged the drain and turned on the tap.

It was freezing cold, because she wouldn't add any hot water. My toes curled like little shrimps and I shivered as the water got higher. The look in her eyes reminded me of the night that Charlene was late from school. She leaned in really close and started screaming that I disgusted her. I backed up in desperation to make space between us. She ordered me to lie down in the water and I was scared to disobey her. I was certain that she would push me under if I refused.

I crouched into a fetal roll and stayed low as the spray prickled my flesh like tiny shards of glass. The water whirled around as I hugged my knees to my chest. The whole time, Wilma was screaming and ranting, and I thought hell was going to freeze over before I got out. My lips were quivering and I couldn't take it any longer. Just then, Charlene appeared in the doorway and I looked at her with pleading eyes.

"Your sister isn't going to save a dirty little pig like you," Wilma lashed out at me and I cringed.

I wished I could cover my ears. Wilma filled Charlene with all the details and I was afraid it would turn into two against one. Charlene stayed out of it and left the room. Finally, Wilma pulled the plug, but by then my body ached and my joints felt knotted and stiff.

"By the end of this day, you are going to know what it's like to suffer from the hand of another. I will show you what it means to live in hell," Wilma said as she put the plug back in and switched to the hot faucet.

As the water raced to the back of the tub, I started hopping from foot to foot like I was dancing on a bed of coals. The numbness in my ankles turned to pins and needles and my feet quickly reddened like two lobsters. Wilma ordered that I lie down in the scalding hot water or she would pull me under.

I couldn't possibly do it, so I backed away using my hands to shield Wilma from reaching me. She screamed that I was a coward and a worthless castaway that deserved to burn. I cried and said that she was right. I was a coward, because I was terrified of her, but I didn't tell her that. I hated living day after day that way.

How could I make her stop? I was beside myself. If ever there was a time that I needed someone to interrupt Wilma, it was right then. It was too early in the day for Regis to come home. In my head, I was pleading for a free pass. Just this once and I would improve and never be bad again.

Suddenly, I heard the jingle of Regis's keys as he entered the house. The squeaky door was music to my ears. Wilma quickly turned off the tap. Then she yanked the chain on the plug and ordered me to get out and dress in my room. I don't know why Regis came home early, but he was my hero. My knight in shining armour. I dropped on my bed in gratitude.

Not long after that day, Wilma's work hours changed to afternoons so I rarely saw her. After the tub incident, I was practically invisible. Without her constant eye, I had a newfound freedom to come and go easily. Not a good thing but at the time it sure felt good. I was often out wandering streets alone and I felt safe until one day I was approached. I was in the same department store where I had stolen the tights. I had stopped to look at some wallets, when I got an eerie feeling that someone was watching me.

Just as my fingers stroked the bonded leather, I felt someone breathing over my shoulder. Before I could move, something slid between the inner side of my arm and upper body. Red flags went up as a hand reached around to the front of my shirt and then to my horror it squeezed my little budding chest. Every fraction of a second seemed timeless; I was like a fly trapped in a web. When the hand finally pulled away, I didn't want to face the attacker, yet I couldn't help from turning.

Right there in the centre aisle, I was looking into the hollow eyes of a child molester. A clean-shaven fresh-out-of-prison look is how I can best describe this lunatic. His crazy devious stare made me feel more tainted than the heinous touch of his icky hand. My mouth dropped and I was about to scream with all the strength I had.

"If you make a noise, I'll kill you," he threatened. He stood dangerously close.

I wanted to gouge out his creepy eyes. I was shocked and furious, but I knew for sure he would hurt me if he had the chance. Without dropping his bogey-man stare, he pulled out his cigarettes and lit up. Was this some kind of a sick joke? What prison did he tunnel his way out of?

"Fuck off, kid," he smugly warned as the smoke filled the space between us. His words came out of nowhere, like he'd gotten bored of his own game. All I could think was, I'm going to die if I don't get away from the filthy pig. I backed away and took my chance to flee. Not knowing if the psycho was following, I made a home run and I didn't stop until I reached my yard.

Once inside the house, I quickly locked the doors and shut the drapes. From behind the curtains, I peered out, but I didn't see any sign of the Grim Reaper. I didn't tell Wilma or anyone, but I wanted someone to talk to. I never saw the man again, but his devilish eyes haunted my nightmares. In public places, I was as jumpy as a skittish little pony that spooked at the slightest twitch.

31: Wilma and Regis, Charlene, and Me

I felt like I was finally out of harm's way when our family—Wilma, Regis, Charlene, and I—went on a trip to Radium Hot Springs and we were gone for a good part of the summer. We usually went there once or twice a year. Radium was so cleansing. It was alive with happy campers, hoteliers, and backpacking hitchhikers. The boardwalks bustled with people buying at the fruit stands and outdoor cafés.

Whenever Regis opened his wallet, he treated Charlene and me to ice cream. Then he would slip us a couple of bucks to go and unleash our shopping bug fever. Best of all, I loved the trail that started at the top of the campground and zigzagged down the side of a cliff to the pool's gate entrance.

Since it only took about fifteen minutes to walk the path, Charlene would race me and win. I would always rise to the occasion and tried to up my game with a head start, but her legs shot right past mine just like all the other times. When I was tired and out of breath, I was rejuvenated by the sweet smell of pine and wild flowers.

From where I stood, I could see down the side of the embankment carpeted in a pile of deep moss. It was fascinating how the natural turf embedded the earth like a thick tousled rug. The forest was well over-grown with no clearing except for the path. I saw disorderly clusters of purple crocuses growing between the timbers. Their heads popped open to the light of the sun strobing through the trees. The tiny droplets of dew sparkled like beads of glass.

It was food for my soul to be surrounded by such enchantment. I was taking it all in because it was so pleasing to my eye. In the trees, the birds chirped over the faint sound of rushing water below. Above all, it brought me inner peace. Later on, Charlene and I spent our lazy afternoons lounging at the pool and pursuing short-term friendships. It was no surprise to find the same friends from the year before.

I never wanted to leave. Going home could too easily turn into a throwback of problems. Trouble somehow always trapped me into something from which I couldn't extricate myself. Such as Wilma's watchdog eyes or the ones she claimed were in the back of her head. Even her nose could target the tiniest omission. It's weird, but I thought I was a master of myself. Yet, I was in that tricky age where it's so easy to get messed up in notions of having to please everyone. I was faking myself into believing that being cool was better than being obedient.

Wilma didn't mess around if she had it out for me; I knew by the icy glares. After we got back from Radium, she rummaged through my stuff. Maybe she got a whiff of my ashtray breath, because it seemed a bit unconventional to see her snooping through my coat pocket. Voila! She found my smokes, so that meant another confession party for two.

At first, she brought over her ashtray and insisted that I light up in front of her, but I couldn't do it, so I was forced to eat them. The taste was disturbingly caustic and dirtier than eating garbage out of the trash.

"I'm going to wash your dirty mouth with soap," Wilma informed me as she went for the dish soap. She pinned my head back and poured the gooey liquid down my throat. My brain and stomach went to mush and I might as well have been drunk, because I didn't have the strength to resist her.

Then, before the soap settled, she grabbed a jug of orange juice from the fridge and poured me a glass. It was raunchy, acidic, and vile beyond my senses of taste and smell. Every swallow burned its way down. When the juice splashed into my gut, it fizzed up like an antacid in water. Regrettably, it rumbled and agitated my stomach like an old washing machine.

As Wilma oversaw every mouthful, I was worried that I would throw up on her slippers. Then I burped and little effervescent bubbles came out of my nose and mouth. I heard Wilma's bray of laughter. Obviously it looked hilarious but it just wasn't funny. A tasteless joke, if you will. The next day, I felt like I had survived a twenty-four-hour flu.

After that wrenching experience, it was time to make some changes. I had turned twelve, so I was old enough to be baptized and I could finally breach the dirty walk of shame. On a quiet Saturday morning, the priest anointed me with my family witnessing. As I left the wooden doors of the church, I was pure in the eyes of God. I was inspired to be a decent Christian girl and determined to stay perfect. I hoped it would raise my stakes for adoption.

For a very limited time, I marked the beginning of a flawless soul. I tried not to flub it up, but it was hard. I wasn't bulletproof, so I was back in the hot seat and stacking up mistakes like a pile of unwanted bills.

When Wilma struck with her hand it was not a smack on the bottom. She would take the wind out of my sails and afterwards she would put a weird spin on it. She said that she didn't want to hit me, but it was for my own good.

"Why can't you have good grades, nice hair, or a boyfriend like your sister?" Wilma asked many times.

Charlene was not a hard act to follow, but I was too much of a tomboy, so it was kind of like trying to compare apples to oranges. My sister liked makeup, short skirts, and heels. I graduated from runners to heels, but I didn't walk like a lady. With a book on my head I got it down in a few steps around the kitchen. Definitely a visible difference on the outside, but inside I was still a kid.

It had been weeks since my baptism, yet lips were sealed tight and no one dropped any hints. It was time to pop the cork and sign the adoption papers. I had no idea that Wilma received an income for my care. It never dawned on me that she was being paid. I just assumed it was "out of the goodness of her heart."

The truth came out when the ministry sent a twenty-five-year achievement award instead of a bonus cheque. She flashed her glossy print at me and cursed that the government had ripped her off. She was a fierce woman when anyone messed with her. She maximized on how she had been stuck with foster kids and barely paid anything, and how it wasn't worth her troubles.

As she ranted on and on, I understood why adoption was always on hold. Right from day one, it was never in the cards. Did she expect to get rich on the backs of foster kids? Maybe there wasn't a grain of truth in it. I hoped that she didn't mean what she said, but it somehow diminished any authenticity I saw in her. I believed I did not deserve the aggravation I felt from her, so I often rolled my eyes in defiance and voiced little sarcasms under my breath.

After that day, I was sick of Wilma's gripes, her flippant remarks, her lies, and trying to dodge her backhand on a daily basis.

32: The Psychiatrist

Wilma arranged for me to see a psychiatrist. The decision had to be finalized by social services, but the brain behind it all was definitely Wilma. So I didn't see that coming until Regis picked me up in the middle of a school day. That afternoon he was just the driver, so he didn't relate any details when I asked where we were going. Regis parked outside an unrecognizable office building and told me to get out of the car. From the side window, he pointed to the entrance door and I knew something fishy was going on.

I got to the glass door with a sign that read, "Psychiatrist." So that's what it was all about. No wonder he was acting so weirdly. I looked back at Regis and could see that he wanted nothing to do with it.

I didn't have to sit in the waiting room because the doctor was ready to see me. I went in the office and sat across from his desk. There was a couch just like in the movies, but I had no intention of lying there. The doctor talked without moving his mouth and he never smiled. He kept poking my thoughts with questions that drove me cuckoo, but I went along with mind-numbing yeses or nos. Quite honestly, I didn't want to give him the time of day. That's how I felt because I was hurt, betrayed, and mad that I was there in the first place.

Go ahead! Judge me as if I am a nut bar, I thought, because I didn't give two cents' worth.

But then, he nailed me with a question that I never dreamed anyone would ever ask.

"Do you feel that everyone in the world is a robot and you are the only real person on earth?"

The shrink stopped looking at his papers and we were eye to eye. I sat there, twiddling my thumbs in my lap and feeling like a misfit. I had convinced myself that I lived within a circle of machines. I had already met my share of rotten people. The voice in my head said "yes," but my lips denied it.

That moment I knew my perception was over-the-top silly, but regardless it somehow reduced the hurt. In the span of an hour, the doctor finished with his questions and I was free to go. On the way home, Regis kept his thoughts to himself; we drove in silence. I hadn't seen Wilma all day so I didn't know what to expect. As we came face to face and our eyes met, there was an unspeakable hurt that hovered in the air. It was like a meeting of our minds.

There was no voice of reason. I couldn't talk or even look at Wilma in the same way. It might have been easier if she would have come with me. Then I would have felt that she was working with me—not against me. Yes, we butted heads a lot, so a mediator might have been ideal if she had thought we were at a dead end.

33: The Boys at School

Home life was often intolerable and I wanted to run away, so I hid extra clothes in a nearby alley. It was a bit of a gamble to hide stuff, because there were four boys that hung around the neighbourhood and I was worried they might vandalize my stuff. In elementary school, they were the bullies. I avoided them because they always had a few tricks up their sleeves.

The ringleader of the boys lived two blocks from my house and went to my school, so it was normal to see him daily. One day as I was on my way to see a friend, I passed by his house. All four boys were busy tinkering inside the motor of a car. Instead of using the driveway, they had moved the car onto the lawn. They put down their tools and began to converse with me. For once in my life they treated me with politeness.

During our easygoing chat, the weather picked up wind so it made sense when they offered me a seat in the warm car. Since all four doors remained open at the time, I took cover on the front passenger side, but I left the door open. The kids hung outside the car but still seemed overly focused on me.

Either way, everything was going great but, in the middle of chatting, I was suddenly blindsided by what happened next. The boys grabbed for a door and they all leaped in at the same time. As soon as the doors slammed shut, they tackled me down on the seat. Instantaneously, my arms and ankles were tightly pinned, so I had no power to fend them off. I thrashed wildly, trying to break free of their grasp, but I really had no leeway because of their crushing hold. As I was being held against my will, I knew the worst was yet to come so I began to scream for help.

"Shut her up!" someone yelled out angrily.

My head flailed about as I tried to get away from the smothering dirty hands. My mouth was clasped so tightly that I could taste the greasy engine oil on their fingers. These stupid boys wanted a fight. Well, they got one! I chomped my teeth into a palm of flesh and one of them howled with pain. For a brief moment, I got my hand free and gouged my nails into oncoming flesh. In anger, the boys jerked my sweater and bra up to my chin and I was completely exposed.

"Let me go," I squealed as the frenzy of icy hands glided over my ribs and seized my chest. It felt like slithering snakes were racing over my body and I couldn't shake them off. Suddenly, I heard the snap on my jeans pop open and my pants were yanked below my knees.

"No!" I screamed, as my thighs were bare to the world. The hands swarmed and brutally groped at my underwear. I could feel the fabric pulling down with so much force that it ripped open.

The shredding sound nearly made me crazy, but I had to keep my head together. There had to be a way to stop this pack of wolves from their mauling, so I pierced their ears with bone-chilling screams.

"Stop! Stop! Let her go before she wakes my Dad," the leader of the boys demanded, and the kids reluctantly released their grip.

With trembling hands and unbearable humiliation, I fought to re-adjust my jumbled outfit as quickly as possible. But my clothes were in such a shamble that I was getting myself caught in them as the boys chuckled shamelessly. They swung open the car doors and I broke away as the laughter trailed behind.

What I should have done was banged on the front door and made that deadbeat father get off the couch and call the police.

No matter how many streets I passed, it felt like I was running on the spot. The sky was as dark and heavy as my heart and I was badly shaken. I couldn't go home, because I just didn't have the will to explain my appearance. I rapped on the door of Claudette's house; she was a school friend. Once inside, I didn't cry on my friend's shoulder—I didn't even tell her and she didn't ask—but she offered me a change of clothes.

Later that day, I climbed over fences and cut through the back roads to foil any chance of being seen by the pack of wolves. Back in the alley I found my stash, but the smart-ass boys had already destroyed everything with marker pens and switch-blade holes. I got home and Wilma wasn't around to eye me over. Thank God, because it would have turned into a blame game and I didn't want my mother to cleanse my body with another tub roasting.

The weekend ended way too fast. I knew that school was going to be dreadful. When I entered my home room, the nitwits were waiting for me. Right off the bat, I noticed two of the boys had red marks slashed over their arms, faces, and hands. They deserved much worse. Jail would have been too nice for them.

They hissed and snickered under their breath, but I went straight to my chair without talking to them. As I was sitting at my desk, they jabbed me in the ribs and I nearly fell out of my seat. They distracted the students with their bragging of how they ruthlessly tattered my alley clothes.

When the teacher left the room, the ringleader leaped from his desk and began pounding the table and chanting loudly so he could get all the students' attention.

"Her boobs are real—they're real," he gloatingly shouted as he pointed to me. By then the entire class was eyeballing my chest.

"Tell them how we know!" he cackled like an idiotic clown and I just wanted to scream in his ugly face what a jerk he was. The teasing and taunting went on for days and I thought it would never pass. It was torture to be the tabloid news at school.

Eventually, it got boring and the story died down, so the idiots channeled their persecution on someone else. Unfortunately, that someone else was my sister. The boys made cheap shots about Charlene's personal life. The poor girl could not shun the limelight that it cast on her. A mother's worst fear is hearing that her child is involved in drugs and sex. The hot topic went viral and spread straight to Wilma's ears.

It pained me to hear Wilma dissecting Charlene with question after question, but my sister was quick to defend herself. I saw Wilma's fear, not anger, as she haggled with Charlene. But Wilma could change so fast that it seemed impossible to come clean with her on anything. Without proof, Wilma let it go, but that didn't mean that she was just going to shake it off like rainwater.

34: Me

It was no secret to me that Charlene dabbled in drugs but I wasn't sure how far. She was the one who introduced me to glue sniffing. It had happened just a few weeks prior. She had invited me to go with her to an out-of-town fairground to watch a band with her friends.

Before the show, we sat cross-legged in the hallway of the arena as her friend produced a bag of glue. When Charlene had finished with the bag, she passed it to me. The fumes went straight to my head and I was instantly hit with the searing pain of a headache. That was the bottom line for me. I would never try it again.

Alcohol was a different bowl of fish. It was a quick fix that numbed my pain, so I didn't see it as a recipe for disaster. A part of me was becoming suicidal. Death was very prevalent in my mind. At the same time I was clinging to life. Yet another part of me was craving love and I was becoming promiscuous. My sister and I were sneaking around doing all the dumb things that teens do.

Then one day I came home hating my life so much that I downed a bottle of household poison from under the kitchen sink. It was a stupid cry for help and I totally regretted it. I did it mostly to get back at my pathetic life and my new boyfriend. He was not supportive when I needed him. He didn't go to my school, but he still knew about the incident with the four boys in the car and he didn't want to stick up for me. I didn't want to die, but it was my first realization that I had the power to end the pain.

I never thought Wilma would find out, because I didn't die or end up in hospital. I simply got sick in the bathroom and that was it. Somehow, Charlene got word and she told Wilma right away. Wilma probed for resolutions like she was trying to talk me back from a ledge. I could not bring myself to tell her; I wanted to spill my guts but I knew it would backfire and she would see me as crazy instead of lost.

Eventually, she loosened up but she didn't get caught up in promises that everything would be all right. I would have been so blessed to hear some kind of assurance. It would have rocked my world and fed my soul. But then, out of nowhere, I got a shot at redemption. Wilma decided that I was going to summer camp if I got passing grades. This was something that I had been waiting for year after year. But then I remembered how she had made that promise before and had never come through on her word.

Fortunately, Wilma registered me into the camp program, so I knew it was for real. I would miss out on our big family trip back east, but Wilma said that it was a better decision all around. It was a long plane ride and she was worried that I would get sick because I often threw up on car trips. I understood, but I was disappointed not to fly with my family.

On the last day of school, I ran home in excitement with my report card and, with pride, I handed it over to Wilma. She didn't pretend to be impressed, but I was gleaming from head to toe. I was in utter joy about going to summer camp, even though I wasn't much of a hiker, but I loved swimming, crafts, and roasting marshmallows on a fire. I had told all my friends that I would be away for the summer.

I could hardly close my eyes at night, especially when it came down to the last two days. I couldn't wait to pack my swimsuit and my summer clothes. I asked Wilma what I should take. She came to my bedroom and stood in the doorway.

As I sat on the bed, Wilma stated there was a change in plans: I wouldn't be going to camp after all. My "sweet Mom" had lied again. She had never signed my name on any list. It had been too good to be true. I should have known better than to fall for it. Just like her yearly promise of a new bike that never happened. It was just the nature of the beast and I would get over it. Disappointing, but not the end of the world.

Then she told me that our family would still be flying back east, and that she had already purchased the tickets for everyone... except for me.

Did she just say what I thought I heard?

"Where am I going?" I was totally stumped.

"You will be staying with another family," she said.

"Who?" I was afraid to ask but Wilma claimed she didn't know, because the social worker was taking care of that.

"When will I come home?"

"Your Dad and I feel that you would be better off living in a home with children your own age. So you won't be coming back here, because it's a permanent move."

"You are sending me away to live with someone else? You want to get rid of me? You mean forever?" I asked, as I shook my head in disbelief.

"You can always come and visit, and we can write letters every week." The volume of Wilma's voice had pumped up as though it was a reason to celebrate. I clutched my head in my hands and my stomach wanted to retch. Suddenly, I had a shelf life with an expired date and I was about to get the boot. So, why was she smiling?

Wilma's knuckles wrapped around my doorknob like an iron fist. She kept one foot inside my room and the other foot never left the hallway.

"You brought this on yourself," she said, as her face dropped the earlier animation and turned unreadable. She didn't flinch when I fell apart. I wanted to rush across the room and clutch her so tightly that nothing could ever pull me away from her. I feared that I would be homeless or go to another home that was worse than the one I was already in. I had no say in the situation. Wilma did not comfort me and over the coming hours, my heart had no peace unless I drifted into sleep.

How had it come to this? All that I ever was or could be was not enough. Even though Wilma wasn't my real Mom, I wanted her love so badly. I thought we were in this together, even when it was hard to see it in a not-so-progressive light. I had barely entered my teens and I would not even have her support during the hardest time of growing up.

Like clockwork, the world went on ticking even though I wished it would stop and give me more time. We couldn't change the past, but we could start with a clean slate. When Wilma put her foot down, she stuck to her guns so there was no hope of changing her mind.

The next morning, I came out of the bedroom and walked to the kitchen. Wilma and her grown daughters sat around the table enjoying a cup of brew. I interjected for permission to keep my bike. She agreed and I left for my room. The kitchen was oddly quiet, so I turned to look back.

Dora, who was the oldest daughter, had gotten up from the chair and was mocking my walk. She put a dumb look on her face. Her arms were swishing back and forth like a stupid ape and they all peeled with laughter. A real vote of confidence for me to see that! Thanks, Dora. They jokingly heckled until someone noticed that I was at the end of the hall. It felt like I was watching a witch-hunt. I thought to myself that they hated me.

Then Wilma called me back to the kitchen.

"How many times have I told you to walk with your shoulders straight? You look like a retarded monkey when you're slouched over. Stand up straight like I taught you and don't be mad at Dora. She is just trying to look out for you."

Trying to look out for me? That's a good laugh, but the joke had worn thin. Good thing Wilma set the record straight. Like her little pep talk was going to make it all better. There were daggers in my eyes and I wanted to smack Dora. I was leaving the next day. Couldn't she save it for when I was gone? I hated her and wished she were dead. My posture was always a pet peeve for Wilma. In the past, she struck with the flat side of her hand in a karate chop action before I even knew that my shoulders were up or stooped or whatever it was that caused her to strike. She would come from behind so I couldn't dodge her. Then she would crack my shoulder like she was axing a log.

When I got back to my room I was so manic that I wanted to smash and destroy everything I owned. My fists clenched so tightly that I shook, because I couldn't let out my anger. It just wasn't worth another blow; it wasn't even worth a lecture. It wasn't long after that Wilma had an idea to memorialize our last day with something more cheerful; she was taking me shopping.

Except for Christmas or birthdays, she never bought me anything but underwear and socks. All my clothes came from the Sally Ann or from Charlene. It was supposed to be a fun afternoon, but it was unbearable. The whole time, Wilma was saying things to cheer me, but nothing she said made a difference. I was at a loss for words. We walked through the department store aisle and passed the spot where the deviant man had put his hands on me. The recap of that day still plagued me, but shopping with Wilma was torture.

After two grim hours, I dragged the shopping bags into my room and dumped them into the suitcase. I took my magazine clips off the bedroom wall and held each one like a piece of priceless art. I loved my colourful handpicked fashion clips, because they displayed beauty and vision.

I piled all the centrefolds and threw them in the garbage. It was a small gesture to acknowledge my exile yet so hard to let go. My room would turn into a guest room once I was gone. These walls had been my little cove, a hideaway that held my dreams, memories, and privacy.

35: Everything I Own Fits in My Suitcase

Whatever didn't fit in my suitcase would have to stay behind. Wilma clicked the locks on my bag and dragged it to the front door. By late morning, the sun was so intense that it was hard to open my eyes. It was already shaping into a warm sunny day, but not to me. I wanted to run back to bed, to hide under the covers, and make the day go away.

Miss Grey the social worker came around with her little car and parked in the driveway. It was impossible not to cry when I saw my suitcase hauled to the trunk. Charlene was crushed to tears and I knew it wasn't her choice to lose her baby sister. After the car was packed, Wilma, Charlene, and I cried together. I didn't know how I would survive such closure. To speak words of goodbye was something I couldn't do.

As the car backed out of the carport, Charlene and Wilma clung together and waved from the porch. I hoped they would rush down the steps and offer a last-minute retraction. I waved frantically as my vision turned murky.

"Will I ever see my family again?"

"I'm sure you will." Miss Grey drove to the freeway and headed north.

"Where am I going?"

"The shelters are full and I don't have a permanent home for you, but I have a temporary placement."

I knew that few families want foster teens. Finding a home would mean that she would have to venture off the beaten path and use her deepest resources.

Miss Grey drove to the other side of town, parked, and knocked on the front door of a polished little rancher home.

Once inside, I met the Taylors and to my surprise I knew their daughter very well. Their adopted daughter, Daphne, was Charlene's best friend, but I had never seen her parents before or known where she lived. I felt certain that Wilma knew where I was. From day one, the Taylors and I didn't hit it off. They didn't like me at all and they didn't mince words.

I did my best to stay out of their face and they didn't pretend to care unless I was late for curfew. There was no parental guidance, so I was hanging out with the worst kind of people. While Miss Grey was making a concerted effort to find a more suitable placement, the damage had been done. My smoking, drinking, and trying to find love in all the wrong places was catastrophic. I couldn't stand the Taylors, so it would be liberating to get away from them.

I was another wild child on the waiting list.

36: Beth

Beth

◄   Eugeanea
◄   4-year-old girl
◄   2-year-old girl

Two weeks later, I was shuttled off to another home.

The new home looked so cute and inviting. Every inch of the yard was surrounded by a picket fence. The flowers arching and turning their faces to the sun made me feel calm inside. I don't remember the introductions of that day, but I will never forget Beth. She was a natural at loving others.

She already had two little foster girls. One was four and the other was two. Beth never raised her voice or hurt them, and I felt safe in her home. It was obvious that the girls loved Beth as their Mom, but she had no plans to adopt or keep them. Regrettably, given their young age, it could so sadly turn out to be a never-ending pursuit to replace their mother.

Every day, I was hanging out or walking around to buy some time. I really felt dismissed by anyone who could give a damn. My anxiety made me feel like I was fighting for air, especially in the night when I was alone to think. Everything was happening so quickly that I did not know if I was going to sink or swim. Some days were good and other days I felt like I was tied to a railroad track and the train was right around the corner.

A thought, memory, or flashback of Wilma would throw me off. In the day, I tried to ignore the absence of my family, but at night when I was in bed, it was all I could think about. One night when I was dealing with my loss, Beth heard me. I thought that I was good at hiding emotions, but Beth was a perceptive mother.

"What's wrong?" she whispered as she opened the door, allowing the light to stream across the room. She inched her way cautiously to the edge of the bed and sat lightly as if I might ask her to go away.

"It's nothing," I retorted quickly, but not fast enough to conceal my wet eyes.

It would be too uncomfortable to allow her to dig in and expose me. I already felt ashamed about the hurdles that left me feeling dead inside.

"Why are you sad?" She looked me in the eyes as she put her hand gently on my cheek and turned my face to hers. Her voice was tranquil and persuasive and, before I knew it, I submitted.

"I just want to go home. I want my family back, but they don't love me and they don't want me anymore." The words were so much more painful out loud than in my head. Of course, my nose got all soppy, so Beth went to get some tissues.

"Why do you think they don't love you?" Beth asked as she came back and sat closer.

"They sent me away. Mom said I lied too many times."

"Why did you feel like you had to lie?" Beth asked.

"My Mom never believed the truth. She would get so furious at me that I was always scared of her. I would lie because I didn't want her to keep doing stuff to hurt me."

I talked on and Beth stayed and listened without putting a negative twist on anything I said. At the time, I only saw the bad in myself. I did not see the horrible damage that Wilma had done.

"It must be so scary not knowing where you are going. It makes me sad to see how much it's hurting you. But you need a family who loves you no matter what mistakes you make. I don't think your Mom was able to do that. It's better that you get another chance with a family who loves you for the girl you are," Beth said. Then she held me and I wanted to stay in her arms all night.

"What will happen to me?" I asked weakly as the words tumbled out of my head.

Beth took her time and I heard a sigh before she spoke. Carefully, she explained that it was perfectly reasonable for me to be scared. Through her own experience and wisdom, she knew there were many people in the world who would open their hearts and doors.

My face was damp and my hair was clingy as she soothed my head against her chest. In those late hours, we achieved a light of hope. She helped me to find strength before I destroyed what little was left of my self-worth. I wasn't any tougher, but somehow I was stronger or, at least, I had enough positive reinforcement to keep myself going.

How could I have tumbled into such an awesome place and not be able to stay longer than two weeks? This was the perfect home.

37: Matilda and Smokey

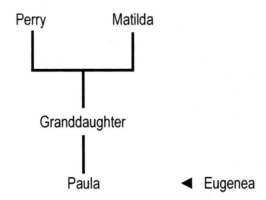

I didn't want to leave , but my social worker was like a rescue dog. She knew when it was time to pull me out of homes that didn't offer long-term security. She had promised firmly and loyally that she would somehow find the right family for me.

So, Miss Grey was back, and she looked amazing as always. Her sun-streaked hair and freshly glowing face seemed to exude her trust in humanity. Her smile was easygoing, and I knew she was anxious to tell me about my next "adventure." We drove out of the city limits and after an hour we arrived in a village. All the way, I heard the exciting news about my new parents and I tried to picture what it would be like to live on a farm.

We pulled into the tiniest town on the planet; it had a population of 300 to be exact. The main road was paved in asphalt and only three blocks long. There was a gas station, a store with mail service, a church, a school, and lots of farmhouses. It looked desolate and I wasn't sure if that was such a good idea after all. The car stopped right out front of a two-storey house. The paint was cracked and peeled, and the grass in the back was knee high.

No matter.

I followed Miss Grey through the gate and along the walkway. I heard a cow bellowing; there were no sounds of city life. It was incredibly quiet and laid back, and certainly something I wasn't used to. In the backyard among the rustle of reeds bobbed a family of long-necked ganders. That was so cool and I couldn't wait to chase them around the barn.

First things first; I needed to meet the parents.

The back door creaked opened and a woman stepped out to greet us.

Yikes! The new mom was much older than any moms I'd had before. Her back was badly hunched over as she peered over the rims of her glasses. It was obvious that the woman named Matilda was in her late senior years of life. I believe that God has a sense of humour, but it didn't seem fair that Matilda would be stuck with a hormonally high-riding teen.

Matilda had something to show me before I unpacked. Near the side of the back porch was a cardboard box that appeared to look empty, so I stepped closer to get a full view. Deep in the corner, I could see a kitten curled in a ball. I looked back at Matilda.

"Oh, she's so adorable." I gushed excitedly as the kitty hissed at me and batted the air with her claws.

"She's all yours." Matilda smiled brightly.

The kitty looked so alone and helpless and my heart ached for her. Instinctively, I loved her like a baby and I wanted to be there for all her needs. I reached in to give her comfort, but I quickly retracted when she fanged and hissed. Her piercing blue eyes were wild and reckless and she was a bit of a rebel.

For a brief second, I hesitated about what to do. Kitty hissed a low cautioning snarl, so I reached in and snatched her before she had a chance to fight back. As I stroked her soft little coat, she let down her guard and purred. I marveled at her ability to adjust and adapt to my touch. I had always wanted a pet of my own. I named her Smokey. It suited her because her fur was a deep shade—the colour of coal.

Miss Grey had to get back to the city, so Matilda and I took the kitten inside.

"I'll show you where your room is," she said as she grabbed my suitcase and I followed behind.

Most of the furnishings inside were old wooden pieces that didn't match. The floor was covered in big leafy green print linoleum that went from wall to wall.

"This will be your room. You can keep your things in here."

Matilda placed my belongings on the bed in the spare room, and I knew the drill from there. As supper approached, so did Perry, Matilda's husband. He was a tall lanky man with a stooped back. Perry was not an audible man, nor did he appear to be a deep listener. It seemed to me that he had developed a way to tune things out selectively.

Matilda was quite a talker. She shared a delusion of shameful tales every night, especially during dinner. I learned why Perry mostly ignored her. On occasion, he would huff, even though he appeared to look tolerable to the situation. Other times he would get mad and storm off, but she would follow him around the house with her endless nattering. Eventually, his escape would be the barn.

Matilda had a few little perks up her sleeve, like teaching me how to cook and sew. She enriched our afternoons with her keep-it-simple learning and I followed along with ease. Naughty stories of the neighbours were a minor distraction, but I laughed them off and over time I could whip up breakfast like a pro.

Whatever Matilda thought or said should have remained at home, but nothing stopped her from running at the mouth. She gave a new meaning to "spreading the word," especially during church. Her mouth spilled ludicrous allegations of love affairs. And it didn't end there. Her claims shocked and riled the accused and it often got ugly during the itinerary of Sunday meetings. She told some real whoppers, which could have caused an angry mob. I kept waiting for the other shoe to drop.

I was scared that she would get her windows smashed or something. Matilda got a lot of tongue-lashings and people called her a crazy old busybody, but that was it.

It wasn't long before I was embarrassed and annoyed by her gossip and we argued many times.

Matilda didn't let our fights clutter up an opportunity to make things better between us. She threw a party and three girls my age came to celebrate my birthday. I didn't know any of them, but I had seen the girls in the neighbourhood. During the hotdogs and cake, we clicked very well. As a result, we ended the party with a sleepover. Inside a wooden-based tent around the side of the house, we shared our secrets and ghost stories.

Matilda was a God-fearing Mormon. I didn't like her bible thumping, because she was too overbearing. She cracked the whip and tried to be a tough cookie, but she had an undeniably soft centre. One minute we were at each other's throats and the next we were buddy-buddy. We had barely gotten acquainted when her youngest grandchild died unexpectedly. It rocked her like a storm and I feared it would be the death of her.

What a woman! Somehow she moved on. She continued with her church activities and did what she could to care for me. She made picnics and arranged for boating on the lake. It was new and exciting as I ventured my luck on water skis. It took three tries before I left the dock and was gliding over the shining water. I was on top of the world.

However, my moment in the fast lane was only a glimpse as I cartwheeled into the air and splashed into the drink. I hadn't let go of the tug ropes so I was pulled in the undertow. What a wild experience. Under the water, I was so thrilled that I had done it. All I needed to do was let go of the ropes and free myself before I drowned!

Being young and foolish, I rebelled a lot. I assumed Perry's gentle demeanor would make him an easy pushover. But there was no way on earth he would tolerate the back talk of a smart-mouthed thirteen-year-old brat. Needless to say, I learned to toe the line around him. My dealings were usually with Matilda, but it was no picnic to scrap with her either. My fast talk couldn't outsmart her old school quick wit and spunk.

Matilda's granddaughter Paula and I shared a common thread: we both loved horses. So Matilda pulled a few strings and set up a time for me to ride with Paula. On our first outing, Paula saddled her horse Star and gave me a pony to ride along. We trailed over the gravel nicely until my horse wandered off the path and down into the ditch. Paula warned me to pull back on the reins, but the harder I tugged the more my horse refused.

"He won't go back on the road," I shouted helplessly.

"You have to stop him or he'll drag you through the trees so he can knock you off." Paula alerted, but it was too late. My horse dropped his head and demonstrated that I was in the back seat. He dove straight under some low-lying branches and he came out untouched. I took a beating from the wiry coil of twigs as I fought the blinding leaves. Amidst all that, my stomach heaved from the thud of a branch when I was knocked to the ground.

With a groan, I looked up to see my proud-as-a-peacock pony eating from the very tree that nearly took my eye out. I sat up and touched my shipwrecked hair. Paula was sitting on her horse, wailing with laughter. I felt like I was in my first class of horse-riding school for dummies. That's what I call "a crash course."

38: Melinda and the Boys

Out of all my friends, there was no one who could hold a candle to Melinda. She lived across the road in a modern rancher house with a double driveway. Ever since the day of my birthday party, we had become best buds. We often did stupid things, like breaking into a closed-down restaurant through the roof and then turning it into a hideout. We were happy-go-lucky to have each other.

At night, we slept in the tent so we could sneak out to meet our friends and raid the farmers' gardens. Let the games begin!

The farmers were angry, so they hid electrical trip wires between the rows of earth. We were completely taken off-guard, and most of us got zapped. No big deal, we made a Plan B and stepped crossways to avoid getting shocked. At the closing of our night shift, we had plucked armfuls of vegetables from the Davies property with no shame at all. As we parted from the land, Farmer Davies caught us off-guard when his door popped open and there he was in his saggy long johns, armed with something that resembled a rifle.

"I hear you out there. Now, get off my property or I'll blow your heads off," he threatened as his eyes scouted around to see who was out there.

We dropped the food and scattered like terrorized chickens. Quick as thieves, we dive-bombed the ditch and lay stiff as carcasses in the rustling reeds. My heart was doing a wild kind of jitterbug dance as I stared at the open door through the blades of grass, but I didn't move a muscle. His scowled face was so scary.

"Don't let me catch you little hellions around my house again," he hollered from under his dully lit porch. His wife shouldered next to him in her knee-length nightie and rolled-up hair. She coaxed him to go back inside. As soon as the porch light flicked off, we scurried over the bank and fled. Farmer Davies's fear tactics worked. It was no laughing matter to any of us. We didn't want to end up dead in the ditch!

Surprisingly, my eavesdropping Mom hadn't caught wind about my unscrupulous night, so I was back on the wild side the following evening. I regrouped with Melinda and the boys and we walked to the water tower. This was our only outlet since we didn't have any arcades or theatres in town. The ladder on the side of the tower wasn't ground level so we had to boost and pull each other up. There were warning signs not to trespass, but we didn't care. At the top we were fearless as we ran the platform that curved around the tank.

Under the moon the boys teased and joked, and didn't seem to have a care in the world. The stars glowed in the dark like the ends of our cigarettes. The boys always had an extra pack of cigarettes as though it were mandatory. I never asked about their upbringing, but when they sat in the same Sunday school they behaved in a totally different manner.

Our compulsions drove us to re-enter the high tower every night. From our lookout post, we could see who was home and what lights were on. I knew Matilda was a heavy sleeper and her bedside lamp never went on after she ascended to her bedroom. The tower was always a peaceful place until the boys got into a scrap that turned into a shouting match and a scuffle.

Had they gone mad? I wondered as they shoved each other. Sheer panic hit me when I saw one of the boys lose his balance. His body crashed the single railing and I caught a mental vision of him spiraling over the edge. He was okay but, after that night, we never went to the tower again.

September mornings had turned to frost so I was no longer allowed to sleep in the tent. I couldn't sneak out of the house because the doors creaked. What an impediment. My friends tapped on my window and promised to wait for me in the tent. I pushed the window pane up, but the wire screen was nailed tight. I tried to pry it open and I was able to make enough room to fling my shoes out on the lawn. I couldn't get it to open any wider so there was no chance I could break free. I finally shut the window and drew the shade down.

In the morning, Matilda walked in without knocking. She insisted I rise, but I ignored her and flipped the blanket over my shoulders. She walked around the bed to the window and yanked on the blind. As it rolled up, she saw the screen partially jutting out on one side.

"What happened here?" She asked and then she spotted the shoes in the grass below. I was busted. "It's you who has been sneaking out at night. You and Melinda," she shrieked and ripped off the blanket as I grumbled. Matilda immediately realized the infamous Night Garden Stalker lived right under her nose. She instantly proposed a punishment of grounding. Big deal, I thought, but then she left the house and went straight to Melinda's house.

From the window, I saw Matilda banging on Melinda's door and that made me insane. How could she do this? Then I saw my friend standing in the doorway with her parents. I was sure that Melinda's parents would flip out and put an end to our friendship.

I couldn't hear, but I could see it sinking in by the way their faces frowned and turned to see me in the window. I wanted to duck out of sight. I hated to be in the spotlight; it made me feel guilty. Melinda's parents didn't care about the raids, our socially unacceptable behaviour, or any other injustice. Suddenly, the front lawn was alive with shouts and pointing fingers. Two against one might come across as a bit unfair, but Matilda didn't back down until she was ordered to leave their property. It was hard for me to watch, because it was my fault in the first place.

During the battle, Melinda came to my gate, so I snubbed the rules momentarily and ran out to hug her. She told me that her parents had never gotten along with Matilda, because my foster Mom had never learned the code of silence. She refused to apologize for snooping into matters that had nothing to do with her. Melinda's parents told Matilda that she was not allowed to set foot on their property.

Matilda and I fought through four emotionally conflicted months and it was time to cease fire and call a spade a spade.

In spite of our battles, Matilda had an impact on me. She taught me some basic needs, but she gave so much more because she gave her heart to me. I could never communicate to her how grateful I would be. It would only come to me decades after her passing as I was in the heart of writing my memoirs.

In the last week of October, life was repeating itself: I was moving again.

39: Martha and Dennis

On my last day at Matild a's, Miss Grey didn't come for me, so I didn't have the slightest heads up on what to expect of the new family. Some time around mid-afternoon, the wheels of a blue station wagon crawled along the gravel out front of Matilda's house. Another move: easy come, easy go. The parents waited in their car with their little offspring in the back.

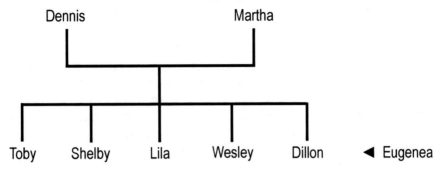

The skies were growing dark early and there was a nip in the air, but it wasn't cold. Matilda trembled and cried as her hands reached for mine. She gifted me with her bible and implored me to be good.

Introductions went around the car as I tried to enter. It was cramped; there were so many little faces and kids sitting on other kids. Kitty was allowed to come too, so she was safe in my arms. I twisted around to look out the back window. Melinda was standing in the middle of the road, between her parents and crying. We had pleaded with her parents to adopt me so we could be sisters. I suddenly felt powerless as if invisible chains and shackles bound my freedom. How was I governed that I had to transfer yet again to another home without anyone hearing my own proposal? When do I get to have a say in this?

In my new home, Martha was the mother of the den. She was a dutiful wife and a hard worker, but she didn't look like she ever enjoyed a second of it. I found the home was unloving and hectic. With kids in every corner of the house, there were lots of needs to fill. I didn't mind the ceaseless chores, but I didn't want to feel like a scullery maid. I felt like I was there for only one purpose when there were nine mouths to feed.

The boys got up at 5:00 a.m. to do the grunt work. They were out in the snow to feed the cows, do the milking, and clean out the barn. For us girls, we slaved over the stove and a stockpile of dishes. When the milk came in from the barn, I climbed a stool and emptied the bucket into the separating machine to separate the cream from the fat. Once that was done, the machine had to be taken apart and washed. It was time consuming.

School sandwiches had to be made and the little ones needed help. The baby had to be fed and changed. If it took too long and I didn't get it all done, then I wasn't allowed to ride the school bus. I would have to walk two miles in the snow and it was impossible to get there on time, so that meant detention at school and more trouble when I got home. Boarding school would have been more fun.

After school came more chores and homework until bedtime. Laundry was done on Saturdays and it had to be dried on a clothesline. I dreaded that the most, because old Jack Frost was so unforgiving in November. The wet linen would freeze my fingers to the bone.

Dennis was such a jerk. But he was my foster parent and I had to respect him. He was a man of minuscule patience. His tall Stetson hat suited his rugged face and gruff voice. I was very cautious around him and the big Mormon household. Practically the entire town seemed to be Mormon and I was Catholic.

At school I fit in right away because I was new. I had many friends and it was very flattering to have a crowd of kids around me. Getting voted for second-most-popular girl in school was a boost to my ego. I felt like a celebrity. But Dennis and Martha had a rule of no dating until the age of sixteen. It was a little late for that, because I already had a boyfriend. Tom and I hung out during lunch, making it obvious that we were an item. He had an impressive James Dean look. His bad-boy image was so cool.

My new foster parents were painfully strict, but when opportunity knocked, I broke some rules. When they went out for an evening I couldn't resist to call my boyfriend. In the pitch black, all I could see was the headlight on his motorbike as he cruised into the driveway. He parked and took off his helmet as I watched from the front window. I knew I was putting myself on the hot seat when we cuddled on the couch and watched TV. He said I was pretty and we kissed, but I was so nervous that it was difficult to welcome his compliment and affections. I kept imagining my foster parents coming through the door as the clock ticked on. I told him to leave.

"I just got here," he said shyly. He looked at me as though I was nuts.

Stay or go? I wanted him to do both.

"Can I see you tomorrow?" Tom asked as he zipped his leather bomber jacket closed. My kiss confirmed a definite yes and we decided to meet at my locker before class. Tom took my hand as we walked around the side of the couch toward the door. My eyes opened wide in shock to find Toby, the oldest son, hiding behind the couch. He said that he was looking for something he'd dropped. I was livid.

"Why are you spying on me?" I snapped as Toby's face reddened.

"I'm sorry. Please don't be mad." Toby was on his feet in seconds.

"Get out of here, Toby," I said, pointing a vexed finger to the door.

He slunk away and I felt a bit shaky. I really wanted Tom to get going before his presence caused a ruckus. Tom's bike pulled out of the driveway and, given the timing, it was more than likely he passed my parents on the road. Toby's little sister Shelby was spying too, but she didn't rat me out, because she was saving it for future blackmail.

Within the week, Shelby made her demands and if I didn't want to comply with her, she would tell her parents about Tom. This went on for months, even after I split up with Tom. As the blackmail worsened, I finally complained to Lila, Shelby's sister. Lila told my foster father Dennis everything and I was scared that I would be punished. To my shock, Shelby got a wicked spanking. I was not happy about it, but I didn't feel sorry for her. She deserved it.

To my heartache, my kitten Smokey got the boot. She had to live in the barn because she wasn't a mouse catcher. She was just a baby—only four months old. I tried to persuade my parents that she was too fragile for Alberta's snowstorms. At night, I heard meowing, but in the day she was nowhere to be found.

"There's a dead cat in the barn," Dennis said in a matter-of-fact smugness as he pulled off his snowy-wet gloves. I dropped what I was doing and ran to the barn. Smokey was glassy-eyed and frozen stiff as a board. Her teeth were fanged and it was obvious that she had suffered in death. I wanted to scream, cry, and swear at my stupid parents.

It was cruel and heartless, and there was no comfort for such a loss. It was then that I knew I didn't have to love my parents, even if I had to live with them. Besides, my friends were far more important than this so-called family. With that attitude, I really wasn't thinking straight when I let myself be influenced by the wrong crowd.

40: The Girls at School

A group of girls skipped out of school for half a day and I was invited to join. The parents of one of the girls had alcohol in the house, so we got drunk. Afterwards, I headed back to school reeking of booze and cigarettes. I just made it back in time for the bus home, but it was quite a blow to find that my little venture was already school news. On the bus ride home, Lila told me that our parents already knew about it.

How was that possible? Wow, no secrets in that town.

The bus pulled up to our house and I was the last to get off. Eyes of anger settled on me as I got in the door. It was time for the talk. It all went down in the music room where family disciplines were usually addressed. I knew that a private meeting in that room was a serious offence.

My foster father Dennis did most of the talking. He interrogated me down to every detail from lunch time onward. After two hours, I just wanted it to be over with, so I confessed to everything and was grounded. Grounded from what? I didn't know, as I had had no life since I moved there. Dennis said that I would have a lot more chores and I would probably be suspended from school as well.

In opening class the next day, I felt a cringe in my stomach as my name was called over the loudspeaker. Where's that drink now when I could really use it?

The principal was not someone to be toyed with. I knew he wouldn't take any patronizing. As a disciplinarian, he demanded respect and I was ready to kiss butt. However, the other three girls would not be worked over so easily and that made him furious.

We didn't get suspended; instead he removed his belt and strapped each of us three times on each hand. That was much more humiliating than a suspension. That was the fork in the road that made me want to get my act together. The good kids no longer wanted to associate with me and my newest boyfriend was a real Goody Two-Shoes. He dumped me immediately. I tried to talk to him, but he sneered and turned his back on me. His groupies that normally fawned around wouldn't give me a second look. From that day, he and his entourage walked through the halls, passing me as if I was invisible.

I didn't want any part of the bad-girl scene, but my past actions were already stacked against me. Unless I took immediate steps, I would be considered as one of them. It's never too late to turn things around, so I wrote the girls and explained. I had resolved to focus on my studies and behave, which meant there was no more hanging out with them. Right off the bat, they twisted my words and left a nasty note inside my desk.

During lunch break, they blocked me so I couldn't pass and knocked my books out of my arms. I was shocked but I quickly dashed around to collect my papers. It was the first of many more such incidents to come. School hallways turned into a catwalk of bullying. The girls travelled in a pack, so it was three against one. I couldn't get from class to class without getting circled and clawed. I took a new route, but the girls caught on. My ex-boyfriend passed by and witnessed the girls trying to make me their sacrificial lamb. I hoped Mr. Most Popular would step in between, but he kept on walking.

I was afraid to use the bathroom, because there I got cornered with fists. I tried to shield myself from the blows, but I was outnumbered. School was Hell. Each time was worse than the last and teachers did nothing to stop it. I thought I was the most hated person in the world. The attacks made me late for class, so my teacher grounded me after school. I would miss the bus and get grounded when I got home. I couldn't win.

Even when I was home, the leader of the girls would call my house. She threatened to stab me to death if she ever saw me alone. I was afraid to leave the house or go to school. I begged my parents to intervene, but bullying was not taken seriously back then. It wasn't their problem, so I had to deal with it on my own.

It went on for another three years.

41: Mr. Hill, Wilma, and Dennis

My parents couldn't care less about my trivial matters, yet they seemed to thrive on the idea of changing my faith from Catholicism to Mormonism. I had an open mind and went along until Dennis condemned my faith with his bible bashing. He drilled it into my head that church attendance and bible study were law. I didn't want it crammed down my throat. He insisted I learn gospel lessons from the missionaries. Although I wasn't a Mormon, I did conform to keep the peace and I attended church.

My one and only male social worker, Mr. Hill, was the first to verbalize compliments and it made me feel good. He noted my progress and never dwelled on anything negative, and I began to trust him. Ultimately I told him that I wanted to go back to live with Wilma. I went on to explain how I was not happy and I had been on my best behaviour and would do anything to be able to go back. I believed that Wilma was the closest thing to a family that I had ever had. Although Wilma was a terrible mother, I accepted whatever shame she inflicted on me even when there was nothing for me to be ashamed about.

Mr. Hill told me that Wilma wanted me back. He promised to call them and make the arrangements for me to return. I was so overwhelmed with happiness that I went to my room and danced around in delight. Life was great and my head was in the clouds as I opened the window to look out. Straight below my window stood Mr. Hill with Dennis. They were outside the back door discussing my conversation.

"She wants to go back and live with Wilma, whom she refers to as her Mom. But I will never let it happen. She will never, ever go back," Mr. Hill told Dennis.

Why would he throw me under the bus? I couldn't believe what I was hearing. Damn him! I was boiling mad and, in one swipe of my hand, I sent everything on the dresser crashing to the floor. In my fury, I tore my bed apart as my eyes flooded with tears. I stayed curled in the sheets until I was able to simmer down.

I thought that there had to be something better than this, as my eyes crusted over with my salty tears. Not one father had ever made an effort to hug me or say the word "love." But Dennis was the worst father figure of all the parents I had encountered. He was a bully.

I remembered when the baby was in her highchair next to Dennis and she was irritable and whiney.

"Shut up." Dennis slammed his fist, causing the dishes to rattle.

The baby whined louder so he swung his big hand straight out and *bam*. He slapped her across the face and she shrieked.

"Shut up," Dennis screamed at her.

Tears were pouring out of her eyes and she was gasping and shaking all over, but she didn't dare to let out a scream. That was more than I could stomach. I wanted to snatch the baby away from him. I was sure that Martha would soothe the baby, but she went on with dinner like nothing had happened. Her baby had beet-red cheeks and swollen eyes, yet Martha didn't do or say a thing. It was so shocking that no one at the table could talk.

I thought I'd seen the worst that Dennis could do, but I was wrong. I was outside weeding with my foster sisters on a baking hot day. There was no shade and we were not allowed to stop working during the day except for lunch.

My eight-year-old foster brother Wesley took our younger brother Dillon outside to work in the yard. The cracked hardened soil had to be plowed. After hours of toiling in the heat, Dillon and Wesley started bickering over the roto-tiller. We had all taken a turn with the rototiller in the past and knew what a pain it was to use. When it worked, it was a powerful groundbreaking machine. But it was loud, big, and awkward to handle, especially for a child. Plus, it was a piece of junk, so it always broke down, causing everyone more work and wasted time.

In the middle of weeding, I looked up and saw Dennis making his way across the lawn. Perspiration was pouring out from under his cowboy hat and his hands were curled into fists. I wished he was going over to calm the boys and help them restart the tiller. That wasn't the case. Dennis went psycho on the boys. He grabbed them and rammed the tip of his cowboy boots into their flesh, repeatedly. He was cussing mad as he gave the little boys a real battering.

"I hate you! I hate you!" my foster brother Wesley screamed bravely as his face reddened against his freckled skin. He pulled away and ran to the house. I was so grateful Dennis didn't go after him. The unspeakable cruelty left me with a stark reality that I was re-living abuse even if it wasn't mine. I was proud of Wesley for having the guts to express his anger. I wanted to share a few choice words for Dennis, but I didn't want to get backhanded like the baby.

From that day, my mind was enamoured with dreams of a way out. I talked to Toby about it because we were very close. During the day we worked, but at night he would sneak into my room. Then we would go downstairs and flop on his bed and talk. He would put on the moves, but I never let him touch me. We kissed a lot, but that was the end of the line. His cuddle was a temporary comfort to coping with loneliness and the overbearing rules of the house. I never once saw any tenderness between our parents, nor did I ever witness Dennis telling his kids that he was proud of them or that he loved them.

My social worker Mr. Hill was transferred to another area and I was glad to get rid of him. I would rather have had the stereotypical social worker than an egotistical liar.

My new social worker Miss Ryder came to the farm to have her first visit with my parents and me. That's when I was able to see beyond the obvious. Somehow, I had to get Miss Ryder alone so I could tell her what was on my mind. But her visit was too short so I missed my chance. Summer passed into fall and Miss Ryder didn't come by, so I had no way to get ahold of her.

Then, at the beginning of winter, I was at school when my name was called over the intercom. It was a bit scary, because I had to go to the Principal's office. My social worker was sitting in the waiting area.

"Here's a thought," I said to myself, "Why don't I take matters into my own hands.?"

I was scared, but I came right out and told her that I didn't want to live with Dennis and Martha. It wasn't in my mind to make a complaint to child-protective services, so I didn't explain why. As I sat across from her, there was no way I could hide that I was truly unhappy. I watched the smile from her face drown into a look of disappointment. She said that it would take some time to find another home for me but she would make it happen. It felt like I was flying by the seat of my pants. I was ecstatic.

Word travelled fast. When I got home from school, Dennis already knew. I barely had my coat off when he singled me out in front of the family. He told his kids that I didn't want to live there because I didn't love them. What a cruel lie! I felt so bad for the kids.

"Who would like to take over her room?" Dennis smirked. He wanted to get even; there was no way he was going to bury the hatchet. Not one of the kids jumped at the offer. Why did he have to use them to hurt me? He kept right on talking about me all through dinner and I wanted to stand up and slap him like the way he had slapped his baby.

However, I would be gone soon and all I needed to do was hang in there. It was hard as I had to stay another month and it dragged right through Christmas. Two days after, I got the best gift of all. On December 27, it was moving day.

42: Gabriella and Howie

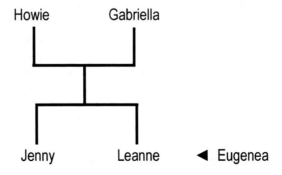

"There is someone here to see you," Martha said, standing in my bedroom door. Nervously, I entered the kitchen to find a woman seated near the living room window. Her face was turned to look over the view of the snow-covered road that led into town. She looked up and smiled, and I wondered what kind of mother she would be. I assumed she would be another typically "nice mother" who would turn on me later.

The two mothers chimed into conversation as I put on my winter gear and set my bags at the door. Until that day, Martha wasn't the touchy-feely type. She wasn't emotionally connected, nor did she show interest in my personal battles. Our journey was over and we cried together for the first and last time.

Gabriella was my new parent. I didn't want to be shy, but I didn't know what to say as Gabriella took the wheel and drove out of the driveway. It was gratifying to just sit and listen to her talk about her family as we travelled along the snow-crusted road.

The frozen ground sparkled like a glitzy skating arena. It was so bright it was hard to see. But the sun went down and it was nearly dark by the time we arrived at Gabriella's house. From the truck, I saw a decorated tree twinkling in the window of her home. Outside, the barn and gates glittered in snow. It looked like an old-fashioned Christmas card.

I felt a tweak of enthusiasm as we stomped the snow off our boots and entered the front door. The cozy interior was sweet comfort to my eyes and I could feel myself unwinding. There was nothing to fear and I wanted to believe that with all my heart. Suddenly, a dreamy scent of oven-baked bread circled the air and filled my nose. What I had longed for was found. I had found my home. My first instincts about Gabriella that she might turn on me later had been totally off.

I looked around as Gabriella took my coat and hung it up. Both her girls rushed to the door and greeted me with their best intentions to make me feel at home. Jenny was my age so she took my bag and led me to the bedroom that we would share. Leanne was the youngest child and she was a doll. Although she was nearly ten or so, she was the baby of the family and I couldn't be happier to have such a cute little sister.

My head was trying to digest it all as Gabriella led the way to the basement. Howie, Gabriella's husband, had his back to us as we entered from the stairwell. He was busy hammering my bed rails together when we entered. As he turned to look over his shoulder, I saw his big smile from under his curly moustache. He made his own introductions and shook my hand. Like many ranchers who lived in southern Alberta, he was a Stetson man. He wore the full regalia of a true cowboy.

By the end of the night, I still had no idea how I would fit in this picture, but

I was feeling good about my decision. I knew I had a thick skin, but my armour seemed less resilient. For some reason, I felt that life was about to take a turn. It was about to become so much better than I could ever dream possible.

As Jenny settled in the bed across from mine, it felt awkward to be sleeping there. Jenny whispered that she was excited to share her room and it would be fun to have a sister to talk to. I was so glad that she said something comforting. Everything was going to be fine.

Conversations with my surrogate parents were light and fun. They liked my stories, so we would sit in the evening just talking and laughing without any heavy demands. With gentle coaxing, they got to know me and I got to know them. Their objective comments kept me in a sort of feeding frenzy to tell more.

Gabriella was compassionate, tender, and a hard-working mother who made every moment count. On top of all that, she would defend me when people treated me unfairly. That was something I had not encountered before. I was still bullied at school. I should have told Gabriella, but I kept it from her. One spring day, my best friend and I left the school grounds to go buy lunch. As we were walking, two of the girls approached out of nowhere and struck me in the back. At the same time, they repeatedly called me a bitch and laughed.

"Don't touch me!" I flipped around to face them. I put on a tough mask and didn't back down. They laughed in my face and I was terrified, but if I packed it in and called it quits, I would always be the punching bag. They backed off and after that day nobody wanted to mess with me and I was known as a tough kid. It was so far from the truth, but the bullying was over.

I saw something more in Gabriella than in all the other mothers I'd lived with. For starters, she was a listener not a talker. She wouldn't make a judgment without using her heart to understand. She could multi-task her chores and delegate responsibilities to her daughters without using force. I could babble for hours and she would never send me away. She knew I was struggling to find myself. It was so comforting how Gabriella always welcomed my freedom of expression without subjecting a punishment. Her optimism, wit, and humanity would inevitably cultivate a better life for me. If by some miracle I could be half of the kind of parent she was, there was a good chance that I would be a decent mom.

I must say that I found Howie fascinating. He loved to poke fun and tease, and that won me over. I laughed at all his silly jokes. Howie pulled quite a few pranks on Leanne, Jenny, and me, so we did our best to get even. Before going to bed, the three of us pretended we were crashing for the night. Then, in our nightgowns we snuck into the master bedroom and scooped a handful of glossy bonbons out of the box that was hidden under the bed. Many years later, he confessed that he found it amusing to watch us sneaking in and out of his room, so he kept refilling the box just to have the pleasure of hearing and watching us from somewhere unseen.

Four months had passed when my social worker came to pay a visit. When we were alone I told Miss Ryder that I loved Howie and Gabriella, but I still wanted to go home to Wilma. It was absurd that I would want to be with a woman who hated me most of the time. I wanted her to see how much I had changed. I was doing whatever it took to prove it, but Wilma had been like fire and ice. Her kind of love comprised fierce judgment and manipulation, and I was so yearning to please that any love was better than no love at all.

Miss Ryder smiled and I saw appraisal in her eyes. She told me that my chances were extremely slim. It was worth a shot: nothing ventured and nothing gained if I didn't ask.

A month later, Miss Ryder came to see me. She had a smile that gleamed from ear to ear. With a grin that wide she could have been a toothpaste model. She announced that Wilma had had a change of heart and wanted me to come home as soon as possible. At first, I choked up and then I shrieked gloriously, like I had just won a lottery.

As soon as my social worker left, I was dying to share the news and hear Gabriella's response. Her face wasn't the least bit excited and she was staring at me like I had broken her best china. Oh, she had insight all right, but it wasn't at all what I expected. For some reason, I concluded that she would be very happy, but that was not the case at all. Gabriella spoke words that made me see things in a whole different light. At the cost of sounding naïve, I wondered how I could have been so dense.

Gabriella resolved that she would never give me up, because I was her daughter now. Wilma couldn't wiggle her finger and expect to me to go running back. It would definitely not be without a fight from Gabriella's end.

"They don't love you or they would not have sent you away," she said.

I knew it was true but the reality of it hurt me deeply. I didn't want to throw myself on my own sword, but my years of wishful thinking had finally come true. Yet, I felt foolish, because the truth of it was I had never made Wilma happy and not from the lack of trying. My dream to become a Charlene was over, and for the first time I realized I did not want to be anyone but me.

How had Gabriella's unconditional love slipped by me without my noticing? I felt a bit dumb. Normally, I was so happy around her but suddenly the room felt uncomfortably hot. Guilt spread over my face. Had my years of insecurity masked my ability to put it all together? I felt like I had cheated on her somehow.

"What are you going to do? Are you planning to stay or move back?"

I could tell by Gabriella's tone that she would not be happy if I chose to leave.

I could barely look at her, but I did and I could not mistake the sheer love in her eyes. How could I say no to that? Her demand for an answer dangled in the air as I grasped at what to do.

"I'm going to stay," I reciprocated. I realized I had just forfeited my other alternative. Gabriella just stared as though she were tongue-tied. Then she turned and went into the kitchen, while I stayed back to lick my wounds. Eventually it all made sense and I was very happy with my decision. It all turned out perfectly.

Unlike my last two foster homes I was not forced to attend church. Howie and Gabriella were Mormons too but they supported whatever I wanted to do. As a result, I wanted to be around them so I went to their church. On a religious level it made the most common sense to any spiritual perception.

I joined the church and at first I was pumped. But I wasn't doing it for myself, so learning the gospel became an exhausting obsession to please others, especially since anyone who was not a Mormon did not fit in well at my school.

43: Kenton and Jenny and Kevin

Howie was usually in the mainstream of any activity regarding horses, so when school let out for summer, he planned to take the family to the Raymond rodeo. There were free pancakes, eggs, and bacon if you were willing to wait in line with your paper plate. The stampede grounds are a dust bowl with the stench of cow pies. Surprisingly, no one cares, because there's music and laughter and so much food that you just can't wait to get started.

The challenge was to find a seat. The bandstands were full. There wasn't even standing room, but our truck was parked in front of the corral gate. I took my plate and sat on the hood of the truck where I could see right into the bullpen. A big black bull was snorting and watching me out of the corner of his dark eye. I'm sure he was raging mad to be held hostage in there with some dumb cowpoke on his back.

He was the first out of the gate and he ran straight into the centre of the ring. What a beast! It was as if he knew that he was the star attraction. He stopped to pound the ground and let out a wet snort. Before the cloud of dust could settle, he whipped around to the left and swerved to the right. In a fit of anger, he booted his hooves like he had a black belt in kickboxing. The event was so engaging that the crowd went crazy, but the poor cowboy could not hold a grasp and was tossed in the air like a Raggedy Anne. He landed with such a thud that I could feel it.

The excitement continued but in the uproar I heard someone shouting my name. It was Kenton, one of the hotties who worked on Howie and Gabriella's ranch. I liked this guy but he had a girlfriend, so I never pursued him by even so much as making eye contact. He climbed up beside me and watched the entries as we chatted it up for about an hour. In the course of conversation, he told me that he was no longer seeing his girlfriend. Our faces were so close that I could feel the warmth of his breath. He was flirting heavily and the chemistry fueled us.

I saw him many times after that day and he was very into me, so I reciprocated. I didn't want to jinx our budding new relationship but I really needed to talk about him, so I shared my heart with Jenny. Her eyes lit up and I could see that she was dying to tell me something too. Bemused, I listened as she told me that she had a thing for Kenton's younger brother Kevin. It was so wonderful to imagine Jenny and me going on double dates with the two brothers. The four of us had a lot of fun together, but the dating part never really got off the ground.

Week after week the boys showed up on the ranch to work and I tried to appear casual even though I was secretly nutty over Kenton. His eyes were always gleaming as though he was looking to see if there was a spark in me. I was totally hopeless at hiding my attraction to him.

All summer long, the boys arrived on Friday and stayed until Sunday night. I didn't have the slightest hope of controlling the pounding love knot in my chest. Kenton was a real sexy beast, but my sparks of love consumed all my heart and nowhere near "the V zone." I wanted him for life and not for some silly fantasy.

But then out of nowhere, the worst thing happened—I had competition. Jenny's cousin, Tessa, came to visit the ranch. At first it was fun to have another girl our age to chum around with and talk about boys. But it seemed like the moment I told Tessa about Kenton, it became her calling card to get her hooks in him. Her flirting strategy was "go big or go home" and she wouldn't leave Kenton alone. The two of them cavorted heavily and I was so darned jealous.

I sure didn't find any peace of mind when we were down at the swimming hole. Tessa was bobbing in the water with her arms dangled around Kenton's neck. Her cherry gloss lipstick was smeared on like varnish and I could see her halter bikini top pressing provocatively against his chest. She pulled him close to her bosom and whispered something in his ear; he grinned like a fool. What a show off! I was so ticked.

Tessa behaved like a floozy and Kenton lapped it up like milk in a bowl. It would have been awesome if I'd had a bucket of ice to chill them off. To add insult to injury, Kenton was openly baiting me with his flirtatious behaviour. After a month of this nonsense, Gabriella's niece went home to her parents and I was so glad to get rid of her. I finally had a chance of turning things around with Kenton. I wanted my dream boy more than anyone could ever know.

When school opened in the fall, Jenny and I didn't think twice about skipping classes so we could visit Kenton and Kevin at their school. Our light bulb idea was purely stupid, but Jenny had her driver's licence so we took the farm truck and turned onto the highway instead of going into town.

School was just letting out when we arrived. Jenny met up with Kevin's class so I stood outside and watched for Kenton to come through the doors. A group of kids left the school and I could see Kenton's head in the middle. I dashed toward him.

As I got closer, I noticed a girl walking and talking with him and that stopped me dead in my tracks. Who is she? I could feel my eyes boring through her head. She was so pretty and he was so close to her that I wished I could evaporate into thin air. But, unfortunately, we had already made eye contact and my stomach had gone from flip-flopping to cringing. Somehow, I knew I couldn't stand in the sidelines and do nothing. After all, there was the possibility that she was just a friend and I would be delighted to push her aside if she wasn't.

There was no time to waste, so I went right up to him. Our conversation began with the usual greetings and social graces, but then just like that, there was nothing to talk about. So he piped up and introduced me to the girl next to him as if I would want her in the conversation. There was no flirting nor any looking into my eyes. He had to rush off somewhere and he wasn't going alone. I was about to lose a man that I was in love with before I even had him. I went back to the truck and waited for Jenny, and tried to figure out what I was going to do. Life is just so damn hard when you are in love with someone who doesn't love you back.

It was a shocker when Kenton showed up on the weekend but he was a total jerk toward me, so that hurt doubly. It would have been better if he'd stayed home. He wouldn't man up and tell me anything, so while he was out haying the fields, I got some answers my own way. Jenny and I snooped through his stuff. I had no business going through his private things, but my hands suggested otherwise.

I found nothing out of the ordinary, except for a small pocket-sized letter on top of the nightstand. In the blink of a second, I had the square unfolded but the message was so shocking that it felt like the floor had fallen out from under my feet. As I read line after line, I knew it came from the girl whom I'd met at Kenton's school.

There was a lot more than kissing going on between those two. Her depressing note confirmed that it was just a matter of time before she would be pregnant. As I continued to read my heart was sneaking up into my esophagus. Nobody wants to feel like they are going down in flames, but that letter incinerated my dreams.

Every time I tried to get over Kenton, he would show a newfound interest in me and it was confusing. To add to the frustration, Kenton was always around to help with the ranch, so I saw him regularly. Then there was the time his parents bought a farmhouse up north and wanted drivers to help with the move. Jenny and Kevin went together in one of the trucks. Kenton asked me to ride with him in the other. It seemed odd that he wasn't taking his girlfriend. But hey, I was happy to take her place.

On the day that we drove out of town, Kenton was in the lead. Kevin and Jenny stayed close behind us and we made sure to not lose sight of them. It was a long haul and I wasn't sure how or what to say for the twelve hours it was going to take to get there. Kenton's flirting had lots of gusto, so I took that as an open invitation. I had him all to myself and I wished the ride would never end. This was my chance to tell him that I loved him, but I couldn't do it. He suggested that I put my head on his lap and sleep, so I tried but all I wanted to do was kiss him.

"Did you sleep?" he asked as I sat up.

"Just a cat nap." I smiled, and melted into the seat when he turned to look at me. It was stifling hot in the truck and even after nightfall we had to drive with the windows open. Somehow in the pitch black, we found the property and lit the house with candles. After saying goodnight to the boys, Jenny and I took our bedrolls and made our way to a bedroom.

My four days with Kenton were so close to being romantic. With all the flirting and fun, I sure didn't want to go home. But I had to. The ride back seemed so long without my love beside me, but I knew I would see him soon.

Sure enough, one morning when I was still asleep, he stopped by. In my dream, I heard his voice and it woke me out of a dead sleep. My eyes lit up like last year's Christmas tree and I bounced out of bed. I rushed around my room trying to look presentable. After a few brush strokes and a hint of lipstick, I had to see him. Kenton was in the kitchen resting on a stool and talking with Gabriella as she rinsed the morning dishes.

"Hi Kenton." I said, dying to see the glow in his eyes.

"Hi," he answered. But he was completely unmoved by my appearance and I felt my cheery smile weaken.

"How are you?" I asked and wondered if something could have possibly gone wrong from the last time we were together.

"Fine," he answered with a tinge of irritation like I had interrupted something real important. I didn't think he was the FBI on a top-secret mission. His eyes stared at the floor with his hands clasped in his lap. He went back to talking with Gabriella like I wasn't there. I waited… nothing. Not even a glance although I was standing directly in front of him.

What was I—chopped liver? At first I didn't want to believe what was happening, but this was the Kenton I'd known all along. I just didn't want to believe it.

"Kent is a jerk."

Jenny comforted me as I sat on my bed.

"I can't understand him. One minute he treats me like I am the girl of his dreams. Then the next time I see him he acts like he doesn't know me," I said through tears.

"Kenton isn't talking to you now because his girlfriend is outside waiting in the truck," Jenny said.

I tried to tell Jenny that I didn't care, but my tears showed the real pain.

"There's more to it than that. She is…" Jenny hesitated and I could see she didn't want to say it.

"What?" I asked as Jenny rolled her hands over her tummy. "Are you sure?"

"Positive. She's huge. I just talked to her. I wish it wasn't true, but she's due any time and she says that after the baby is born, Kenton will marry her."

No wonder he was so insensitive and cold as cement in winter. Nothing would have pleased me more than to walk back into the kitchen and kick his ass out the door.

"I don't care. I hope I never see that man again," I said as my eyes narrowed. I meant every word. The thought of Kenton having a shotgun wedding was maddening. It was the straw that broke the camel's back and I had had enough.

Over the days, I thought about his new life with a wife and a baby. I wondered how it would be to have a baby screaming in the night. I babysat often and found it hard to tolerate the screams and cries when they went on for a long time. It bothered my mind. One night I had some time alone with Howie, so I opened up and told him that I was afraid of becoming a parent.

"What if I hurt my children?" I asked. "I'm scared that I will be a bad mother." My bottom lip quivered at the thought. Tears rolled from my eyes and Howie quickly took me into his big arms.

"It's different when they are your children. When the time comes, I know that you will be a terrific mother. They will be your world. Every parent makes mistakes, but you will figure it out as you go along," he promised and I trusted his wisdom. In truth, I loved Howie's gentle heart and his encouraging persuasion.

44: Howie and Smokey

I had countless opportunities to see Howie's good deeds. He could calm the most stubborn horse. In a soft voice, Howie would brush them down and slip a saddle over their back. It's quite a thing to see a wild beast pacified by one man.

One night I went out with Howie when it was dark and snowy. A cow was standing out in the cold and she was in labour. Howie walked around to the back of the cow so he could get a closer look. She bellowed and I saw her baby coming out from under her. A thin opaque sack slid down the back of her legs. The bag was still intact, but it had stretched so thin that it looked like the calf's hooves had been sealed in plastic wrap. The cow had had a long labour and was distressed, so Howie secured a large chain around the hooves and pulled the fetus out with the tractor. I was worried that the heavy chain would break the delicate little legs of our unborn calf. But Howie told me not to worry because the hooves were hard as a rock. The sack slid out, causing the bag of water to burst as it hit the mud. Howie reached down and pulled away the sack that clung to the wet calf. He looked over at me and smiled, and I knew that calf was lucky to be alive.

Everyone knew I was one of the boss's daughters, so I proudly stalked around the ranch in my tattered jeans and Howie's old shirts. My manly looking western boots had worn a quarter size hole through the soles, but I wouldn't trade them in for new ones.

Whenever Howie wanted me to be involved with the ranching, I got into my riding gear and tried to help. During weaning season, Jenny and I missed a couple days of school to help with the roundup. We saddled the horses and separated the cows from their babies. The cows and calves suffered anxiety detachment and grew frantic as they tried to reunite. With a thousand calves there was a lot of bawling and mooing from both sides of the wire fence. The crying went all night and carried on to the next day. It was heartbreaking. I couldn't stand to watch. It reminded me of the terrible loneliness I felt for my mother. Especially the second time when I was in the orphanage waiting day after day to go home to my family.

On the second day, I followed Howie out to the barn. The men were rounding up the calves into a pen. Howie mounted his big sorrel horse and lassoed the calves one by one as they ran out of the gate. The poor little critters had no idea what was about to happen. The calves tried to escape, but the hired hands wrestled them and branded each one. No one likes to be the bad guy, but that's how cattle are identified and protected from theft. My job was earmarking and that was enough for me. The jobs of castrating, dehorning, vaccinating, and branding were meant for the men folk as far as I was concerned.

The ranch had big beautiful horses but I was only allowed to ride certain ones. Often, I was a little ahead of myself—a bit too ambitious, some would say. I wanted to be a full-fledged rider who could handle some of the more aggressive horses. A grey spotted horse named Smokey was hot-tempered; he had a reputation for causing trouble. He was all horse and muscle, but he acted more like a stubborn mule. So I challenged Howie for permission to prove I was cowgirl material. Howie warned that I was playing with fire so I needed to keep in mind there was no room for second-guessing. He had barely said yes and I was gone. I yanked the big barn door open and prepared to meet my maker.

The horse eyed me down but didn't seem to care when I dragged the saddle over his back. He peered over his shoulder and went back to eating from the trough. I cinched the belt under his belly and put a bridle on him without any fuss. What a good boy, I thought. I took him by the reins and he walked gingerly alongside me. I began to think that he had been given a bad rap. Outside the barn, two farm men idled next to Howie as they watched me come through the doors. All three tried to keep a straight face as I mounted my foot in the stirrup and lowered myself into the saddle.

I took Smokey through the gate and he ambled to an open field of fresh grass and warm sun. Smokey seemed totally carefree as he passively trotted over the rolling hills. His head swayed from side to side, so I knew I was in his peripheral view. Another fifty yards, my horse would be over the last green slope and the barn would be out of sight. One thing I had overlooked was Smokey's desire to see his domain.

In a flash, the horse did a hairpin turn and whipped around so fast that I lost the reins. I screamed at him to stop, but it's hard to quarrel with an animal. That horse stampeded all the way back to the barn. With every gallop I was tossed from side to side. I held onto his mane for dear life as my legs flapped like a pair of jeans on a clothesline.

He soared past the gate, ran across the gravel yard, and swerved around the corner of the barn door. His inner speedometer didn't drop a point until he came to a dead halt in his stall. He stopped so suddenly that I was flipped over the top of his head and hurled into his trough. As I scrambled my way out of the box I could hear the Stetson clan howling in laughter.

I was not ready to call it a day though. I picked the straw out of my clothes and hair, and smacked the dirt off my jeans. Smokey was busily gobbling down his hay when I intervened and took him by the reins. Outside, I ignored all the chortles as I slumped back into the saddle. I waved to the men and rode away. I was sure there would be no more funny business.

When Smokey neared the last hill I pulled up the reins so he couldn't ambush me. But before I got the upper hand, Smokey turned a U-shaped curve and fired off at full pace. In the twist of a second, I felt my body flipping in the air like a kite in the wind. It was hard not to feel a little hot under the collar as I wriggled out of the food bin for the second time. I heard the jokers whooping it up outside.

Part three of the live comedy show was about to close down. The gig was up. As Smokey and I rolled over that last stretch, I quickly pulled the reins and wrapped them around the horn of the saddle. That anchored him so he couldn't drop his head down or turn around and run. Instead, that cantankerous steed reared up and twirled around on his hind legs, trying to buck me off. He would have made a great circus horse with all that spinning and twirling.

It took several minutes of dancing around before he accepted his defeat. Once he got back on all fours, we moved on. So, after a while, it was a no-brainer and I had him pegged. It was a sobering moment to be confident enough that I would not give up, no matter how difficult. He was a good horse but very stubborn like me. Through the course of our ride, Smokey was on a mission to return home. I felt soul to soul with him. The beginning of the ride was rough, but in the end it was very rewarding. Whenever there was a slight pause in his hoofbeat, I knew he was up to no-good. Although I had earned his respect, he would act up once in a while but he never got the better of me again. We cruised in harmony and later that day I proudly rode along with confidence. I passed Howie and the men, and they were impressed.

Although I loved Howie and Gabriella with all my heart, I still felt a void. Up to that point, I was missing the essence of my own identity. It was like the blood in my veins had no matching DNA. I was stamped as a "Ward of the Government," but I had a real family out there. My biological siblings, the two unmentionables, had become the marrow in my bones. I rarely spoke of them because it was too painful. There was an infinite love that emerged from the past and nothing could ever replace the timeless bond that began so long ago.

I desperately missed them and I was often distracted over their whereabouts, but I did not want to dishonour my foster family or lose their trust.

45: My Sister Sheila

At times, my love for Howie and Gabriella made me feel a bit guilty, as though I was betraying my own blood. I didn't want to cause a rift. However, it was daunting to wake in the night and feel such alienation from Josh, Sheila, and my real mother. At the age of sixteen, I wanted to know something about them—anything to feel a connection. All I knew was my name. I didn't even have a picture of my mother or Josh and Sheila.

From my bed, I was sometimes awakened by the sound of a train. Although the train was a long distance off, I could feel a humming vibration as the engine rolled its wheels across the tracks. I thought of my mother and my siblings.

I didn't have any memory of riding a train, but every time I saw a Murphy bed on TV it seemed so strangely familiar, like a kind of déjà vu. A haze of faces etched my mind like an old black and white movie. I wanted to know what my mother's voice sounded like. Did I have a living grandmother or a cousin? Did anyone remember me?

My life felt insignificant without them. I thought about all the attempts that government bodies and foster parents created to disunite a family and deter a reunion. I hated the reckless words about my parents being physically and mentally abusive. The stories varied, so it was time to reclaim my family and hear their side of the truth. Until that day arrived I would not leave it alone.

Seldom did I ask for help from my social workers, but I wondered what could be the harm in meeting my siblings. I took the question to my social worker and she took it to her boss. It was a tall order, but I got permission to reunite with my birth sister Sheila.

Nearly a month later, my social worker showed up with great news. She had met my sister Sheila and got an address where I could write to her. My foster mother Gabriella was just as excited as I was. She suggested that I write my sister and ask her to come for a visit. Suddenly, my life had turned another corner and I was in my glory.

That same summer, Jenny and I worked in town at a chocolate factory. On our first week we got stuck with scrubbing out the messy resin of fudge that stuck to the stainless steel tubs. It was tedious, but the second week was better because we moved to a higher position. We were instructed to operate the conveyor belts. There was no training; it was a mindless job that just required speed.

All we had to do was scoop up four rows of chocolate bonbons and stack two layers per box. Sounds easy enough. But the chocolates were moving along the conveyer belt on a timer.

The whole process was a bit too rushed and, before I knew it, some of the chocolates teetered over the edge. We scrambled to catch them, but the conveyor was dropping more and more chocolates; the stupid belt was on autopilot and we couldn't lower the speed. Jenny and I were ducking and grabbing as the chocolates pelted the floor like fallen soldiers. In a desperate measure to avoid tossing the damaged bonbons, we quickly stuffed the irresistible freebies into our pie-holes.

In the middle of the flurry, our boss entered the room. He was a stalky man with a balding head and a chubby face. I felt a little inadequate when he had to side step to dodge a rolling bonbon. At the flick of a switch, he simply shut the machine down and looked at us like we were two big dummies. Jen and I exchanged a guilty glance and I stifled the urge to giggle. In the metal machinery, I saw my reflection.

My hair net was lopsided and when I moved it back, there was a big raised line across my brow. Our cheeks were so lumpy and full that we looked like *I Love Lucy* and Ethel in their famous conveyer-belt chocolate scene. I was surprised he didn't fire us on the spot. Our boss lectured us that speed and time were money. We both nodded and got back to work.

We lasted two weeks. I don't know what the problem was, but we got a pay-cheque and a free ice-cream bucket of fudge. The new five-pound battle of the bulge and the consistent nightmares of chocolates marching toward me lasted much longer.

So it was official. My sister Sheila had replied to my letter and she was willing to come and visit. On my last day of work, Sheila was sitting on the couch in our basement. She stood as I entered the room and I saw a face similar to my own. It was indisputable; this girl was my biological sibling. Like looking in a mirror, the resemblance was incredible and we both talked and laughed in the same fashion.

Sheila's complexion was deeper than mine with an olive tone, and she had exotic almond-shaped eyes. Her thick hair fell in waves over her shoulders and she looked like a native princess. We were awkwardly shy because it was so new and hard to believe that we were finally together. We knew nothing about each other's lives. We had so much to learn.

At first, it was a delicate transformation to speak with each other. Gradually, we opened up and she told me about her journey. I told Sheila everything I could remember of our parents and Josh. Because she'd been a baby at the time, my memories sparked no memories for her. With no history to fall back on, it would be hard for us to find family. We had a fun reunion, but our days went by fast and she had to return to her foster family in Calgary. My first night alone was really hard, but I knew I would see her soon. My social worker dropped by to hear about the reunion and she was so thrilled for my sister and me.

"It was difficult to find any information about your parents, but I wrote a few notes for you from your file."

She held out two small sheets of paper. The first paper had a history of my medical data from birth. The second paper had my parents' given names—Karina and Louis—along with their birth dates and places of birth. On the bottom of the second paper was the name of the city where my Dad had resided when I was born. Hours after my social worker had gone, I was reading it over and over. For some people that wouldn't be much, but for me it was a sacred link that could help me find my blood relatives.

46: Louis and Karina

One evening when I was alone, I studied the two sheets that I had been carrying around for days. I figured that my mother had probably divorced and remarried so she wouldn't be listed in the white pages. I knew it would be better to search for my father and maybe he could lead me in the right direction to finding Karina.

The information was at least fifteen years old. A lot could have happened since then. I pressed the papers out on the table and went over the details. I picked up the phone and called a toll free operator, but I had no real expectations. Then an operator said she'd found one listing in Langley and a pang of excitement grew in my stomach.

I felt the pins and needles in my chest as I picked up the phone and quickly put it back down. I was breathing hard and feeling the adrenaline as I picked it up again. It seemed essential to go with my heart, so I dialed and waited to hear a voice connect at the other end.

"Hello? Hello?" I heard a man's voice and I gasped in shock, because I knew it had to be my father. My imagination was trying to put a face to his voice.

"Hello. Could I please speak to Louis?" I spoke so fast that it sounded nervous, but I didn't want to scare him off.

"Speaking," he answered lightly, and I felt a bit more relaxed. I told myself to just breathe.

"I'm a long-time friend of Karina and I am trying to find her. Do you know where she is?" I managed to get my question out and I hoped the "friend" bit didn't sound like some kind of phony-baloney story.

"Are you one of my daughters?" he asked.

All my strategy of thoughtful wording had gone out the window. I was afraid that he might not want to hear from his kids. If I answered "yes," would he hang up on me?

"Because I have been looking for you for a long time." His voice was sincere and I was instantly relieved. It was great to hear him say that.

"Yes." My voice hoisted with cheeriness.

"Is this Sheila?" he asked.

"No, it's Eugenea." I responded.

"Oh," he said.

That didn't sound right. I didn't like the vibe I was getting from him.

"You seem surprised that it is me. Are you disappointed?" I asked.

"No, not at all. But I was told by the government that you…" He paused.

"What?"

"I was told that you were mentally retarded, so I never expected to hear from you."

What a blow! I was speechless. How was I supposed to answer that? I felt outraged, but I exhaled slowly to get my bearings. It was pretty nasty that my Dad had had to endure such crap. Sure it was a cheap shot, but it shook him off and he stopped trying to find us. So why am I so shocked? The stupid government was so desensitized from the children they were supposed to protect and nurture. To put it bluntly, children have been ripped from their roots, stuffed into foster homes, and forced into clinical programs for psychological evaluation. It made perfect sense as to why I had thought people were like robots when I was little.

On the lighter side, my Dad invested his conversation with questions to learn more about my life. We both had questions and answers regarding our separation. It was happy and painful to put some stuff together.

"Do you know where my mother is?" I asked eagerly.

"Yes, she lives in Surrey," he said.

"Where's that?" I asked, curious to know her exact location.

"It's a suburb of Vancouver. She lives in a trailer court with her husband and her two daughters. She's about twenty minutes from me."

I never thought about my biological Mom having more kids, so that was quite a surprise. Our conversation continued and I learned that Louis had had a couple more marriages and a handful of daughters.

"I kept in touch with your mother and we are friends." Louis said. He told me Karina's number.

Wow! It had happened so fast. Just minutes before I had nothing and then it all rolled out before me like a red carpet. But what should I say? How would I talk to her? My mind was fixed on what to do, so I asked Louis to help.

"Could you call Karina and tell her that I want to make contact with her?"

"I can do that. I know she will be so happy to hear from you. I will let her know that she will be getting a call in ten minutes. Would that work?"

I agreed and we hung up. As the phone rested back on the hook, I thought ten minutes would be easy to handle, but then I found myself watching the clock hands move from second to second. A minute felt like an hour.

So many things went through my mind. How was Louis going to tell her? What if she didn't answer or didn't want to talk? It never struck me that she might not be home. I had to channel my inner voice and keep it calm.

Done. The waiting game was over. Someone picked up the phone on the second ring and a woman answered with a sketchy, "Hello?"

It's her! My ears perked up. I knew every decibel in her voice.

"Hello, may I speak to Karina?" I asked politely, even though I wanted to scream out, "Mommy is that you?"

"This is Karina." Her voice was rehearsed and rhythmic, yet I sensed some fear in there. She was just as terrified as I was.

"Do you know who this is?" I asked, hoping the groundbreaking question would bring us ultimate happiness. But instead, I heard sniffles. A big lump formed in my throat. I was terrified that she might not want me.

"Is this Eugenea? Is this my little girl?" She was smitten by emotion when I said yes. It took a moment before she could go on. She kept repeating the words, "It's my baby. I have my darling baby again."

Her voice took me back to that day in the basement suite. I remembered my mother's scolding us over the peanut butter and the mess of the broken jar. I remembered the babysitter coming but I could not remember the black car that took Josh, Sheila, and me from our mother.

Neither one of us knew what to say. We both wanted to speak, but there were so many tears in the way.

"Are you okay?" she finally asked.

"Yes. I'm okay... I just don't know what to say."

"You can ask me anything. I don't want to hide anything from you. I'm so sorry, I am crying, because I never expected to hear from you. I prayed so hard for this day to come, but I thought you kids would never want to talk to me," she said, and I knew she was still picturing us as her three little ones.

"I just wanted to hear your voice," I said, feeling more shaken than before.

"Can I ask where you are living? I want to know what has happened to you. I mean, I haven't seen you since you were a baby," she tearfully apologized over and over.

"I live on a ranch in Alberta."

"Were you adopted?" she asked.

"No. I still have the same last name I was born with."

"Did you have many foster homes?"

"Yes," I told her and it made her very sad.

"Please tell me where you are. I promise I will leave you alone if you don't want to see me." Karina begged but I didn't give in to her pressure.

"You don't want to see me?"

"No, it's not that. My foster family... they don't know yet. I don't want to hurt them."

"I understand. Any time you want to talk you can call me collect. When you were small, you had fair hair and big brown eyes. You were so pretty. Tell me. What do you look like now?" she asked, so I gave a short description of my looks, height, and build.

"Are you happy?" she asked. I knew that was a crucial question—one that could heal or hurt.

"Yes, my foster family are very good people," I assured her.

"That is such good news. I'm so happy to hear that. I know that you must have gone through some terrible experiences," she commiserated, but I didn't want to bring her down with guilt. I told her about my hobbies and how I loved to draw.

"Really? That's great. I do lots of painting. It seems to run in the family," she sounded more optimistic. "I never stopped loving any of my children." Her voice grew thick with emotion again. "My biggest mistake in life was losing you kids. I have never forgiven myself."

I didn't know what to say. I was still getting used to the idea that she was really my mother was on the other end of the line.

"It's okay. Please don't cry." My voice crackled.

"Honey, do you know every time I walk past kids your age I look very closely to see if there's a chance that it is one of my own? I have spent all these years praying that I would get my children back." Karina's love was very clear and I was quite relieved to learn that she was always hoping to reunite. As she struggled to talk, I could see in my mind a mother walking the streets desperately searching every child's face. Not for one baby but for three.

"Are you Christian?" she asked.

"I believe in God. My family is Mormon and so am I," I told her.

"Mormon? That's unreal. I am Mormon too. It's incredible that we are both in the same religion."

"Are you an active member?" I asked.

"No, I don't go much, but I do believe in it. I have always believed in God. I've done a lot of things that I regret; I have made a lot of mistakes."

"We all make mistakes," I said with sympathy so she would know that I wasn't judging her. I wondered if she was going to get into all the details of what had happened. We didn't have that kind of time; that was a subject that should wait until we met.

"What should I call you?" I popped the question that had been on my mind since the second I heard her voice.

"You can call me Karina or Mom if you like."

"You don't mind if I call you Karina?" I wasn't ready to give her the Mommy title yet.

"Okay." She sounded a bit disappointed. "You have a grandmother living in Alberta. She's on a farm ten miles outside Lethbridge. She would be so happy to see you."

"I lived in Lethbridge for six years. We probably crossed paths and never knew," I told Karina. It saddened me to know that my grandma had been practically a stone's throw away. Karina spoke about her awkward divorce from

Louis and about her second marriage to Bart. It was mostly factual, just so I would know what had happened after I'd been taken. I also had two half-sisters.

In a matter of minutes, I had gone from no family to unearthing a whole bucketful. Finally, I said I had to go and promised to call her as soon as there was an opportunity.

"I want to see you. I know you are not ready now, but I hope that we will meet."

"I want to see you too, but it's too soon. I have to go now." I didn't want to say goodbye, because our talk had barely scratched the surface, but time was moving on.

"Will you please call me soon?"

"I promise to call as soon as I can. Goodbye, Karina."

"Goodbye, my sweet girl. I love you so much. Call me soon." She would not hang up so I had to do it. It was over and she was gone, but not forever.

47: My Two Families

It was weird to keep such a big secret. I wanted to share the wonderful news with my foster parents, but it would be terrible if they thought I had betrayed them. Suppressing my secret gave me a fuzzy feeling of elation, but it was a burden not to share the most exciting thing in my life.

Finally, I had to clear the air so I took the plunge and told them everything. They stared at me with an expression as though that I had done something sneaky right under their nose, but they said nothing. The silence was worse than a punishment. I felt ashamed. What kind of stupid mess have I gotten into? I bit my lip. I wanted to take it all back, but it was too late.

"That's quite a... shocker," Gabriella spoke out. I saw her look over to Howie for help, inspiration, or anything to be supportive.

"That's great! We are so happy for you," he jumped in.

"It must feel really wonderful to know who your parents are." Gabriella glowed with happiness and I knew she only wanted the best for my future.

"It's so hard for me to believe I found them," I said lightly. My attempt was to downplay it by trying not to sound too excited. But they were genuinely thrilled and wanted to know everything, so we had a heart-to-heart talk. No matter what, they had my back. We laughed and cried and celebrated and it was a big weight off my shoulders. I had found my real parents, but Howie and Gabriella were the cornerstones to my steps in life. They had used tools of love to help me find myself.

"You don't have to call them collect. It's important for you to get to know them," Gabriella insisted.

"Call them and give them our number so they know where you are," Howie added.

Why did I wait so long to tell them?

Once the story was out, I was on cloud nine. At school it was a big deal and my friends were so inspired. On lunch break I ran every day to the post office. Upon the opening of my first letter, I found a picture of my father. His face was gentle. He had bright blue eyes and a funny animated smile and I liked what I saw. I held a picture of my mother. I could see the Métis genes, yet she looked Mexican because of her curly long black hair.

Karina could hardly wait to see me, so she took the first opportunity to fly out for a visit. Before her flight, she called and announced that my grandmother would also be waiting at the airport. We would have to drive to the airport in Lethbridge to meet her.

The day I had been dreaming about and waiting for had finally come. My restless sleep didn't cause my heart to slow down one bit. I didn't waste a minute as I hurried into the shower and scrubbed every pore. I wanted to be perfect.

Wrapped in a towel, I stood in front of my closet and scanned my wardrobe to find the right dress. I wanted something modest and pretty that would give me a skinny mini look. A soft knit dress in pink with brown angled stripes hung limp on the rack. I tugged it off the hanger and slipped it over my head.

It didn't look dowdy or sensual or too made up. I paraded over to the mirror and turned sideways to see if it would pass the test. Nice curves in all the right places. The dress was slightly hugging without being too fitted. What would my mother think? The young girl in the reflection stared back at me. Butterflies fluttered in my tummy as I thought about what would be taking place in a couple of hours.

I missed Gabriella. I wanted her reassurance because she always knew what to say. Her smile didn't need words to build my courage. At the time though, she was not home, because she had booked airline tickets long before I knew about Karina. Gabriella had gone to the United States to see her relatives, but I would be okay, because Howie was happy to go to the airport with me. The drive to Lethbridge would take us an hour, so I tried to relax. But it was hard because every mile was closer than the last. As Howie drove to the city, I chattered nervously about what questions I should ask.

As we walked into the one-room airport, it was empty except for an old couple sitting and waiting for a plane to arrive. The old woman had strong na-tive features and she was old enough to be my grandmother. She wore a bright yellow dress with a line of daisies down the front and a white knit poncho clocked around her shoulders. She sat arm-in-arm with the man beside her and I knew without asking directly that she was Elaine, my Grandmother.

Her man wore his cowboy hat low, so I couldn't see his forehead. But I saw his face and he could have passed for a John Wayne double. The couple huddled together even though there was plenty of room on each side of the bench. Suddenly, it came to my attention they were whispering and watching me. I pretended not to notice. Howie and I sat across the room and I impatiently fidgeted next to him. Whenever I glanced around, the woman was staring back. She had an eager smile but I just couldn't bring myself to talk to her.

"I think that could be your grandmother," Howie said in a whisper.

"Yes, I think so, too," I said, as I stole a quick browse to see if there was anything familiar about her. I didn't remember her at all.

"Why don't you go over and talk to her? Maybe introduce yourself?"

I jerked my head up as I felt my cheeks flush. He couldn't be serious! He must be crazy to expect me to have the guts to do that!

"No! What if she's the wrong person?" I asked, feeling stunned at how he had sprung that on me.

"Go on," he nudged. "Go over and say hello."

He gave me the eye that assured me everything would be okay. I peered over to see if that cute old lady was still watching. Her deep button eyes never wavered and I wondered if she was really seeing me as her grandchild. Then, she made the first move and stood up, and I saw her feet coming in my direction. The closer she came, the antsier I got.

"Hi. You must be my granddaughter," the woman said in the sweetest little granny voice.

"Yes, I think so." My voice squeaked like a duck's and I was at a loss for what to say, so Howie stood up and broke the ice with introductions and shook my grandma's hand.

"It's nice to meet you," she said with a smile as I got up and stood next to Howie.

Her eyes coasted over me and I had this ridiculous urge to step back and hide behind Howie's back.

"We finally meet after all these years," she smiled and her wide eyes twinkled. Her infectious happiness rubbed me with the same enthusiasm. Then, with her purse still hanging off the crook of her arm, she embraced me.

"Your mother will be here soon. She is so excited to see you. I'm sure you must be nervous. Are you okay?" She pulled back and looked me in the face.

"Yes. Thank you," I answered in a refined manner of gratitude, but really I was in shock. The John Wayne look-a-like came to my Grandma's side and introduced himself as Gordon.

"I remember you!" Gordon's gruff voice matched his crooked sneer and tar-stained lips. He had a uniqueness that was very interesting, but just as we started to converse, the plane landed and that took precedence over everything.

A sleek white jet taxied over the runway and through the window we could see it rolling to a stop. The passengers made their exit and headed down the metal steps, but I couldn't see my Mom in the crowd. For some reason, I knew that she would be the last person to poke her head out of the plane door. My eyes felt hot as I watched her leave the exit.

Karina's long hair whipped her face and danced uncontrollably in the wind. It was obvious that it was hard for her to see. With her suitcase in her hand, she carefully steadied her footing down the long narrow stairs to the pavement below. Then she crossed the landing strip and entered through the glass doors. She was right in front of me, just steps away from my touch. Our eyes glued and instinctively my emotional state evolved to exhilaration, a joy beyond anything I had ever known.

"Here's my baby, my little girl," she whispered to me, but I was numb. I couldn't move or talk. My mind was chattering with excitement: that's her! That's my real Mom and… here she is! My brain was repeating the same sentence over and over like an old doll with a string in its back. Karina dropped her bags and gently pulled me to her. She wept on my neck and her arms trembled as she cuddled me like I was still a baby.

My hands were sweating and shaking at the same time. I saw the long-held-back tears in Karina's eyes and when her lips quivered for words, I knew I belonged to her. All the years that had stolen us apart had finally ended.

"You are so beautiful. My baby is so beautiful," she said proudly.

It was the first time I had ever been told that, and I felt foolish from such an exaggeration of words.

"I have waited a long time for this day," she whispered as she glided her fingers over my cheek. She reached up to brush a strand of my hair but it rebelled against her touch and twisted back toward my face. With her makeup smeared and eyes swollen, she shared the immeasurable love in her heart. My eyes burned with tears.

My Grandmother Elaine stood in the shadows watching and listening. I was totally absorbed in my mother's arms, but I still remember how my grandma glowed with happiness. She looked as though her heart had filled beyond its capacity. She couldn't ask for anything greater than the gift that her daughter had just received.

I never dreamed at that time that she had been dealt the same hand as my mother.

The exiting passengers had slowed down and some were clapping. A few gathered around and became teary-eyed like us. Nothing could distract me from my mother's face, so I did not remember that until much later in my life. I couldn't imagine how strange it had to be for my mother to meet Howie. How could she know what to say when she didn't even know how to face the man who had become the parent to her own child?

"How can I ever make this up to you?" she asked Howie.

"How about I take your bags?" he insisted and Karina nodded her head, like she was too weak to argue.

"Hello, Mom." Karina dabbed her eyes with tissue and hugged Elaine.

The men carried the luggage as Karina and Elaine walked me to the truck. There was a lot more conversation, but I don't remember what was said. I knew Gordon went home alone and the rest of us left all together. As Howie drove, I sat between Karina and Elaine. My mother had her arm around my shoulder and couldn't resist holding me tight.

"You are so grown up," said Karina and Elaine nodded in agreement. I had to admit, it was a bit suffocating. I wasn't used to receiving all that attention. Occasionally, I got a little overwhelmed by all the tears and words. It was a lot to take in.

Jenny gave up her bed so my mother and I could be in the same room together. Elaine slept in the guest room next to us. Karina and I didn't get much sleep the first night. There were so many stories to tell and questions that needed to come out. Long after Elaine had gone to bed, I wanted to know why social services had intervened and taken me away.

Karina left Jenny's bed and came over to mine. She lay down beside me and we snuggled together. I could hear and feel her heart beating and I loved her more than I ever thought possible. It hurt her to talk about that New Year's Day back in 1963, when she came home to find her children gone. Her finger brushed away a fallen tear as she confessed that she hadn't always been a good mother, but she loved us more than anything in her life. She stayed in my bed every night of her visit and held me close. She couldn't sleep without touching my arm, my face, or my head.

If I moved over she would search for me and would not rest until she knew physically that I was still there. It felt unnatural; I had never been in this situation, but I happily reciprocated. We spent our days reconnecting, taking long walks along the gravel road that led away from the ranch. We walked arm in arm and sometimes Karina would switch to putting her arm across my back.

"I love you, my wonderful girl." Karina turned to face me and her eyes didn't lie. She'd already said it a dozen times or more, but I still couldn't hear it enough. I loved her too, but the words didn't come as easily. I didn't know her the same way she knew me.

When we came back to my house, my Grandmother Elaine had been telling Howie about our family. He was just as surprised as I was when she told us that I had distant relatives all over town. I even had many cousins in my school!

"You have cousins on the Stand Off Reserve, too," she said. It had crossed my mind that maybe some of the kids who bused in from the reserve could be blood relatives. Although I was blonde, Wilma called me her "little Indian foster child" so many times that it just made sense. Even more exciting was to find out that Howie and Gabriella's son-in-law was my second cousin! It was the first time that I knew I belonged somewhere in the world and it was practically happening in my own backyard. I was part of a real existing family and through marriage I was a part of Howie and Gabriella's family too!

My Grandmother was also pleased to tell me that one of our relatives was in government; James Gladstone had become the first Status Indian in Canadian history to be named a federal senator. The Late Senator's son, grandsons, and granddaughter had also had made history. Later I found an entry on the Internet (www.canada.com) about the granddaughter June Willms,

> *"the first female inducted into the Volleyball Canada Hall of Fame. ... Willms was born in 1941 in Cardston, on the Blood Reserve. She was the granddaughter of Senator James Gladstone, the first Status Indian to be appointed to the Canadian Senate; daughter of calf roper Fred Gladstone, who won the Canadian calf-roping championship in 1948 and 1950, and sister of Jim Gladstone, who in 1969, 1971, and 1973 won the Canadian calf-roping championships. In 1977, Jim also became the first Canadian to win a world title in a timed rodeo event and is a member of the Alberta Hall of Fame."*

At school, I had heard about Jim and his brother but I didn't know them because they were a lot older than me. I didn't know I was related to them.

Elaine talked about her days when she was a young horseback rider in the Calgary Stampede and how she had won first prize in the barrel racing competition. It was so wonderful to hear all these stories about my relatives. I never dreamed it could be so exciting.

Three days passed and my mother Karina had to take Elaine back to her farm. I pleaded with Karina to stay longer, but she couldn't. I was still a young adolescent who was terribly insecure; I feared that my mother would walk through the door and out of my life again. I would have leaped at the opportunity to go with her but it wasn't an option because I was still in school. I felt like I couldn't go another minute without her touch.

"I'm not leaving you forever, sweetheart," she vowed as she snapped her bags closed. Then she added, "I have to take your Grandma home because she needs to tend to her farm. And your little sisters need me."

She tried to give comfort as she stroked my hair as though I was a child, but

I was inconsolable. I couldn't comprehend that she would leave me, especially after all the things we had shared.

After Mom and Grandma had gone, Howie was there to pick up the pieces. Even after I unloaded my emotional baggage on him.

I never imagined that I would be bitter and resent Karina when it was time for her to leave, yet there I was feeling cut off from her life again. Karina went to the farm and stayed with Elaine, and she made time to see some of her old friends. Then she boarded a flight back to the coast. The plane flew over the horizon, taking my mother with it.

Part Four: Finding Myself

48: Mr. Atkins

At school, I had turned into a mail junkie. I would skip lunch and rush off to the post office to find all kinds of goodies. Sometimes there were long letters with words of deep emotion from my parents. Other times, it was short and sweet with a card or pictures of family members. Occasionally, my mother sent me a gift and that made me feel special. Along with that came a steady flow of calls from Elaine, Karina, Louis, and some of my half-sisters.

My parents wanted to contact Sheila, but there was a problem: she had run away.

My social worker dropped in for a visit and was quite shocked to hear that I had already made contact with my parents. I asked for her support in my search for my brother Josh. Unfortunately, Josh had been adopted and his records were sealed, so the social worker had no way to access that information.

I felt I had a really good shot at finding Josh, so I wrote a letter to the Revenue Canada Taxation Office to see whether Josh might be listed under his biological name. I got a reply but there was no record of such a person. I had nothing. I mean nothing!

My mind was set to fix this problem, but how could I solve such a problem if there were no leads? I decided the best option was legal advice. Mission accomplished! On my lunch break, I didn't have to make a trip around the globe to find an attorney. I walked right off Main Street into an office holding the papers that covered bits of Josh's history. I had envisioned a puffed-up lawyer who would scoff and tell me to take a hike. But the man spoke in easy tones as he introduced himself. Mr. Atkins didn't sit across from me; instead, he pulled a chair around and took a seat next to mine.

"What brings you here?" he asked in a professional manner.

I told him about my brother's adoption, how we had been separated, that I loved my brother, and couldn't imagine a life without him, but that his records were sealed. Mr. Atkins looked a bit baffled, but as I told him everything I remembered, he jotted some notes.

He got right to the point. "How are you planning to pay expenses?" Business is business, so I understood.

"Occasionally I do some babysitting and I could pay whatever I make," I offered. But I didn't have any kind of extra money to burn, so he wasn't going to get much of a bang from my buck. I didn't know that lawyers were so costly. I explained that my foster parents had no idea that I had pursued a lawyer, because I didn't want to upset them.

He was willing to act as my lawyer and do it as a service, but it would be on his time and conditions—pro bono. What a generous man! He took my case because he believed that I should be entitled to know my roots. In the closing of our meeting he promised to retain my privacy on the issue. He said he would call or write about any progress in finding Josh. I got up and thanked him for everything he was willing to do. I walked outside, headed up the street and traced my steps back to class. Mr. Atkins had given me a new hope.

Mr. Atkins made several attempts to reach my social worker, but she did not return his calls. Finally, he wrote a letter requesting information on the identity and location of my brother Josh. A reply came at the end of November 1976 stating that Mr. Atkins' client would need a court order to make such a request and that the court order was still no guarantee of permission to receive the requested information.

My lawyer's only statement in his return letter was simple: "Expect that we will be seeking a court order."

The following January, Mr. Atkins wrote to the Honourable E. Helen Holton asking for help to trace the file containing an adoption name for my brother Josh. Mr. Atkins received a letter from the legislation building. The Honourable E. Helen Holton stated that she had accepted our request and would bring it to the attention of the Minister of Social Services.

49: Louis

The Christmas holidays were right around the corner and Louis wanted me to come out to British Columbia and meet him. He offered to buy plane tickets for me, but I didn't feel right about taking his money. I did not expect him to pay my way. Even though I was biologically his daughter, I didn't know him.

Instead, on Boxing Day, I got on the Greyhound bus and took the twenty-hour trip. It was long and boring, and I began to wonder why I made it so difficult for myself. I could have flown!

It was shortly after six in the morning when the bus arrived in the City of Langley. I rubbed the sleep from my eyes and did whatever it took to look presentable. From the window, I could see a man waiting nearby.

I told my brain and heart to stay calm.

"Hello, it's me, Louis… your Dad."

His words were plain and simple. The morning frost prickled my skin as we stood face to face on the sidewalk.

"Here we are," he said with an unruffled voice and a straight face.

My gust of excitement was big enough for the two of us. He reached out with his arms in a way that assured me he wasn't holding a gun to my head. He didn't come with bursts of joy or any kind of mushy words and it almost seemed like he was trying to downplay what should have been the most memorable moment.

How did he keep such a cool head? He had come straight from his job working the graveyard shift; he might have been exhausted. He was still in his work clothes and his hair was a choppy mess, but he wasn't apologetic for his appearance. I sensed he was the kind of person who didn't waste time apologizing for past mistakes.

"How was the trip?" he asked as he took my luggage.

"Too long."

"You should have taken my offer." He smiled and shrugged his shoulders.

We walked in silence, but my thoughts were rolling around like cannon balls in my head. I had a lot of things I wanted to say.

"I call this car my little hot rod," he beamed as he opened the door for me. "I have put a lot of sweat and work into fixing the engines of old cars. They're my hobby," he said proudly.

I took that as his way of connecting with me. Morning rush hour hadn't picked up yet, so it was fairly easy to cut through traffic. From the passenger window, I could see nothing flashy about the city. I felt a million miles away as we passed the cars going in the opposite direction.

"I want to make a quick stop at the mill where I work," he said, cutting into my thoughts. He pulled into a big empty lot and shut off the motor.

"I won't be long."

He got out and walked toward a large steel complex. The area was near to desolate except for a few seagulls that guarded from the top of the buildings. The wind howled outside but the car stood rigid against the elements. It was cold and the air was damp, so I sank low into the bucket seat and waited with apprehension. I didn't feel comfortable waiting alone in a strange place. It was eerie, like I had travelled into a twilight zone. It was a good ten minutes, but it felt like an hour before Louis reappeared and I was more than thankful that he was back.

"Where are we going?" I asked as I studied him. I saw how my eyes and the shape of my face were so much like his.

"We're going home." He raised his brow and smiled. He turned the key in the ignition and off we went. We left the industrial area and gradually made our way into the residential community. It was a dreary morning, but I didn't want the weather to shake my spirits. My father's house sat on a big shaded lot that was overrun with trees and old cars. Inside, the furnishings were plain and comfortable. I remember standing on the top of the landing and seeing a fake Christmas tree with sparkly tinsel and multi-coloured lights. There wasn't anything underneath except for one small gift.

"Hi. I'm Lindsey," said my father's girlfriend. Her head popped around the corner of the kitchen doorway.

"Hi. I've heard so many great things about you," I told her and she looked amused. She smiled bashfully, but she couldn't resist the urge to stare.

"Wow! You look so much like your father." She spoke as though her eyes alone could establish a gene pool connection.

"Really?" I looked at Louis. Yep, it's legitimate! I'm the female version of my father.

Lindsey's daughter made her way in to see what all the fuss was about.

"This is Marley; she is nine." Lindsey brightened as she pulled her little pride and joy into the conversation.

"Hi," Marley chimed in with a lively little hand wave. She wasn't shy and she didn't look anything like her mother. What a contented child, I thought, as she bounced off to play.

"You have half-sisters whom I want you to meet while you are here." Dad stated the facts so easily and maybe that was a good thing. Straight forward and get it out so I wouldn't be confused. I followed him into the kitchen and we sat around the table as Lindsey poured coffee and put out a plate of sandwiches.

"I've got something for you," Louis said. Then he pushed himself away from the table and went into the living room. He reached under the tree and came back with a present. "I hope you like it."

"Oh. Thank you," I marveled as he placed it on the table before me. It was my first gift from him, so I was excited.

"Go ahead. Open it!" he urged, so I tugged the ribbon loose and tore away the wrapping. Inside, I found a classy black chain with emerald beads randomly placed.

"It's so pretty," I gushed. I knew he was trying to get me to open up and get back in touch with him. We were off to a good start!

Louis insisted on keeping it light. He kept me in the game with his generic questions about school, friends, musical preferences, and hobbies. At times, I really had a thirst to know everything. I didn't want anything to delay us from having a wonderful meeting, so I pitched in with plenty of questions.

But Louis didn't want to get knee deep in the details. Maybe he felt it was

128

more important that we savour our first visit with good memories to fall back on. From my view, I didn't want anything to be saved for a later date. As a seventeen year old, I had missed so much already.

Louis set up times for family get-togethers so I could be reacquainted with the older generation of my family. We went to the old folks home to visit my great grandmother. She was close to a century old, so Louis warned that she had lost much of her memory.

"She probably won't remember you. She doesn't remember me and I see her all the time," he said. We both chuckled.

Louis was right. She didn't know me at all. I wondered if she had ever cuddled me in her arms. Had she indulged herself with the idea of a search for her great grandbabies when she was of sound mind? She was adoringly childlike as Louis tried to stir her memories. Her silver blue eyes shone like two nickels and she talked incessantly—I think more to herself than to us. Her typical granny appearance was comforting, but her vacant eyes held no stories of the old days. As we were about to leave, I turned to wave goodbye. She smiled and our eyes held as though she had had a brief epiphany. On our way back to the car, Louis was already talking about our next reunion.

"I want you to meet my Dad—your Grandfather Leroy," he said it with such conviction that I sensed it was going to change the whole flavour of reuniting with my family. I got a gut feeling that it was going to be weird. We set out for New Westminster where many of the old historical buildings had taverns. Although it was already dark out, I could see the city was mostly brick and stone. I didn't like the area. It was grungy and smelled like garbage. It didn't feel safe, yet I wasn't scared, because Louis was right by my side.

We turned onto Front Street and continued along the sidewalk that ran horizontal with the CP Rail tracks. On the other side of the track was the Fraser River where hobos hid in the darkness.

It was getting close to nine in the evening so the bars were filling up with partygoers. Louis poked his head in the bars as we passed along and finally he spotted what we had come for. He pointed my grandfather out to me and we proceeded to walk through a throng of people. As we moved across the bar, I couldn't see a single woman anywhere. The place was buzzing and I felt a bit too dressy as eyes shifted from my leather coat down to my black strappy heels.

"Hello, Dad." Louis nudged his father's arm as I waited respectfully, trying to be ladylike. It was standing room only, unless a man was willing to part with his chair. I wasn't sure what the house rules were, but as I searched for a chair it seemed that it was every man for himself.

"Who ah, what'cha doing here?" Grandfather Leroy wasn't tipsy—he was sloshed, and I was worried that he might black out. I noticed that Louis was not surprised to see his father slumped over a bar table, cradling his beer. Grandfather was completely unplugged from the world around him, but that didn't stop Louis. His mind was set on making the moment memorable.

"I came to see you." Louis stood close to me and I could feel his pride. "There is someone I want you to meet. Do you know who this lady is?" Louis asked as his finger gestured in my direction.

We both gleamed at each other and I felt quite pleased to be his daughter. The old man rolled his heavy eyes in my direction.

"No. Should I?" Grandfather Leroy spoke off-handedly and took a swig.

"You don't recognize her? Well, I'll give you a clue… you haven't seen her in a long time. Not since she was a baby." Louis's persistence didn't seem to get my Grandfather to focus, so he added, "She is your granddaughter, Eugenea."

Not a word was passed—just a big long stare.

I told myself to breathe as the man's eyes bulged with shock. His nose was red and pitted by pores and he looked like he had given up on life many years earlier. With rumpled hair and the task of holding himself upright, he eyeballed every speck of me. I wanted to behave naturally, but it was hard not to be a ball of nerves when Grandfather Leroy had gone from a slurring, sloppy mess to what I would call stone-cold sober.

"Where have you been, child?" he asked as he rose to his feet. His eyes were soulful and my head began to spin like I had been on a momentary bender. I was so happy to meet my Grandfather Leroy. I felt saturated in happiness. There was a short recess of silence as we embraced.

"I never believed that I would ever see you again. "

He smiled and I smiled too. There was more silence.

"You are so grown up—a lady now. I have a beautiful grandchild," he raved under his façade of liquor and I flushed at his approval. "Where have you been all this time? I mean… well I know what happened but…" He didn't finish.

I quickly gave him an update of my years in Alberta and explained that I was only visiting for the holidays and would be going back after New Year's.

"I hope I see you again real soon."

"I hope so too," I conceded.

Drunk or sober, he loved me. The sky had no limits and I took for granted that my Grandfather would be here for years to come. I thanked my lucky stars that Louis did everything he could to make it possible for me to meet a vital member of my family. My Grandfather Leroy passed away a year and a half later.

Throughout my visit, I met more family. I had half-sisters from Louis's second and third marriages whom I wanted to get to know. I also met Louis's Mom, Norina. She was strong in a proper queen-like way and yet she carried an exuberance that showed her enjoyment of life. She was not the kiss-and-hug type, but she was nice. She didn't use the terms of endearment such as "I love you."

50: Karina and Bart, Chloe and Iona

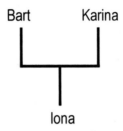

As I had anticipated, Karina couldn't wait to integrate me with my two half-sisters, so Louis volunteered to drive me there. For twenty minutes or so, I had to sit patiently in the car while Louis drove, but in my mind I was doing acrobats. I could hardly catch my breath as we entered the city of Surrey. However, the view was a bit daunting. So many houses were spoiled by rotting piles of firewood, garbage bags, and broken pieces of furniture that had been left in the rain. The road flew under us as Louis ignored the speed limit. He pulled the car into a trailer park and backed into a visitor's spot.

As I got out of the car, I heard a growling and I quickly turned to look. It wasn't the kind of welcome I'd expected. Karina's Doberman set his evil eyes on me like I was a steak bone. He barked madly as slobber and spit glistened on his fangs. Although the dog was tethered to a big chain, he had full range of the deck. With all the force of his weight, he pulled so hard it was a miracle that he didn't break loose. I didn't want to be devoured by his razor-edged teeth. Karina quickly came to my rescue. As she attempted to drag her dog inside, I could see right into the gully of his throat.

"Hello, sweetheart. Hello, Louis. Come in." She smiled and waited for me, but I wasn't moving. "Don't worry about the dog. He gets a little hotheaded, but he won't bite you. He is a big sap and barks for attention."

I didn't really find Karina's voice of reason to be much comfort. Again I heard a low warning growl as we hugged for the first time in months. Before I could look, the dog had pushed his wet snout against my bottom and practically lifted me off the floor. I wasn't going to let that beast rip the hide off my backside, so I mustered some courage and smacked his nose. To my relief it worked. His claws clicked noisily on the floor as he backed away. He lay down and curled up in front of the sofa. After the dog had settled, Karina was very excited to get on with the introductions.

My two half-sisters, Chloe and Iona, had a hard time absorbing the news flash of a half-sister. Chloe hadn't grown up with her father Andrew. When Karina married Bart, she moved on; she never talked about Josh, Sheila, or me. It was just too hard to explain—too unbearable. Chloe didn't take the reunion as a celebration. On the contrary. That day she stayed in her room, ignoring her mother's pleas.

"Eugenea came all the way from Alberta just to see you," Karina said as she popped her head in the bedroom doorway.

"Whatever."

"You are being very rude to Eugenea. She is your big sister," Karina whispered, but her voice carried down the hall and everyone heard.

Chloe mumbled something like, "She's not my sister."

I knew Karina was mortified but this was Chloe's way of letting us know that she was hurt and angry. She was used to being the older sibling. Finally, when she decided to come out of her room, it was on her time... not ours. She walked out wearing pyjamas with her hair still matted. She wasn't making a fuss like everyone else.

"Hi," I smiled.

"Hi," she groaned as her brown eyes rolled.

"I'm Jeanie. That's my foster name. You can call me Eugenea if you want."

"Sure." She snubbed me.

I didn't want to appear uneasy but the issues at hand were getting more and more unpleasant. It was so obvious that Chloe was trying to make everyone feel uncomfortable, so maybe then I would go away and she could have her life back. Karina was appalled and made excuses for Chloe's behaviour but that only added fuel to the fire. Chloe accused Mom of putting up a front by making such a big deal out of the reunion.

Chloe was flat-out jealous of all the attention I was getting and Karina looked as though she had been slapped. Her face was red and I hoped that she would just let it go. My sister looked a bit like I had when I was her age. She was blonde and brown-eyed with similar features to mine, but in her thirteen years Chloe had sprouted like a bean and towered over me. I suspected that my sister was quite a handful long before I came into the picture.

All the while, Iona was standing in Chloe's shadow. She was nothing like her. She didn't have a rebellious bone in her body. Her soft-spoken voice and gentle manner was so attractive that it was hard to take my eyes off her. She was still at that age where Barbie dolls and skipping ropes were a big part of her day. Her tender heart and warm eyes showed an old soul, and I sensed that she might be open to the idea of a new sister.

"This must be quite different from your life in Alberta. Do you think you would like to live in British Columbia some day?" Karina's husband Bart snatched my attention from the girls. The room fell quiet. The look on Karina's face showed signs of a desperate "Yes." As for Chloe, her loud telepathic brain waves screamed a big fat "No!"

"Maybe." I ignored Chloe's burning glare.

"Karina, do you still want to take the girls to Vancouver for the day?" Bart asked lazily from his recliner. I could see that he was ready to nod off at any moment. I was thankful that he had switched to another subject.

"Of course. We should go soon." Karina took his cue and got Iona ready. As we got our coats on, Karina quickly combed the knots out of Iona's glossy strands. The tugging and pulling hurt and Iona whined a lot. The squabbling got awkward. My Dad wasn't keen to hang around any longer so he went home and the rest of us went shopping.

The after-Christmas sales had caused a flock of buyers to come into the city. Some of the store displays were massive. A big corner window featured a Victorian carriage with a red velvet seat piled with gifts wrapped in shimmering foil. I saw families bundled together, who were awed over a display of tiny city replicas and a miniature train rumbling around a track.

For me, the entire day was magical. I wanted Chloe to join in and have fun, but she refused to walk with us and often strayed off to the nearest pay phone. Chloe knew how to push her mother's buttons. We continued on with our shopping and didn't make an issue out of it.

"I want to get a special belated Christmas gift for my girl," Karina offered.

"But you already got me a gift," I said as we entered the double-wide doors and passed under a gleaming chandelier.

"I know, Honey, but this is something special." Karina cast her eyes toward a rack of floor-length gowns.

"Your Dad and his girlfriend want to take you to a New Year's event so I would love to buy you something to wear. Look at the dresses in here!" She chirped with excitement as we looked around at the endless stream of clothes.

Karina had missed out on any shopping sprees for me, so I knew she'd been dreaming of this day. It meant everything to her.

"Honey, you must try this on." She clutched an eye-catching slinky red gown.

Heck, yeah! She's too cool, I thought to myself.

"Come on, try it. If you don't like the style, we'll find something else." Karina held up the dress so I could see the bodice. It was slightly gathered with a pretty empire waist and it was definitely the style I would go for.

Inside the fitting room, I slipped off my clothes and wiggled into the dress. In the gilded mirror, I turned sideways and tied the sash in the back. When I pulled back the curtain, Karina gasped.

"It's gorgeous! What a dress! You will be the belle of the ball for sure."

Karina was pulling out her wallet already. "Tell me that you love it." She got all starry-eyed.

"It's so pretty. You have such good taste, Mom," I said and I noticed her emotions were suddenly a bit rocky. Then it hit me—I had called her "Mom" for the first time.

"Will that be all?" The woman was waiting over at the cash register next to a glass showcase filled with rows of sparkling jewelry.

"Yes. I think so," Mom said.

Chloe snubbed me all day and made it clear that I was cramping her life. I tried to make conversation with her, but she would snap her gum and scoff. She had a total hissy fit when her black raccoon eyes caught sight of my shopping bag. At the end of the day, Chloe hadn't ironed out her problems with me. Our relationship was going to be a steep hill to climb.

51: Louis and Lindsey

The New Year's party was at a singles club for adults so it wasn't going to be anything like my school dances. I felt honoured to go as a guest but as the hours in the day progressed to evening, I felt a little giddy. Then Louis emerged in the living room and he was dressed up with his hair slicked back. I'm pretty sure that my cheeks had turned the same red as my dress. I hated to get carried away, but I got misty eyed and my throat choked up. He looked so dapper in his savvy blue suit. It's incredible how his striking outfit could suddenly make his eyes bluer. The man had swagger! Louis knew how to pull it together and he made it look so effortless.

When we arrived at the party the dancing had already began. Louis and Lindsey mingled me in with their friends and I was soon deep in conversation. Through the course of the night, the music varied between classic, disco, and rock. I never refused an invitation to get a dance on the floor. As the night went on, Louis joined me at the serving table with a big grin and raised eyebrows.

"Would you like to go and shake off some energy?"

"Sure," I cooperated, thrilled at the chance of our first father-daughter dance. He took me by the arm and we moved into the middle of the crowd. Louis shuffled his feet and swirled, and I could tell he liked the lyrics. He was a typical freestyle dancer; he didn't have any special kind of moves and I knew he wouldn't need to resist any urges to show off.

He caught me staring and he did an amusing twist. I let out a lighthearted giggle and he chuckled back. Although I didn't quite fit in with all the divorcees and singles, I felt grown up. It was certainly a far cry from my rock 'n' roll high school dances.

When it was time to ring in the New Year, everyone gathered together and chimed in on the countdown. "Three... Two... One! Happy New Year!" we shouted in unison at the stroke of midnight.

"Happy New Year!" Louis shouted over the lively party and gave me a wonderful hug as I yelled back. Everyone was getting ready to do a toast. I dipped a ladle into a large tiffany bowl and poured some punch into a glass-handled cup. Glasses were raised and clinked together and then we all took a sip. As I daintily sipped, I noticed Louis holding Lindsey in his arms and I wished the night would never end.

I could tell that Louis took the lead when it came to planning family events. He organized a night out for dinner at a swanky Italian restaurant and we all went, including the youngest child in the pack. At five years old, Shauna was the spitting image of how I had looked at that age. Her short flyaway hair reminded me of my own tresses when I was a child. This kid had a real spark about her. She was feisty and talkative and she knew how to pitch a fit if she was misunderstood. Over dinner, her angelic voice lit our conversation. Her dazzling eyes and spunkiness were heart-warming and sweet to watch.

Louis treated me very well. He had the gift of the gab, but not in a derogatory way. He would talk about politics, religion, and music, and it was so interesting that I wanted to hear more. Some of his views seemed a bit eccentric, but I found that to be the best part.

During my visit I had been surrounded by so many loved ones. It was an emotional and humbling day when my family gathered around to say goodbye. As I parted with hugs and entered the bus, I wondered if I was losing out. Given the timeframe, I might not see my family for a long time. I had to go back and finish another semester of school.

Plus I had to find Sheila again and Josh for the first time.

52: Mom and Grandma Elaine

January rolled in with chilling news. Grandma Elaine was very ill and she was taken to the hospital in Lethbridge. Immediately, I set out from Gabriella and Howie's and went to visit her. She didn't seem sick from her appearance. Her curtain was pulled open and she was sitting up as if she was ready to go home. She spread her arms wide and I got a full dose of her love.

"How are you feeling?" I asked with great concern.

"I'm doing fine—there is no need to worry. That's the doctor's job." Elaine's voice grew serious.

She wanted to hear all about my trip. I told her everything and she praised me for my courage. She was very proud of me for not giving up on my family.

"We have to stick together. Do you think you could find Sheila so I could see her too?" Elaine asked as she took my hand and pressed it against her cheek.

"I'm working on it." I assured her that I would do whatever it took.

When my semester ended, I packed up and moved to Calgary where I could be in the general area of my siblings. It was extremely important that I reconnect with Sheila and find Josh. I would be forever grateful that I had the best years of my adolescence with Howie and Gabriella. I could not express how much they meant to me but I have loved them all my life. At the same time, I was grateful to be independent and lose the stigma of being a foster child. I could erase what many foster children account as a mark of disgrace. From then on, I called the shots and made my own decisions.

Karina was always enthusiastic and positive but then I saw that her writings began to change. She was having a lot of problems with Bart's drinking habit and Chloe was skipping school.

"There is something I need to tell you and I can't write what I need to say in a letter," Mom said as we talked over the phone. "Your Grandmother is not getting better." Mom was stalling and I could tell she was crying. "She... has stomach cancer. It's not good."

"I'm so sorry, Mom. What can I do?"

"Honey, I need you to pray for her and ask God to help her. Continue to visit her. She loves to see you."

"How long has she been sick?" I asked.

"She was sick when she met you, but she made me promise not to say anything. She didn't want to spoil our reunion." Her voice cracked and I understood why Mom had had to leave the ranch that day.

As soon as I could, I went back to the Lethbridge Hospital to visit Elaine, but as I came toward the door of her room, I heard a moaning sound. A curtain was drawn around the bed so she didn't know I was there. The doctor was resetting a tube that was inserted in her stomach. I could tell by her cries that the pain was eating her alive. Up to that moment, I didn't want to believe how gravely ill she was. The most I could do was run to the nearest exit. I hid in the stairway, trying to compose myself. I prayed harder than I had ever prayed in my life. I pleaded with God to stop her from suffering and begged him not to take her away from me.

When I came back to her room, I didn't want her to know that I had been there earlier. It would have upset her so much. The doctor had gone, but there was an empty paper cup on the side table with a tray of food, untouched.

"How is my sweet granddaughter?" Elaine tried to sit up, but not without difficulty.

I moved closer, willing to do anything I could to lessen her discomfort. Her elbows pressed into the mattress as she tried to drag herself upwards. Frail and exhausted, she lay back against the pillow.

"I'm in good company. I know the doctors are doing the best they can." Elaine patted my hand with reassurance. "I love you." Her words were as soft as a whisper and I responded with the same message. "Your mom loves you very much. I think you know that. Right, Honey?"

"Yes, I do, and I love her too." I stared at the floor. My head was heavy with thoughts about my mother. We were miles apart and I was suffering from separation anxiety. I also found that it was hard to hold down my resentment about what had happened to our family. I had never thought I would ever hold it against Mom, but I was seeing her in a light that wasn't as forgiving. Without Karina, I had endured so much pain at the hands of so many foster parents. The sexual, physical, and mental abuse were traumas that I couldn't erase. I think Elaine knew that something was a little off between Karina and me.

"Karina needs you and you need her. Both of you have been through some rough times, so I'm asking you to be patient with her. She is ashamed and embarrassed about what happened. Karina has never gotten over it. She has been saddled with guilt for many years from her mistakes. In time, you will come to know your Mom and I think you will see that she has a big heart and is a good person. Please try not to be too hard on her."

My Grandma was right and I respected her opinion, so I took her words of counsel very seriously. I wouldn't let her down because I couldn't refuse the only promise that she had ever asked of me. I didn't want to let my Mom down either.

In Grandma's final days, she was trying to tie up any loose ends. She was not thinking about her pain and agony, but doing her motherly duties. She was making sure that all was taken care of before she left her nest to soar the skies.

Elaine at the Rodeo

53: Sheila and Carlton

Meanwhile, I was busting my chops trying to find Sheila and getting nowhere. She had run away and was living with her boyfriend on the other side of town. After a considerable amount of difficulty, I got a tip from the boyfriend's relative. It took some pressure, but eventually the woman admitted that Sheila was living with her boyfriend Carlton and they were renting her basement. I stuck around and waited, and in less than an hour Sheila arrived with Carlton. When I finally saw her, my heart was at peace. It was the best moment ever! It felt so good to hug her.

"I missed you so much! I was so afraid that I would never see you again," I said with a sigh of relief.

Her boyfriend Carlton had a biker-like way about him. His hair was bushy and he was so husky that my sister looked small beside him. As we got better acquainted, he couldn't resist the urge to tease.

"Don't pay any attention to him. Carlton's full of jokes, but he's harmless," Sheila comforted.

I knew that Carlton and I would get along. I liked his cheesy puns.

"Can you make your awesome spaghetti? He's such a good cook," Sheila boasted.

"Sure, I know you both have some catching up to do." Carlton rummaged through the cupboard for a pan. While he concentrated on making supper, I told Sheila about our parents, siblings, and grandparents. She was so surprised at how much I had accomplished in such a short time. She wanted to know if our mother asked about her or wanted to meet her. Her face was very serious.

"Oh yes! She wants to know everything about you," I told Sheila and her eyes sparkled. I was very excited for my sister, but I held back. From experience, I knew that meeting family was not a one-size-fits-all situation. I didn't want to storm in like a force of nature. I saw in her eyes that she was contemplating what to do.

"Do you think she would come here?" Sheila asked quietly.

"Yes, I do. She wants to see Josh too. Both our parents have waited all these years."

"Where is she?"

I told her that our Mom was in Lethbridge visiting our sick Grandmother. I believed my sister had the right to know everything about her family and what was happening to our Grandmother. If she decided to reunite with her family, I would support her any way I could.

Carlton drained the noodles and covered the pot with a lid while Sheila and I set the plates around the table.

"Alas! Dinner is served." Carlton gave Sheila a saucy grin. Then he served it up like a waiter. Sheila was a teeny bit wrong. It wasn't good; it was scrumptious.

54: Nur

I'm not sure if it was Carlton's Italian cuisine or just a fluke, but that week I got my first job in a little Italian café. My first day was a joke. With a tray in hand, I bumped around and scurried between the boss and the chef. The food was late and my service was too slow. I was nervous and I spilled a chocolate milkshake on a customer's lap. My boss was furious.

Great, I thought gloomily. I have totally screwed up this job.

A voice came from behind me. "Can I make a bold suggestion?" It was Felicia, one of the cooks. In her heavy Arabic accent, she told me not to be so nervous. I was happy that she was on my side.

"Clean the mess, then go and serve those men at the door. Be good to them. The tall one is my little brother." She waved her hand in their direction and tossed me a rag. I saw a man in a suit waving back.

That's what she refers to as a little brother! He had to be a foot and a half taller than her. I realized that I was staring and he was staring too. I quickly turned away and mopped the table. The two men didn't wait to be seated. Felicia's brother ordered a coffee and watched my every move. I couldn't stop myself from looking back to see what he was doing. The other waitresses were checking him, out but he didn't drop the stare.

"Nur!" Felicia's voice got his attention and they spoke in a foreign language so I didn't know what was being said until he went back to speaking English.

"Who is that woman?" He put it so boldly to his sister that I knew he was referring to me.

"Eugenea. It's her first day," Felicia acknowledged and then she went back to speaking in her native tongue. I sure wished I could understand what they were talking about. Felicia went back to work, so Nur and his friend finished their coffee, paid up, and left. I knew absolutely zero about Nur, yet he wasn't leaving until he'd made eye contact with me. He wasn't like the pubescent high school boys I had known.

After a stressed out day, I tugged my coat on and got out of there. It was incredibly cold and I hadn't taken more than five steps when I heard a voice calling my name. There was a man in the distance waving his arm high above his head and I recognized the smile. It was Nur. He strutted with confidence and had his hands buried in his pocket pants like he was the stud of *Saturday Night Fever*. His suit jacket was open and revealed a silky shirt. His friend was there and he was dressed in a similar fashion. I slowed down as they approached.

"Hi. Eugenea. Right?" He was very happy. Too happy. It felt like a put-on. It's not like he had struck oil or something.

"Right, and you are Nur." I wondered why a parent would give a baby such a boring name.

"How did you like your new job?" he asked, but he wasn't interested in my job.

"It's okay," I answered as I thought back to that stupid moment with the chocolate shake. He must have heard about that. How embarrassing! I said hello to his friend and he reciprocated with a smile.

"He doesn't speak English," Nur said and turned to his friend. They talked for a moment and then the man left.

"He's going to work," Nur said. "It's too cold out here. Why don't we go for a coffee?"

"I don't drink coffee," I said coolly, but it was frigidly cold, so I wondered why I was giving Nur the brush off. I didn't plan to get weak in the knees like the other waitresses.

"There's the mall entrance. Let's go in and warm up." My heels tapped over the cobblestones as I made my way to the glass doors. Nur was right beside me, taking my arm.

"You must be freezing," Nur said as we glided up an escalator. It was the perfect space where he could make his move. I quickly moved up a step and he followed. He didn't seem to care if I snubbed him.

"Hungry?"

"Yes," I laughed and he leaned so close that I could smell his aftershave. As we stepped off the escalator he suggested that we go for dinner on the corner of Eighth Street, but it was getting late so I told him that I didn't want to miss my bus.

"Well, I am taking a bus too, so I will walk with you." Nur wasn't discouraged for a second. He was quite the Cat's Meow and he wasn't afraid to speak his mind. I liked the way his eyes searched my face.

"You are so transparent," I teased, but I could see by Nur's expression that he didn't understand what I meant.

"I don't speak English as good as you," he shrugged with a dreamy smile. We walked through the mall and all the while he was trying to carry a conversation. I didn't want to miss my bus because it would be another hour before the next one and it would be dark by then. We left the mall together, but I was in a hurry; I could see the bus was coming.

"That's my ride," I interrupted and quickened the pace. The brakes hissed as the side doors unfolded. People rushed out and I tried to hurry in. "Bye, I must go. I'll see you tomorrow," I yelled over my shoulder.

"Wait for me." Nur's legs took only half as many steps as mine. He caught up and grabbed my hand and we got on the bus. I entered first with my hand still caught in his. I pulled my hand away as he pointed to an empty row of seats.

"What are you doing?" I asked as I took a seat first.

"I am trying to be a gentleman. I want to make sure you get home safely," Nur said with a condescending wink. "How else am I going to get your number?"

With that he pulled out a pen from his jacket and scrawled my number on the palm of his hand.

"Would you go out with me on Friday? We could see a show or go to the disco."

"I'm not sure if I can make it."

"Is your life so full?" he challenged.

"You don't believe me?" I asked.

"I didn't say that. I know you are busy, but I bet you have time for me." He held up his hand and curled his thumb to his pointer finger, meaning okay. He left a half-inch of space in between. What a joker! He was crooning me with his teasing and flirting and I was taking the bait. But at the same time I was making sure he didn't see me as a victory.

"This is my stop. Would you like to meet my roommates?"

"No, I go home. I live on the north side, so I have a long way to go."

"I can make you a hot drink. At least come in and get warm," I urged. He did. My roomies tried to make friendly conversation, but Nur was not friendly and wasn't interested in small talk. How awkward!

"I should go." Nur couldn't seem to get comfortable on the sofa, so I suggested we go outside.

"I don't like crowds," Nur said as we walked toward the bus stop. "I really want to see you again." Nur's eyes were demanding and overly serious and it didn't seem like he was willing to take no for an answer.

"I'm not sure. It depends on what time I get off work," I said. In my head, I was thinking I want to play hard to get, because it was obvious that Nur was used to getting any girl that he wanted.

"I'll see you tomorrow." Nur pulled me into his arms before I got a chance to reject him. The bus sloshed through the snow and came to a stop as Nur sealed a passionate kiss on my lips. I was breathless. As the wheels pulled away from the curb, I watched Nur take a seat near the window. Then he lifted his arm and waved until the bus was out of sight.

I ran all the way up the stairs and into the apartment. I liked Nur a lot. He made me feel beautiful. My roomies thought he was hot, but they didn't like his vibe.

Straight away as I came in the door, the phone rang.

"Hello?" I was slightly out of breath.

"Hello. I want to speak to Eugenea," said an unknown voice.

"Speaking," I replied, but there was no response and the line went dead. The phone rang again and I picked up.

"Hello," I spoke.

"Eugenea?" It was the same voice as before.

"Speaking. Who is this?"

"Did you have a good time tonight?"

"Pardon?" I asked, but the caller was gone. I knew it wasn't Nur, because he would still be riding home. I hoped it was just a one-time prank, but the phone rang again and it was the mystery man.

"Stop calling here, please." I hung up but in less than ten seconds he called back.

"What do you want?" I answered sharply and he was gone.

As a young woman fresh off the farm, I was a bit timid. I realized that I was not very street savvy in the big city. How did he know my name? Had he overheard me giving my number to Nur?

55: Sheila and Carlton, and Grandma

I got up to go into my room when the phone rang again and somehow I knew it wasn't going to be the mysterious caller.

"Hello, Honey," Mom said and I was so relieved it was her. But there was something very sad in her greeting.

"What is it, Mom? Tell me."

"Grandma has taken a turn for the worse… the doctors don't think she will make it through the next twenty-four hours."

"That's horrible." I couldn't bear it. "I'm so sorry, Mom. Are you okay?" It was impossible to hold back from crying.

"No… I'm not… but I have to be strong." Mom was falling apart. "Sweetheart, is there any way that you can go to see her? I know it's a lot to ask, but it could be… your last time."

"I'm supposed to work tomorrow and it's only my second day. If I take it off I'll get fired." My throat was thick with tears, because I was ashamed to say that.

How could I be thinking about my trivial little job in comparison with the price of a life at stake? I had to go and be with Elaine immediately, but there wasn't even a bus leaving that late.

"Maybe I should call Sheila and Carlton. If Carlton drove, we could be there in three hours. We could go tonight and Sheila would see her Grandmother before it's too late."

"Do you think Sheila is ready to meet her?" Mom asked.

"If she's not ready, she won't go," I stated.

By 10:30 p.m., Sheila and Carlton were at my place so we rushed out to the car and drove to Lethbridge.

"Hang in there, Elaine," I thought to myself.

We drove straight through and fortunately traffic was minimal, so we arrived shortly after midnight.

We entered Elaine's room and quietly tiptoed around the bed. Although Elaine didn't open her eyes, I knew she was alive. Her room was squeaky-clean and there was no sign of activity. The nurse on duty had been at Elaine's beck and call, so she knew that our Grandmother had been unconscious for quite a while. It was shocking to see how much Elaine had weakened since the last time I was there. Without a doubt, it would take nothing short of a miracle to reach her.

"Grandma, it's me Eugenea." I leaned over the metal frame of the bed and stared into her face. She didn't move. "I have someone here to see you." I desperately hoped my voice would stimulate her.

I would have been gloriously relieved to see a wave of her hand or a twitch of a finger. Anything. Give me anything!

"Grandma, remember Sheila? She is here to see you," I said. That seemed to revive Elaine, because she woke up. Her eyes opened momentarily.

"Hi." Sheila spoke softly and inched her way into Grandma's view. I choked up with tears as Sheila spoke sweetly into her ear. What a brave girl! I was so touched by Sheila's compassion and unconditional kindness to a woman she'd never known. Elaine's glossy eyes rolled in Sheila's direction and she made a gurgling sound, but the words wouldn't come. I truly believe that emotions can speak louder than words. The cancer had spread like wildfire and there was barely any life in Elaine. Her IV was disconnected. Nothing could make her thrive—not even Sheila.

Among the "Get Well" cards that stood on Elaine's night table was a card unlike the others. It had a different heading altogether: "Congratulations on your Wedding Day!"

Confused, I flipped it open and read the contents inside.

Dear Mom and Gordon,

Congratulations, I am so happy for both of you.

I love you with all my heart and I am here for you, whenever you need me.

Love, your daughter,

Karina

I was still confused.

Although Sheila was able to see her Grandmother, she hadn't met our Mom Karina. I kept hoping that Mom would come through that door. I knew she was just a short drive away, but she did not come that night.

56: Karina, Grandma and Gordon

When I got back to Calgary, I returned to my job and told my boss what happened. He didn't believe the sick grandma story and I was fired. Three days after my return, Elaine succumbed to her death. She was finally set free from her prison of pain. I went to visit my mother while she was preparing for Elaine's funeral. There was to be an open casket at the wake. It was my first time to attend a funeral and I had never seen a dead person before.

It was all too much. I moved about in a trance, not believing what had transpired in such a short time. Mom stayed close beside me like we were the last two people on earth. She walked up the aisle and stopped beside the coffin. She cried so hard it took a while to pull herself together. Then she bent over the casket and kissed Elaine on the forehead. I had never seen such love so, when it was my turn to view the casket, I kissed Elaine too.

She looked so different in death. The makeup was very heavy and her lipstick was too pink. She never wore pink lipstick, because all the women in Hollywood wore red.

When the service was over, the family and friends went to Gordon and Grandma's farm. My Auntie Latisha was dressed in a gorgeous gown that looked like it came from Paris. Elaine's three sons—my uncles—came for the funeral, but they sported a weird arrogance from too much testosterone and not enough time to let go of past issues.

I told Mom that I had seen the wedding card and in return she told me a remarkable story.

"Your Grandma was terrified to die because she believed that she would go to Hell."

Mom said Elaine was very unhappy, because she was unable to see all the good things that she had done. She had no peace in her soul. In the hours before her death, a priest visited her. Mom listened as Elaine talked with her priest. For some reason only known to Elaine, it seemed imperative that she talk about the sequence of her life. She wanted a clean slate.

She started with her memories as a child. It had been an easy life compared to what lay ahead. As a young girl, she rode horses and had a passion for clothing design. She opened up about her marriage to Lloyd and how quickly it turned into a loveless sham and how it became a living Hell when her first baby died in infancy.

When Elaine saw her baby's coffin she had wished she could die right then.

"My poor little baby still lies in an unmarked grave." Grandma never recovered from that awful day. Elaine was going through the confession mode—the part that makes dying so horrible. She told the priest that she had committed adultery and had never found a way to forgive herself. "My husband disowned me and got revenge. He took away my babies… all five… and hid them. Now, my kids are grown up strangers who look at me with disgust."

Mom and I cried as she recalled the details of Elaine's final admissions and how her life had literally crumbled after the loss of her children. Elaine and Lloyd had wasted all those years with hate and revenge and created a terrible outcome for Mom and her siblings. But Elaine found love when she met Gordon and moved in with him.

The priest took Elaine's hands in his and prayed for her soul to find peace with God. He asked Elaine if she had ever considered marriage.

"Marriage?" Both Elaine and Mom were shocked. "Marriage shows that you are taking the steps toward perfection in the eyes of God."

Elaine understood what her priest was saying, but she couldn't get out of bed so how could she walk up the aisle? The only way to make it official was to have a ceremony right there in her hospital room. Mom could sign as a witness. The priest suggested Elaine and Gordon seek penance with the Lord. He read parts of the bible to help them realize that sin is reversible: "God has a merciful and forgiving heart." He read the scriptures and taught them how to become unchained from guilt.

Gordon didn't reject the idea of marriage. He stood up from a nearby chair and slid off his hat and held it in his big callused hands. His thinning hair was flat and dull, but his eyes shone as he knelt by Elaine's bedside.

"Sweetheart, we never had much, but you have stayed with me through it all. I do regret many things, but I have never regretted my love for you. Please give me the one thing I have wanted most in this life. I ask you to marry me." Gordon took Elaine's shaky hands and kissed them. Mom was sad and happy all at the same time.

It was beautiful how love could outshine the worst possible circumstances.

"Will it matter that I don't have a ring?" Gordon turned to the priest.

"I have one," Mom piped in. "You can use mine for now and we will get a new one later." She tugged at the band until it gave way. "Take it please."

Mom waited, holding out the ring to Gordon. In honour of the bride and groom, the priest held an informal and private service. There wasn't enough time for a ceremonial fuss or the traditional setting of a church filled with guests. Mom watched as the Priest's long robes swished with his steps. His rosary made a soft tinkle as the beads shifted in his hand. He faced the couple and opened his scriptures and read a passage about the sanctity of marriage.

"Dearly Beloved. We are gathered here to witness the love and dedication between this man and this woman. Do you, Elaine, promise to love and obey your husband in sickness and health, for rich or for poor until death do you part?"

"Yes, I do." Elaine showed great strength. The priest repeated the question to Gordon.

"Yes. Elaine, you are my girl. I will always love you and I will never part from you." Gordon was miserably happy. Sadly Gordon would never carry his bride over the threshold. No honeymoon. Not even a chance of consummating the nuptials. Gordon took the shiny ring and slid it along Elaine's finger. The ring fit loosely, but it didn't matter. Gordon kissed his bride and the priest pronounced that it was official.

Mom said it all happened quite fast and she had a hard time telling me everything without crying. She heard the priest consoling Elaine with a promise that the Lord would receive her.

"The next day I went to visit the newlyweds," Mom said. "I wanted to bring a wedding card so I could congratulate them, but your Grandmother was so sick that she didn't respond to my voice or my hugs or anything. It broke my heart. No one should have to die that way. I wish I could have taken her home so she could have the support of her family. Instead she was full of morphine for the pain, with a priest reading her last rites. I came just hours before you and Sheila, but it was so unbearable that I couldn't stay. I had to leave even though I knew there was hope that I might be able to see my other baby for the first time. But I was not at all emotionally prepared for that."

Mom wiped her eyes as she told me how she had struggled with what to do. In the end, she put Sheila's feelings as a priority. There was no way she could justify hurting her baby girl by putting her in a compromising reunion no matter how desperately she wanted to have Sheila there in her arms.

Once inside the tiny farmhouse, the memorial took place. I was surrounded with new faces. A death in the family doesn't create an easy opportunity for getting acquainted with aunties and uncles. It was super scary to mix in with relatives that I didn't know.

My Grandma's home was sparsely furnished but she had lots of family pictures to make up for it. The house was a shack, but to my Grandma, it was her palace and she never turned people away. Because of its condition, her home had little value and would not even qualify as a fixer-upper. The kitchen and bathroom had been added on, but not integrated into the construction, so each room was a separate building. The place was pieced together so the plank flooring didn't match up. I doubt it conformed to any of the building codes.

"Your Grandma lived a simple life. She didn't have a TV or material things except for her Singer sewing machine. For many years, she didn't have electricity or running water. She would heat the well water on a cast-iron stove. In the summer, she dragged her washtub outside and she would pretend it was a pool. We watched the three of you splashing in your birthday suits and running barefoot through the grass."

Mom wiped away her tears as I tried to imagine myself so young and carefree.

"She never got tired of that," Mom remembered and glanced idly around the room.

"Do you think Grandma was happy?"

"Oh, Honey, your Grandmother had hard times, but she was at her happiest when she got to see her children again."

I watched my mother as she studied a picture resting on top of a small china cabinet.

"That's your Grandmother and Buddy. She loved that horse." Mom wiped away the dust that had settled against the glass.

"I want this picture to remember her by." She pressed the frame to her chest.

"I have something for you."

Mom pulled out an old wooden trunk that was buried under the cabinet. She lifted the lid and dug through old photos, letters, and papers.

"I have all the letters that your Grandma wrote the government."

She handed me a little stack of mail that was bundled together with an elastic band.

"Your Grandma wanted you to have these. Keep them. Someday, you might need these letters to help in your search for Josh."

Gordon didn't get much sympathy from the family. Don, Geo, and Eddie had little to say, so it was hard to be there.

Later that day, I took the bus back to Calgary. During the bus ride, I read the letters that Elaine had received from the government. When Mom lost her kids, Elaine wrote many letters to find out what was happening to her grandkids, but there was nothing she could do. As I read the letters of rejection, I felt sad for her and cried easily. But it was time to yo-yo back to my old self and create some good out of a tough situation. I would find Josh. I loved him and needed him and my parents couldn't live day after day without their son.

57: Nur and Sam

When I returned to the fold, my roommates were upset about the ongoing prank calls. What an intimidation and super annoying to say the least! I promised to do what I could to get to the bottom of it.

I believed that life would return to a certain amount of normalcy once I had a job. I would never forget my Grandma but she would want me to get back on the horse, so to speak. I applied at an office and got hired as a filing clerk. Most days, Nur met me for lunch or after work.

Although Nur was a bit obsessive, I didn't find it offensive. It was great the way he introduced me as his girlfriend, so everyone knew we were a couple. But I was uncomfortable with the way women stared at him. He reassured me that I was the only girl for him. Nur was a steamy passionate man and we were wildly attracted to each other. It was hard to keep our amorous feelings in check, but somehow I was incredibly disciplined and showed self-restraint.

"Come with me."

Nur tucked my arm in his. We strolled up one street and down the next.

"Where are we going?" I asked.

"It's a surprise. I can't tell you now." I didn't like surprises, but I thought Nur was taking me to meet his parents.

"We are here," Nur said at last. "This is where I live."

He took out his keys and opened the door. No one was home, not even Felicia, his sister. He showed me every room in the house and saved his room for last. We went in his room. He sat on the bed and clutched me around the waist. His hands pulled me down onto the sheets. His kisses were convincing and exciting, but I didn't let them rule my head.

"Do you love me the way I love you?" he whispered as he held me tightly in his arms. That was unexpected. I had never had a boyfriend talk to me that way. He took my fingers and kissed them tenderly.

"I think so, maybe." I was tempted to say, "Yes." My heart was definitely going there, but my head was yelling, "Stop!"

My conscience was demanding that I make a clean getaway immediately.

"Please take me home."

He laughed as though I was mocking him.

"I have to go."

"Stay with me. Please, Baby, I don't want you to leave," he murmured as he cuddled his face into my neck. His voice was romantic and sexy. "Honey, I know you want to be here with me."

"I can't," I said. He moaned disapprovingly as I pulled away from his reach.

"I need to go."

He dropped his arms and I knew he was upset. When he realized I was not staying, he got up and called a cab. He hardly said a word and I felt like the Wicked Ice Queen. When I got back to the apartment, the phone was ringing before I could get my coat off.

"You had a late night. I have been waiting for you."

I knew that voice. I was sick and tired of hearing it. I pulled the phone cord all the way to the window and peeked out from behind the drape.

"Look as long as you like, but you won't find me."

I hung up and disconnected the line until morning. On my way to work, I knew I was being followed, but I didn't see anything unusual, and I didn't know what to look for. That evening when I finished at the office, Nur was waiting outside the building.

"We need to talk." No greeting, no kiss. Nur took my hand in his, but it was clear that he wasn't at all happy. We walked in silence as we crossed the road and stepped inside the mall entrance.

"Let's sit here," I beckoned to a long bench away from onlookers. After we sat, I noticed that Nur was rigid as a post, keeping an arm's length away from me.

"We have been seeing each other almost every day for a while, so you know my feelings are very strong for you and I told you what I felt in my heart."

I loved what he way saying, but I knew it was too premature to cross "the bedroom line."

"You think our relationship is some kind of game, don't you?" He was so sarcastic that it pained me.

"You tell me you love me and now you are mad because I didn't sleep with you?" I was taken aback and insulted. I didn't like his attack. "Who do you think you are?"

"Do you think that you are the only woman in the world?"

"What do you mean by that?" I asked in defence. I was flummoxed that Nur talked to me that way.

"I am a man, not a child… not something for you to toy with."

Okay, I got it. Poor baby. I had deeply wounded his ego.

"Nur, I really like you a lot, but last night was too fast. I think we need to slow it down. I'm not going to sleep with you. I'm just getting to know you, so please don't rush things along."

"I don't need you. I can have any woman I want and sleep with her. No woman has ever turned me away."

His words stung like a slap in the face. It was all about sex and nothing more. I had unintentionally battered his ego.

"So that's what this is all about! Well, I guess there's a first for everything," I snickered.

"You don't understand. In my country back home, the women would give money to have me."

"They pay you? Really? You are such a liar," I laughed.

"Whether you believe it or not, you've seen the way that women look at me," Nur defended himself lightly, as though it was an inside joke.

"So you are insulted that I refused to be another notch on your headboard."

"If you want to put it that way, yes," he said and lifted his chin to me. His eyes were bitterly cool.

"You're despicable! I can't believe that I almost fell for your sweet-talking crap."

"I don't want you."

"You can't have me," I blasted back.

"Good, then we're finished," he said.

"It's over," I added. "Are we done now? I want to go home."

"That's right. Go home." Nur dared. "We are finished, but I promise you, you will regret it, because you will want me back."

"When pigs fly."

Well said, I thought to myself as I stood up. Courtship was over. Time to put one foot in front of the other and get out of there. If Nur had given me some understanding, love, and time, I could have loved him and he might have persuaded me to do something that I would have regretted. Lucky for me that Nur was too obvious; he was big trouble. I had spent enough time on this person. I needed to save my energy for something better.

"Nur, you are a real piece of work. I will always be proud to say that you never had a chance with me."

Mighty Nur didn't apologize; he just went on his way and I went mine. From that day Nur's dark side had no disguise. He was a backstabbing wolf with a vicious bite. The guy was a liar and I didn't want him anywhere near me.

Around the same time I was racking my brain and doing everything in my power to put a stop to the prank calls. Every time the guy—who called himself Sam—phoned, I let him do all the talking and pretty soon I figured out that he was from the downtown core. The problem was, I didn't know how to confront him. I wasn't sure how much of a threat he would be. But I still had to deal with him somehow, or it would never end. My friends suggested setting him up for a face to face. One Saturday afternoon, they saw someone they thought was Sam in the mall and kept a watch on him. I hurried to the mall and took the escalator to the second level where my friends waited.

"Where is he?" I asked, feeling brave yet nervous.

"Over there! That's him, the man in the grey puffy coat." They pointed and I saw Sam leaning against a railing that overlooked the level below. He was distracted by the bustle of shoppers and hadn't noticed the watching eyes.

"Are you sure that's the man?" I was surprised at how tiny he was. It was hard to believe this was the stalker who kept me awake at night.

"That's the guy. We saw him outside your place and we saw him waiting for you to catch your bus. Do you want us to come with you?"

There was no need for all of us to corner the guy.

"Hello, Sam," I said boldly. I had the right man. I could tell because his eyes revealed an undeniable truth that he recognized my face.

"Can I help you?" He quickly put on an act.

"Don't pretend that you don't know who I am."

"So you finally figured it out. What now? What do you want?" He kept his voice low.

"I want you to leave me alone. Stop following me and calling my apartment," I said crisply. My anger was rising, so I kept it short and to the point. I put it straight on the line. I would press charges if he made contact with me again. Sam seemed to be socially conscious of shoppers passing by, but I didn't care if they heard. I kept a marginal distance between us so he couldn't touch me.

"You had so much to say on the phone. How come you can't speak in person? Are you scared of me?" I asked, using his own words to refresh his memory.

"Okay, I'll leave you alone… it was only a joke. No harm done," Sam said in a low voice. His shoes slyly inched away.

"That's a lie. You wanted to scare me. You are a real creep."

Sam didn't wait for another word. He turned his back and went down the escalator that took him out of view. I never saw or heard from him again.

58: Alastaire

Living in Calgary was not the easy glide I thought it would be. I had everything I needed, yet I felt lost. The nightlife looked more and more attractive, because it was easy to make friends there and the disco scene was becoming my style.

One night while I was at one of the clubs, I met a sporty-looking gentleman named Alastaire. I have always been a lover of style, so I noticed right away that his flare was unique. He was decked out in a yellow dinner jacket with cream linen pants and two-tone Oxfords. Such panache! He would have looked awesome playing cricket.

He wasn't a flirtatious, silly adolescent, nor did he make advances. He was gracious and I found him to be very cordial, which put him in an attractive league. But as luck would have it, he was way too mature for me.

After a few dances under the spectacular lighting, he told me that it was his last night in town. He was leaving in the morning to travel for a month in Europe and he tried to convince me to go with him.

"If you join me, we will go straight to the airport and I'll buy everything you need when we arrive. You don't even have to pack." It seemed pretty evident that he was living a yacht-style life of beaches and martinis.

"Are you crazy?" I asked, realizing that he didn't even know my name yet.

"I'm not asking you to do anything bad," he said.

At the time, I was too young for him.

"I can't do that," I said.

"Sure, you can." His smile looked harmless.

Yikes, I didn't want to be arm candy for some rich old tycoon.

"Think how wonderful it would be to see the Greek islands, tour France, and visit Rome. Can you imagine the beautiful lights of Morocco at night?" he asked.

My thoughts were swirling with visions of a chateau lined with rows of wrought-iron balconies. I was momentarily dazzled at the idea of living in ritzy hotel rooms with maids serving caviar. I could be swept off my feet while sipping champagne out of a fluted glass. Had I just hit the jackpot? I confess that it was very tempting. Europe was definitely something I really hoped to cross off my to-do list, but not with a stranger.

"It's one chance in a million. I'll show you places you might never see in your lifetime."

"Thanks, anyway," I said as the dream in my head popped like a balloon. He walked me back to my seat and before the night was over, he was at it again. I had declined his ever-so-dreamy offer and, wouldn't you know it, he had found someone else. I saw him dancing with a young woman about my own age.

For me, the situation was obviously dangerous. I realized there are some people who lead others into dangerous situations for their own gain. In my community, there were a lot of immigrants waiting to get their citizenship.

The fear of deportation was enough to push strangers into quick-fix weddings. I was one of many Canadian girls who were offered marriage in exchange for a big payout. I would only have to stick it out until my spouse was legally accepted as a Canadian. Then, after six months, I could apply for a divorce.

After much prompting from co-workers, I was introduced to a man who was anxiously looking for a woman to marry so he could become a Canadian Citizen. I was living paycheque to paycheque but I was getting by. I declined. I did not want to be a glutton for punishment. It was obvious that too many things could go wrong and I could be putting my whole future on the line.

A six-month marriage just might turn into a life sentence. Between jobs, it was hard to make ends meet, but I had my freedom. No one could put a price on that. I didn't need to be scared. I just had to be aware and cautious. When I was feeling down or lonely, I had a tendency to be impulsive. I thrived in the city, but at times I missed having a family.

59: Mr. Atkins

My lawyer was doing everything to help me find my brother so I believed that it wouldn't be too long before Josh and I could reunite. Mr. Atkins wrote the government and requested the social services ministry grant an order to allow access to the adoption file so he could determine Josh's new surname and address. A few weeks later, my lawyer received a call from social services in regard to setting up a screening before a sibling reunion could be allowed. Everything was going forward and it seemed almost too good to be true.

A reply confirmed that the adoptive mother had died and the father had remarried. Josh wasn't living at home, but he was still under his father's influence. Josh's adoptive father was considering a possible reunion, but he hadn't reached a decision yet. The ministry was optimistic that a positive resolution would come in the following month.

Another message was sent to my lawyer and he mailed a copy to me. One of my roommates had put the letter on the kitchen counter where I could see it as I entered the apartment. I couldn't wait to open it. Josh and his adoptive father had had a difficult time in determining their feeling regarding any contact with his biological family. They had finally agreed that such contact would be undesirable. Their closing remark for my lawyer was to please advise his client in this regard.

It never occurred to me that Josh would not want a reunion. How could I have been so sure—so positive that Josh would want to see me?

I felt heartsick inside as I read it again. Whose feelings are they referring to? Did Josh object to a meeting or was it the workings of his father? I stood there for a long time, wondering how it had gone so sour so fast.

At first I blamed myself. Then I blamed the system that had failed me in the past. And finally, I was sure it had to be the adoptive father's negative influence. Simply put, I didn't want to believe that Josh had no interest or desire to see me. But then I wondered if he remembered me at all. Or maybe Josh felt enslaved and didn't want to dishonour his guardian father.

The letter was a done deal but I couldn't give up. I had to prove that Josh's father had not informed Josh about me.

My lawyer couldn't do anything more. He had tried and failed, so how would I measure up to that? I didn't have the tools or the information to access a search. On top of that, Mom couldn't remember the name of the orphanage or where it was located. Luckily, she could recall that she'd had to cross the Bow River Bridge because we were staying somewhere on the north side of Calgary, and the orphanage was in the south.

In the phonebook, I found an orphanage that was in southern Calgary, but I wasn't sure if it was the right place. I told the woman on the phone that I would like to come and take a look around. It was my way to resurface the past. I wanted to awaken the sleeping ghosts of my memory. I hoped that my senses of sight and smell might help me put a face on the past and… who knows? It's possible that someone there might have known me from back then.

On the day of my visit the weather didn't comply. It was overcast and I could feel the cold through all my layers of clothing. By the time I arrived, my fingertips were stinging so badly that I wished they were numb. I had waited for two buses and walked quite a distance, so it took two hours to get to the orphanage. I don't remember much about the building, except that it was old on the outside and it had the classical heritage stairs made of concrete and stone. The steps were wide and large but not as intimidatingly grand as they had seemed when I was small. I was not even sure if they were the same steps as I quickly sought refuge from the cold inside.

But the woman I spoke with on the phone was no longer allowing me to enter.

My trip was a complete waste of time. I couldn't possibly have crossed any boundaries, because I never made it past the front desk. The staff had made a decision that my visit was a breach of security for the children who were living there. They didn't care what bumpy road I wished to unravel and they were not sympathetic about sending me back out into the cold. I had been "dog-piled" by the rules in the system.

Without entry, I couldn't see if that was the shelter where I had boarded. The dining area and all the rooms were out of view. Maybe it was just as well. No matter how many years had passed, it was still a dismal institution that emitted a feeling of incarceration. Once I got outside, I looked back at the building. I saw it was just as alien then as it had been fifteen years earlier. As I walked away, I felt sad that I hadn't found what I was looking for. That day depressed me a lot.

60: Joel

To top my disappointment from visiting the orphanage, I got "foxed" by my boyfriend. I was really fired up about Joel. At first, he was like a hero on a life raft. A man ready to save a damsel from a life of loneliness. Joel was what I refer to as a hit-and-run. He was my first intimate love since my precarious and promiscuous age of fourteen. I thought we were made for each other, but it all turned to hell when we had a pregnancy scare. During our relationship, I stayed with Joel one night. I felt badly about it and when I didn't get my period, I was worried. Our workday schedules were fairly equal, so we had decided to meet at the pinball arcade near Calgary's city centre.

At noon I rushed off to see Joel. As I turned the last corner I could see him entering the doors of the arcade with two other men. I had squeezed into a fitted pencil skirt and Joel was sporting a suit as usual, so we were both over-dressed. As I opened the door, it felt like I had crossed into the twilight zone. The arcade was like a circus without the tents. I could hear the coins dropping into the slots as tabletops magically lit up.

Ding, ding, ding… the steel balls shot over the sensory buttons causing the flashy spinners to blink on and off. It's okay if you like that theatrical kind of entertainment, but if not, then you need your shades and some cotton batten for your ears, because it's a madhouse.

Joel grabbed a table for two and we shared a soda, but it was not the place to talk.

His colleagues drifted through the throng of players to see what machines were available and Joel was distracted, because a winner wanted to challenge him. I suggested we go outside and talk. We finished our drinks and snuck out the side door where the noise changed to car engines and stereos.

"What's wrong?" He buttoned his suit to keep warm.

"I know we have only had one night together, but I think I'm pregnant."

Joel stayed silent as his eyes pinned me without expression. I chewed on my bottom lip like a nervous little kid getting sent for a spank.

"Get an abortion," he said, with obvious annoyance.

"Abortion?" Ouch. I didn't expect Joel to blow it off so easily.

"Don't be stupid. Go get it done." For the first time Joel was demeaning. Maybe I'd picked the wrong day to tell him, but I felt that he would want to know.

"Joel, I can't do that." I answered. I expected so much better from him. At the very least I hoped to hear, "It's okay. We will figure this out" or, "Don't worry, I am here for you." Obviously he wasn't going to play Dad and that was okay.

"There are other options besides termination, Joel."

"No, there are not. You are going to get an abortion. I'm not going to let you destroy my life. End of story."

That cut me deeply. I had to take a gulp of air to breathe.

"Joel, I can't. That's so final and so…"

"You're not listening." He cut me off. "I'm not going to tell you again. If you don't do what I tell you, then I will settle this score myself."

"What score? Are you threatening me?"

"I will kill you or have you killed." Joel had gone from sweet and loving to downright corrosive.

"You should hear yourself. You're not the Mafia!" It was not one of his playful teases that would end with a kiss to assure me that he was just kidding. He was dead serious.

What frame of mind makes a man verbalize such crap? That big black heart in Joel's chest was causing lots of childish paranoia. That is… if he even had a heart! Knowing that I might be on Joel's hit list scared the daylights out of me. I was not going to be slaughtered like a lamb, so I was out of his sight forever. Fortunately I was not pregnant and Joel never got a chance to track me down. To this day, it is still a dark memory to think about, let alone write about.

61: Elias

Well, I had strayed off the path, and I felt a lot of remorse, but in time I would mend and get on with something else. I signed up for evening classes in dance and modelling to lighten things up and do something fun. Because of money issues, I wasn't there for long, but I learned how to wiggle walk with one foot in front of the other, with my toes slightly turned out and my figure ready on demand to pose for a photo shoot.

I stayed away from Joel; my friends didn't like him so I felt safe when I was with them. At night, I took a cab instead of the bus, because I didn't want to walk alone. It wasn't coincidental that my friends and I had the same cab driver, Elias. He was on our regular route so we relied on him especially on the weekend. Because of my previous experience, I didn't want to blow this out of proportion, but there was no dirt on this guy.

Everyone liked Elias because he was a funny decent kind of person. I had come to learn that his kooky sense of humour and charming nature gave him a leg up with girls like me. He was every girl's dream and he was the kind of man that Moms would beg their daughters to marry. His mischievous voice and curly espresso hair reminded me of the Arabian actor Omar Sharif. When I let that slip out, Elias blushed and said he had heard it before. We began dating and I had no complaints as he seemed like such a genuine person.

One late afternoon when we were walking back from an outdoor pool, Elias teased me about who would do the vacuuming after we married. I suggested that we take turns and he agreed and smiled, as though he was seeing our future. Without actually hearing the words, I knew Elias loved me. When my roommates finished college, our apartment lease ended so I had to find another place real fast. Rental costs were steep and my wages as a filing clerk were low, so Elias let me crash on his couch until there was an opening for a rental.

A big parking-lot slab of grey concrete ruined the view of Elias's ninth-floor apartment window, but I loved his meticulous one-bedroom flat. The only downside was it didn't have a spacious walk-in closet for my obsessive mass of diva shoes. Elias didn't care that his high-rise was smaller than a nutshell, because that's what made it cozy.

Another suite was going to be available in his building in two months, so I suggested that we keep it nonsexual and Elias respected my wishes. He behaved, but every now and then, I would see a twinkle in his eyes like he wanted to play cop so he could pat me down. My choice to avoid entangled feet under the sheets was driving him nuts.

I often wonder how love can make you so dumb and smart at the same time. I guess it's because I was trying to decide what I wanted. Was it love or lust or both or… neither? The most confusing part was trying to figure out what was really going on in the emotional rollercoaster driven by my head and my heart. My boyfriend had no privacy. He couldn't burp or have an off night of bachelor's gas from a couple of beers, because I was there.

Elias might not have understood why I was tighter than a clamshell, but when it came to romance, he really knocked it out of the park. He was an open book like Romeo and he was never on the sly. He would go the extra mile with evenings of to-die-for Greek dishes at Roma's Disco or he would plan something sweet and simple, like a moonlight stroll under the stars.

I couldn't seem to open up and tell him about my background. I didn't share the indescribable story of finding my mother, even though it had changed my life forever. To avoid any bedroom activity, I told Elias that I was waiting for the right man. I didn't tell him about the mistakes I had made in the past, because he believed I was the perfect girl for him. I didn't know how to measure up to what I thought was his view of me. Without talking to Elias, I did the unthinkable and asked Mom if I could have Chloe visit for a while.

62: Elias and Chloe

Stupid! Stupid! Stupid! I'm not a moron, so why would I do that? I wasn't asexual and I certainly wasn't afraid of Elias, yet I had cold feet. So much so that I was willing to harbour a reckless teen. It all boiled down to my fear of getting hurt again. With Chloe in the mix, I thought it would save me from making another mistake. Seemed logical. Two's company and three's a mood killer. I don't know if Elias knew that I was avoiding paradise with him, but he didn't shake his fist and shout war.

Chloe was a troublemaker. I thought for sure that Elias would be at the end of his rope when his miniature bottles of airplane liquor vanished. He didn't throw a fit when Chloe would forget to pick up her dirty undies after her shower. Most of the time, she was a pain in the neck.

Chloe was under my watch for almost a month when she dropped a bomb on me about Elias. She told me that he had sexually harassed her. Did Elias have his own agenda for this third party?

She was a child, not just a pretty face to be pawned off like a doll. It was hard to be calm. Chloe couldn't wait to tell me that Elias was a cheater, because he pulled her into his room and pinned her down on the bed.

When Elias entered the apartment, I attacked him with Chloe's accusations. I wanted answers ASAP! Elias was not baffled. His expression showed that he was expecting a blowout and that really took me for a loop. He wrung his hands through his hair as I angrily waited for an explanation.

"When I came home from work, your sister was here alone and she said that you were still at work. She started asking me questions about our relationship. I told her it was none of her business, but that only made it worse."

"What did you do, Elias?"

"Nothing! She followed me around and asked me if I like her and if I think she's pretty. Then she started probing for some insight about our sex life."

"And…?" I could feel my eyes growing wide with shock. I really didn't know Chloe at all.

"She was egging me on and I was fed up with her teasing and her stupid questions. I told her to stop it and she just laughed in my face." Elias stared at me with that look of innocence, but I didn't believe him. My perfect man had done something insidious to my sister and it was my fault. I felt like I had just been pushed off a cliff.

"Why does Chloe tell me that you pulled her into your room, because you wanted to sleep with her?"

"When you are at work, Chloe is always coming on to me. I am constantly pushing her away, but she won't leave me alone."

"I don't believe that," I shouted.

"Whenever you leave the room or go to the store, she is on the prowl. She grabs me around the neck and hangs on me, wanting attention. I push her away. I ignore her, but she does it more. I don't know what to do."

"Why didn't you tell me?"

"How could I tell you? She's your sister."

"You should have told me. Now, I don't know who to believe."

"Can't you see that she wants to break us up? Your sister is jealous of you. I know this is a bitter pill to swallow, but Chloe doesn't want us to be together, because she wants you for herself and she will do just about anything to get what she wants."

"Stop it, Elias!" I couldn't hold my hysteria any longer. "Did you sleep with her?"

"No. Chloe was hanging on my neck and I pulled her off. Then I threw her on the bed. She didn't try to fight me off. She was looking into my eyes, waiting for me to make a move, so I asked myself, why not?"

"You disgust me." I wanted to kick him.

"Please, let me finish. I looked into her face and I thought about you and that's when I told Chloe she wasn't worth it. It made her mad and she got pissed off and swore at me. I refused to play her game so she threatened to tell you." Elias's eyes were blurry. The grief in his voice caused him to choke up. Who was holding the smoking gun? Was it Elias or Chloe?

"I wanted to tell you, but I was afraid that you wouldn't believe me."

Chloe was not as good at keeping her story straight. That's how I knew Elias was telling the truth but it put our relationship on the line. He had fought Chloe off, but I was afraid my sister would try again. It was a lot to digest.

"Chloe, Elias is my boyfriend, not yours." I warned Chloe to keep her hands to herself. There was an icy stare between us. The look on her face confirmed that I didn't own him… or her. She finally admitted that she was sick-to-death of our "cutesy wooing." It was not in those words exactly, but I knew she felt a lot of resentment. I did not doubt that she pushed Elias over the brink, but Chloe was my kid sister and Elias was an adult.

Right there and then, Elias and I were over. I was ready to take a hike, so I grabbed Chloe and left. We were waiting for the elevator when I realized my sister had no shoes on. We were two for the road with nowhere to go. How dumb, I thought. In less than an hour, it would be dark. But then I remembered my neighbour who lived on the same floor just six doors down, so I thought I should ask if I could use his phone.

I knocked three times and I heard Parker coming to his door. I waved at the peephole just in case he was looking out.

"Can I talk to you?" I asked as Parker opened the door. I looked behind me, and Elias was out in the hall begging to talk, but I just wanted to get away from him.

"Sure." Parker caught on quickly. He stepped aside and waved his arm in the direction of the living room. I told Parker that Elias and I had had a falling out. Parker was shocked when I told him what had happened. I was still in tears when I asked to use the phone. Minutes later, I was crying to Mom as I rehashed the situation.

Mom told me that she was moving to Calgary without Bart, her husband. She couldn't live with an alcoholic anymore, but she still had a few things to wrap up before she could leave. Mom warned that Chloe's craving for attention was a huge stumbling block as Chloe would say anything to make ears perk up.

I promised to keep a more vigilant eye on Chloe. I asked Parker if we could stay with him for two days. Parker didn't treat us as though we were a burden. He seemed to welcome the company. The day before Mom arrived, I was going for the elevator and so was Elias. Bad timing! We rode down without a word. I was such a drama queen.

By the time Mom and Iona arrived, I was very agitated with Chloe. It was a huge relief when she took my half-sister off my hands and set up house for her children in the suburbs of Calgary. I moved into a studio suite in another apartment building. It was a one-room shoebox with a trailer size kitchen and a mini fridge.

In the meantime, when the time was right, I was fairly confident that Sheila would meet our Mom. That day came and I was overjoyed just to be a part of it. It was a moment that is hard to put into words. No matter what misfortunes had monopolized our family history, I felt confident that the search for Josh would soon have closure.

Mom never turned down an opportunity to do things with me, so I hung around a lot. Overall, we both liked a lot of the same things.

One night I was out with Mom and we saw Elias at a dance hall. It was packed with lots of people, but he saw me and came to say hello.

"I've missed you so much. I never knew that I could love you so much." He looked into my face striving to see beyond my mask. His pleading eyes searched for some kind of sign. "I'm asking you to give me a chance to show you," he blurted out, with watery eyes. I had never seen a man cry before, much less display such feelings for me. I was overcome. How could I be so cold to him?

The hours passed as Elias gave me his whole heart. He knew that I had strong feelings for him, but I wasn't ready for marriage. In one way, I felt sure that he was my prince, but in another, I needed time. We began dating again right away and seemed to be off to a great start.

63: Howie and Gabriella, Louis and Lindsey

By December I was dying to go home to Howie and Gabriella.

Once I was home, I kicked off my city clothes and nestled into my comfy old jeans. I still loved the serenity of the ranch, but cows and horses were boys' play. I had become a completely different species of person, but Howie got me back in the saddle and down to earth again.

During my visit, Howie and Gabriella heard the details of my endeavors in work, talents, and love. Somehow, they could tell when I was lost and trying to fake that everything was going great. They worried just as parents do.

They proposed that I move to Vancouver and start a new life, suggesting I could stay with Louis until I got set up. I agreed and promised to look into it, but I was grateful when they dropped the subject. I had found some of Calgary's dark sides, but the city had my vote, so I had no intention of moving anywhere. And besides, I was falling in love again. Christmas was over and it was time for me to head back to the city. I dropped my luggage outside the bus, and gave Howie and Gabriella a big squeeze.

"Have you thought any more about moving to Vancouver?" Howie asked again.

"Yeah, I'll look into it," I said as I came to grips with that annoying idea of his.

Had he not heard me when I talked incessantly of my love for Elias and for Calgary? I tried to appease Howie, but he was like a dog on a scent and could sniff out a bluffer.

"You are just telling us what we want to hear; you have no intentions of following through."

How dare Howie assume to know me so well?

Two weeks into January, I took Howie's dare and moved to Canada's West Coast. It wasn't a smooth transition as I left behind my mom; she was very sad at my decision. I would also have to adapt to a long-distance relationship with Elias.

Plus, it was a big adjustment living with a parent again, especially with someone I hardly knew. Dad had some interesting personality quirks, but he was easy to get along with. He wasn't the type to pour out his soul and so I needed to do my part by listening. But unfortunately, Lindsey—Dad's girlfriend—wasn't comfortable with me taking up my father's time. Right from the get go, her good intentions sifted away as jealousy with a capital J somersaulted into motion. She would sulk around the house, causing fights and crying about nothing.

She made stupid innuendos that I found repulsive. Lindsey was not my first rodeo. I'd already gone through this with Chloe, so I was not going to pussyfoot around a woman on the warpath. Dad told me that she was often jealous when he was around other women. I wasn't any woman; I was his child. Best way to resolve the problem was to leave. I needed to hit the trail and live somewhere else.

64: Maureen

In order to move, I needed work but it wasn't like Calgary where opportunity knocked at every corner. Job hunting was tedious and I wasn't having any luck until I got a call from a relative, my mother's brother's wife, Breanne. She put in a good word at a Cuban store and I got hired. It went so well that I was able to move into a room at the downtown YWCA. In April, my boss sent me to work in the hotel gift shops where I could start doing what I had always wanted to do: be my own boss.

In the spring, I upgraded to an apartment with Maureen. I knew her from the YWCA. From the moment we moved into our tiny apartment, it felt like a palace in comparison to the Y. It was only two blocks from some waterfront properties, so we had really lucked out on a great deal.

I thought all cities were the same, but boy was I wrong. Vancouver is a rain-forest so it's wet for a good part of the year but I liked the well-kept endless clean-and-green environment. It was bizarre how the weather could go from downpour to sunny and then sleeting hail to dumps of snow all in a day's work. This all-inclusive city had everything. Every corner had a different element of surprise with sailboat harbours, majestic mountains, and long-stretching beaches. The ethnic diversity was all part of what made my Vancouver home outshine any other place that I had lived. It's almost the norm here to lose your head in the clouds. No wonder Howie was so persistent. Maybe... just maybe, he was right.

My roomie Maureen was born to a privileged black family from Minnesota. Her parents sent her to Canada so she could get a fresh start in the modelling field. Because her family was far away, she didn't have a lot of social interaction; but she was working hard to make it big. I could see that. Fortunately, with her elite upbringing and her gorgeous Nefertiti cheekbones, Maureen could be the next model swishing in silk under the catwalk lights.

At some point in Maureen's teen life, she had been institutionalized. She told me that she had been poisoned with LSD hidden inside a chocolate bar. The drug overdose was so debauching that her parents had had her hospitalized for two years. It seemed to be out of her system now; except for her occasional lows, there were no issues whatsoever.

At first, we got along great. But then, out of nowhere, her hallucinations fired up and she seemed to be crisscrossing through a time zone with the devil.

On one workday, I was home earlier than expected, so I thought we could grab our towels and head to the beach. Maureen was sitting at the table staring out the window. Two cups and a teapot sat on the table. Maureen was still sipping from her cup but the other one was bone dry. I could see that someone had been there before I came in. I suggested my idea as I grabbed my swimsuit bag, but Maureen barely responded.

"No, I'm tired," she said, without turning from the window.

"Who was here?" I asked curiously as I passed the table to get the cokes out of the fridge. Aside from parties, Maureen wasn't a social type, so I assumed that she had made a new friend.

"Satan."

"Who?" Normally, Maureen wasn't too slick at being condescending, so I wasn't expecting a joke.

"Satan." Odd remark for such a refined person, but I chuckled.

"Oh, the Devil. Of course, did he stay for tea?"

Maureen didn't laugh.

"Yes. Satan was here."

At that moment, I wasn't sure if it was wishful thinking or if she had gone mad.

"I know it sounds weird, but he's my only friend and he loves me."

"The Devil only loves himself." Apparently Maureen's mind hadn't quite descrambled after all. I'd say she still needed some work.

"It's not the first time he has been here for tea." There wasn't a hint of playacting in her voice. Her stare was so hollow and unhappy that I could see she believed her words.

"Maureen, do you hear what you're saying?"

"Yes, I know, but he is good not bad, like you believe." My roommate was off her meds and her eyes were in a trance like she was lost in space.

"Maureen, you know that's crazy talk. The Devil is… well, the Devil! He's bad."

"Please don't say that. He loves me and I want to be with him."

Well, this conversation was certainly not for the weak of heart. No exaggeration, I was weirded out by her. But it was pointless to poke any holes in her theory of the truth. Different strokes for different folks! She can believe whatever she wants. Later that evening, her parents called and Maureen didn't tell them about her delusions. After Maureen got off the phone, she said she feared her family might send her back to the hospital if they got wind of what was happening.

The bedroom was her domain, but I didn't mind sleeping in the living room. Clearly, I didn't have the luxury of privacy, but that wasn't a problem until she made it one. In the middle of the night, I woke up because Maureen flicked on the hall light and started calling me.

"Wake up, Eugenea! Wake up now!" Maureen wasn't asking; she was demanding. I was trying to come out of my dreamy state of mind when she booted my rollout mattress. Through the slits of my eyes, I saw the light glowing around her silhouette. It was hard to make out her face, so I couldn't tell if she was crying, scared, or seeing things again.

"What is it? What's wrong, Maureen?" Groggily I reached out to calm her, but she jumped back.

"Don't touch me," she screeched like a seagull. "If you touch me, I'm going to kill you."

"You know what, Maureen? You're crazy!" I had had enough of her nuttiness so I rolled over, but she didn't leave.

"I'm not finished talking, so you'd better listen to me!"

Sure, I would be happy to hear more crazy talk. But at 3:00 a.m., patience was not a quality I had, so I played possum.

"Your hand touched me. No one is allowed to touch me. If you touch me again, I will kill you. You understand?" Maureen wasn't making any sense. I knew we had made contact as we crossed paths through the door at times, but this was ridiculous.

"Get away from me, Maureen. Get away from my bed," I hollered into the blinding light.

She stared down at me for what seemed like a fortnight. *Tic, tic, tic…* Finally, she stomped to her room like a child.

"And, don't you ever threaten me again!" I shrieked as the bedroom door slammed. "Damn it Maureen. Turn the stupid light off," I yelled down the empty hall.

We had never fought before and, after that night, I didn't want another catfight. Maureen's invisible friend had damaged our friendship. When she was home, I didn't hang around trying to strike a conversation with her and the Devil.

65: Tory

No more freak shows. On my days off I was at the beach. No drama—just relaxation with a good book and the feel of the sun on my skin. I had barely opened the pages one day when I had an encounter with a Frisbee. It dropped down out of nowhere and tapped the side of my leg. I looked around and saw a guy running over to retrieve it.

"Sorry. Are you okay?" He looked embarrassed, so I knew it was an accident but if that was a hidden agenda to spark a conversation, I was game. I put my book aside and looked for any signs of harm.

"Whew, no visible damage. Lucky me! I must have been blessed with good dodging skills," I humoured.

He laughed at my little witticism and identified himself as Tory. I, in turn, gave him my name. Once the pleasantries were done, he asked if he could sit and join me. I liked that idea, so we had a short get-to-know-each-other chat. I noticed Tory's opponent was lingering on the sand waiting patiently for a rematch.

As I watched Tory the Sun-Seeker run off to rejoin the game, I never dreamed that he would become the father to my baby. I found his "high on life" energy to be very attractive. I loved his messy dark curls and the way his jeans fit so perfectly.

While we were dating, Tory went to Montreal to find us work. During that time, he made some connections with some modelling agencies. Every night, we talked for hours and Tory promised that he was coming to get me, but I didn't believe him. He was not the everyday run-of-the-mill type; he was flighty and always on the go. He had big dreams for our careers.

Two weeks later, he was back and wanted to sweep me away to live in Montreal, where models and actors were lining up for auditions. At first, I didn't want to go because I loved Vancouver, but Tory was talking circles around me with a promise that Montreal would be our best chance at a future together and I was buying into it.

My man was hyped! He was pushing me to go beyond my limits and seize the moment. Was I prone to be on the move after all the moving I had done in the past? Was this a pattern that I couldn't see? But with all that young blood looking for a challenge, how could I turn down such a golden opportunity? Tory's Frisbee pal Andy and his girlfriend Liz were planning to go as well. So, maybe it was good to toss away my comforts and release my inner restlessness for the unknown. Despite the fact that Liz and I had jobs and apartments, we did not tell our families about our plans to go to Montreal.

The four of us sat down, mapped out a route, and packed only the bare essentials. We pooled our money together. Then we made a decision to hitch rides and stay in hostels so we could use our cash for food. I was shocked at myself for having the courage to go through with it. But if worse came to the worst, and modelling was not my passion, we could always move back.

66: Tory, Liz and Andy, and Ollie

On our first day out, we rode the bus to Hastings Street and got off at the end of the line. Travelling by thumb was easy for the boys, but Liz and I weren't the thrill-seeker types so we couldn't have done it on our own. Cramming into a stranger's car was definitely not a luxury and using our thumbs gave a new meaning to the term "public transport." At the end of the day's travel, we had got as far as Kamloops and stayed with Tory's sister, Carla. She didn't look anything like Tory. She was a short full-figured girl with bleached hair and heavy make-up. We stayed another night so Tory could have more time with Carla.

In the morning, we got our first ride of the day within twenty minutes. As the miles faded behind us, it was mysteriously lonely to be passing city after city.

Our next drop was in a logging town called Revelstoke. The presence of logging trucks and semi-trailers was killing our chances of a ride. There was nowhere to duck from the shivering rain. Four pathetic-looking people with mops of wet hair and mud-peppered clothes would be a significant reason to keep driving. I was betting that truck drivers thought we were bad news.

Tory's ideals seemed so wonderful and I was trying to please him, but I felt I was drifting as though I was still in foster care. It seemed like one place was as good as the next. I had moved all my life, but I was still searching for something to grab onto. I wanted to believe that going back east was the answer. My goal was to build a future with Tory.

We waited and waited, and finally a car slid to a stop. The woman in the four-door rolled down her window.

"Are you all together?"

"Yes," I said, as a huge glob of water dripped off the end of my nose. The woman behind the wheel stared in disbelief. Her expression was more priceless than a credit card commercial.

"Quick! Go around and get in!" the woman hollered over the pounding rain as she cranked the window back up. Going, going, gone! We were out of Revelstoke.

"How far are you going?" she inquired as she drove.

"Montreal," Andy answered from the back.

She glanced around at us like we were nuts.

"Why on earth would you go there?" she asked.

"Better jobs in the east." Liz spoke up and added that we were from Vancouver.

"I can take you to Cranston; that's my stop," she smiled and remarked on how tough it was for kids to find steady work on the coast.

"My name is Olivia, but you can call me Ollie," she said, so we introduced ourselves. The wiper blades swished back and forth in a kind of rhythm with the rain. It was dark and mesmerizing as the gullies of water bucketed over the windshield. The road lines smeared as the rain doused the pavement. Ollie liked our company and we liked her. The ride was so comfortable that I drifted off to sleep and woke up later to the sun's heat on my face.

"Liz, where are we?" I looked out through the car windows trying to make sense of my surroundings.

"Cranston," she said. As we drove through the streets, the midday sun penetrated the arch of trees that bowed overhead. The leaves shadowed the glass like lacey curtains twisting in the wind. No matter which way I looked, properties were lined with hedges, accent walkways, and stone paths.

"The neighbours are very friendly here. Everybody knows everybody, so people are good. Otherwise, you become the talk of the town," Ollie laughed as we passed a community church. "I think you kids should come to my house and meet my family." She said it so gingerly that it would have been presumptuous to say no. Tory looked back at me and I shrugged my shoulders. As I turned and looked through the glass, I felt comfort in Ollie's invitation, and I wished we could take a break and hang out for a couple days.

"My husband and I have lived here since we were kids, and our children are all grown up now, but they live only a few blocks away so we get to see them all the time." Ollie smiled at me through the rearview mirror.

"That's the school my husband and I attended, and my kids too. The green house on the corner is my home."

I watched as Ollie angled her car into a double-wide driveway. From there, we followed her into the house, where her husband and kids waited as though they were expecting guests. We gathered under the patio umbrella to feast on barbequed chicken and summer salads.

Everyone was chatting like the way families do at a Sunday dinner. I looked at Ollie's children and saw how they had been brought up. They were so down to earth and open to loving others. There was no conflict of interest between any of us. Such humanity was so wonderful to find. I would always remember how their stories inspired us and how they engaged with our stories with pure enthusiasm.

67: Tory, Liz and Andy, and Dinah

By early evening, we were back on the road with our thumbs waving high. Within a few hours we had made it to Calgary and I was excited to see my old stomping grounds. My boyfriend Tory knew his old chums would make room for us. He used a pay phone while the rest of us tried to figure out an alternative plan.

"I have good news," Tory announced as his hands slapped loudly to get our attention. "I just talked to my surrogate mom, Dinah, and she is making space for us."

"You have a surrogate mom?" I could feel my face scrunching up. "Odd, you never mentioned her before."

"Well, she's like a second Mom to me."

That sounded weird; something wasn't right. It became obvious that Tory had done this many times before. Nevertheless, we raced to get there before Dinah had time to change her mind.

Good thing it was a hot night, because Dinah didn't have bedding to spare. We had to roll up our coats for pillows and share a sleeping bag on the living room floor. Dinah's little boy was sleeping in the next room, so we laid out the bedding with as little noise as possible.

Dinah's goodnight voice carried as she walked to the master bedroom. As she went into her room and closed the door, I heard Tory's feet shuffle along in the dark.

"Dinah?" Tory whispered. "Can I talk to you?" He asked so softly that I could barely hear him. They exchanged muffled words, but I couldn't make out what they were saying. I realized that I had no business being there, but it was too late for me to undo my choice. Minutes later, he was creeping around the living room really slowly, trying not to wake me.

"What's going on?" I asked, feeling cynical.

"Oh, you're still awake," he said and crawled under the cover. "I just wanted to thank Dinah for letting us stay here."

"That's all?" I gave him a look that said there is more to this than he's telling.

"Well, I asked her if we could stay another night."

"Why?"

"Why not? Are we in a hurry?" Tory's expression was as unreadable as his words.

"You are so nonchalant. What am I missing here?" I was clearly upset about his sudden game change. "You're holding out on me." I looked at him with suspicion.

"I guess it's kind of senseless to hide anything from you. We need money so I asked Dinah to spare a few bucks and she gave it to me."

"Why would you do that?" I asked as my voice broke from a whisper to anger.

"We will need it and she is a long-time friend. I knew I could count on her." Tory's reply was justifiable, but I wasn't happy.

"Well, that's just great. Did you forget that she's a single parent, Tory?" I said.

169

"So what? She has money and I don't want to keep talking about this right now." Tory ignored me and turned over.

Long after Tory had passed out, I was still wrestling with his comments. I was upset that he hadn't talked to me first. The next day, Tory was in Dinah's room for almost an hour with the door shut. I didn't believe the "surrogate mother" crap for a second. Dinah was very overweight and not at all good looking. Her face was round and it melted into her neck and her neck melted into a double-E bosom.

The chemistry between Tory and Dinah went beyond normal; it was weird. I didn't see any canoodling or anything, but they were too friendly. Finally, I had had enough and demanded some answers. Tory admitted that he had had a prior relationship with Dinah that fell into a category of convenience and support; but it was not for love. Unreal! Well, the past was gone and we were gone from Dinah.

Next stop would be Regina. It should have taken two days tops, but the lack of rides was so ridiculous that we could have crawled there faster. To add to the frustration, we got the boot in the middle of a drought. The blistering heat wave made the road look like a mirage. Or maybe the heat was frying our brains. We were trying to be world travellers yet not one of us had brought any water. Smart! Somewhere around the halfway point between Calgary and Regina is where we got trapped.

"We have to split up in twos, because it's the only way we are going to get anywhere," said Tory. His plan made no sense to me at all.

"No. We have come so far! It's a bad idea to split up now," I said. "No matter how bleak it looks, giving up is out of the equation," I defended.

"It's just temporary. We can meet in Regina and in two days we will be back together." Andy supported Tory, but I shook my head with disapproval.

"I don't want to take that chance, especially when we don't know anything about Regina."

"We have no other choice," Liz cut in impatiently.

I didn't want to admit it but we were choking in the dust. Andy and Liz kissed us goodbye, then turned on their heels and went on their way. I knew we were hooped when a car stopped in front of them. Andy opened the car door and gave us two fingers up. I yelled goodbye and good luck, but they were out of earshot. For two hours, we sat on our trunks like a couple of hobos.

68: Tory, a Roach, a Kind Woman, Monty, and John

My goal to broaden my horizons seemed unreachable. We had to get out of there before we turned into rambling nomads. All I could see was a wide stretch of freeway dotted by road signs and exit ramps. There was nothing but pavement as far as our eyes could see.

Surprisingly, we made record time considering our waits were long in between rides. It was exhausting. From one town to the next, the weather would change. In Regina, it was pouring as we dragged our luggage along the wet streets until we found a dirt-cheap hotel to rent. Our money was spreading thin so it was a luxury we couldn't afford.

Some luxury! What a dive! Every inch of the place smelled like old carpets and cigarettes. The manager behind the counter took our money and passed Tory a key. I asked the manager if he had seen our travelling companions and he said "no."

"Nobody here by that name. You're in room 510. There's only one bathroom on every floor and it's at the end of every hallway. Rules are you must be out by 11:00 a.m., unless you plan to pay for an extra night." The manager turned back to his veneer-panelled office where he could watch his portable TV in privacy. The elevator took so long that I wanted to take the stairs, but it would have been insane to drag our bags to the fifth floor.

Tory twisted the key in the lock and opened the door. I looked over the dimly lit room. No wonder it was so cheap. Next to the bed was a cracked porcelain basin with a mirror that hung on a nail. The room was so cramped that the bed seemed much larger than its actual size and there was nowhere to store anything. It was no palace, but a lot better than sleeping in a car.

Tory shed his jacket and draped it over a wooden chair to dry. I left the room and walked to the end of the hallway looking for the bathroom. The door was closed but there wasn't even the slightest bit of sound coming from inside. I tapped lightly and waited. What kind of hotel has one bathroom per floor?

The door finally opened and a tubby old guy with grey stubble pushed his way out. He glared in annoyance as he folded up his newspaper and passed me with a grunt. I didn't wait for conversation. I quickly slipped in and locked the door. The crapper stunk so badly I couldn't breathe.

"I want to find Andy and Liz tomorrow," I said to Tory as I re-entered our room. He stood around the other side of the bed facing the window.

"Maybe they didn't make it," he said without looking back.

"We have to wait for them," I said as I shuffled through my bag until I found a toothbrush and paste. I squeezed a generous amount onto my brush and walked over to the basin. I nearly screamed as a large thumb-size beetle scuttled across the bowl of the sink. Tory saw my panic and came at once.

"Wow, that thing is huge." Tory's head turned sideways as he tried to size it up from an angle. He was totally fascinated as the creature moved swiftly over the edge.

"It's a cockroach, isn't it?" I asked, still standing at a safe distance, as though the bug might leap at me and suddenly tear off my face.

"I think so—same colour anyway."

"Stop looking at it and get rid of it," I pleaded.

"Relax, I'll get some tissue and flush it," Tory said and left me alone with the man-eating monster. He came back with a wad of Kleenex over his nose.

"Was that you?" he asked, remembering that I had come from the toilet end of the hallway.

"No! Please, Tory." I shook my finger in the direction of the intruder, which had now crawled under the bowl. "You have to get it before it falls on the bed." I stared wildly as the bug glided along like a tiny motorized car.

Tory laughed, but in a split second, he struck and the bug never knew what hit him. It was over so fast.

"I can't stay in this rundown roach house," I vented at Tory.

"It'll be fine. We'll leave tomorrow and I'm betting that anywhere we stay will be no better than here."

Before I was willing to climb between the sheets, I analyzed the bed. Giving it a one out of ten, it passed my eyeball inspection. No sign of a bug napping anywhere! That night, Tory opened up and told me that he missed his parents, and we talked more freely than at any other time. While he had lived at home, there were a lot of heated arguments and beatings, so Tory was living on the streets by the age of fourteen. His family had become phantoms of his past.

It reminded me of my own experiences as a child. In a way, it was not such a big surprise that we had ended up together. As Tory fell asleep, I closed my eyes but I didn't sleep very well as I was terrified that something might crawl up my leg.

In the morning, I looked out at the streets below. Unfamiliar faces passed, but I didn't see Andy or Liz. We cleared out of the room by 10:00 a.m. and searched all day for our travelling companions. Another unrewarding day left me with nagging doubts that we would ever see them again. By nightfall, we had reached Regina's hostel, and it was a castle in comparison to the fleabag hotel. It was smaller, but the guest rooms were bug-free, clean, and fresh with plenty of washrooms.

On the third day, we let go of any hope in finding Andy and Liz. Our bags were packed and by early morning, there was a steady flow of rides so we were making progress. The rain had subsided for a long period and one of our lifts gave us money. That had never happened before so we were completely surprised. The woman driver did not give us her name or tell us where she was from. As we got out of the car, she just pulled out a ten-dollar bill.

"You might need it to get food or a room."

"Thank you," I said as Tory stuffed the money in his jeans. What a gal! We were at the mercy and kindness of so many wonderful people. But then, we met Monty who was totally out of the ordinary. He was our entertainment. Monty was pure manic, panic, and non-stop chatter, like he was on steroids or something. He was on a roll about all the stupid things he had done in his life and we were cracking up with laughter.

At two in the morning, our trip with Monty was over. He was turning to go to a different town so we parted outside a gas station. Tory and I watched helplessly as Monty's backlights seared through the rain like dragon's eyes. We went inside the gas station. It was raining so hard that we couldn't go out to the road to hitch, so we stopped drivers as they came in to pay for gas. The night dragged on like a ball and chain around our ankles.

Around 4:00 a.m., a kind old man who spoke little English drove us to a roadside diner. We were bagged from no sleep, but our appetites were instantly aroused by the smell of bacon and eggs. We took a booth seat by the window and scanned the drivers to see what direction they were coming from. After all we'd been through, Tory and I both knew it was just a matter of waiting for the right one. The waitress came over to offer us a menu just as a loud white semi rambled into the gravel parking lot.

"Coffee, black," Tory said, not taking his eyes off the truck. As the door of the cab swung open I could tell Tory had a plan.

"Don't order yet. I'll be back in a minute," Tory said and off he went. He went straight to the driver and approached him. I couldn't tell what was being said, but I had a pretty good idea.

They had a smoke and talked for less than it takes to drink a coffee. They entered the café together, so Tory was in good standing with this guy. To me it indicated that we would be on route soon. The man sat somewhere else as Tory came back to our table and slid into his seat.

"I got us a ride all the way to Winnipeg," Tory whispered as he brought me up to speed. The truck driver was willing to take us all the way. We stared at each other with a silly grin on our faces.

I had never been in a semi, so that was way beyond my scope of travel adventures. In the beginning, it was fun, but the eight-hour stretch of flatland was a killer. There was nothing but tarmac and the occasional gas station.

When we got to Winnipeg, the driver John handed us the keys to his truck so we could use the sleeper cab instead of forking out a bunch of money for a hotel. We were stunned that he would take such a burden off our shoulders.

"You're not worried that we might steal it?" Tory looked surprised.

"That would be stupid." John eyed us with confidence. "Truckers from one end of the coast to the other know my semi. Every driver would be waiting to kick your teeth in." He was speaking the truth.

The next morning, I got out of the cab and stretched with ease as I had slept very well, considering I was still in my halter top and cut-offs. By noon John was back and ready to roll, so we wished him well and went on our way.

69: Tory and His Friends

I wanted to head straight out of town, but Tory suggested we stop and say hello to some friends who lived just a few blocks away. He had mentioned it earlier, but I didn't push the idea because it would delay us. We walked along the littered streets and passed the old spackled homes that should have been demolished. Downy-white dandelion seeds floated softly in the air like falling feathers. There were so many that it looked like it was snowing.

"This is it. We're here," Tory said as he pushed his way through a rusted metal gate.

"Who are these people? I mean how do you know them?"

"I used to live here so I stayed in contact with my friends. You never know who your real friends are until you need them," Tory explained as he thumped on the door. A young man heard our knock and opened the door.

"Tory, my friend!" His eyes twinkled with surprise as he shouted happily. "What happened to you?" He slapped his arms around Tory's neck and pulled him close like a brother.

"Look everyone. Tory's home," the kid hollered. Well, I hate to stick my neck out, but my home wasn't anywhere near Winnipeg. Suddenly, we were surrounded by a group of happy faces and the room vibrated with excitement. From every corner of the house there were young people gathering to say "hi." The house was so packed that we were lucky to get standing room. I had the feeling that most of them had been through the foster-care system or run away in childhood.

"Cheers to Tory's return!"

Bottles opened and glasses clinked, and the party went all day and on through the night. At first, I was happy for Tory. But the next day led into more drinking and before I knew it we had lost a week. For the first time, I was cut off from Tory; he was trying to appease his friends. On September 2, we woke up to a dump of snow. Because the rooms were full, Tory and I had nowhere to crash, so we had to sleep on the veranda. It was glass-enclosed, but there was no heat.

We buried ourselves under quilts, wearing double pairs of socks and coats, but it was awfully cold. I hated every minute; I was desperate to get out of there. Tory wouldn't get his act together but I took action and packed up. I was not going to Montreal; I was going back to Vancouver with or without him.

Tory tried to reason, but I was not going to stay another day.

70: Tory

Tory gave in, but he wasn't himself. He was crabby and despondent as we back-tracked over the miles. Suffice it to say, we got to Calgary where the weather was as hot as summer. What a country! We made an agreement that we wouldn't budge another step until we made some cash so we could travel in comfort.

Most waitresses and hostesses made good tips, so I applied at the nightclubs. Nothing was available, but there was a job selling roses. It wasn't my first choice, but beggars can't always be choosers.

That job turned out to be better than most people would expect. On top of my wage, I was tripling that money in tips. Every night, I made my rounds through three or four discos. For my protection, the owner of the club hired a personal driver to chauffeur the company limo, so I went to work in style.

Tory got a job working part-time as a bartender. That kind of work was right up his alley. We were so happy that money was pouring in and our situation was a lot more stable. But Tory was always one to rock the boat with new ideas. Somewhere in his mind, he had developed the white-picket-fence syndrome. He wanted a wife and family whom he could call his own. His career-minded avenue had switched as though he were clicking through the TV channels. During our stay in Calgary, he talked about "us" having a baby. I was thrilled that he loved me that way.

In my brain, Tory's desire to play Daddy equated with a huge billboard sign that read, "Commitment." I loved Tory more than ever. I wanted him, so I was ready to give him what he wanted and nothing would change my mind.

In childhood, we had both gone through inner loathing and self-abnegation due to abuse. With so many inadequacies, we were both terribly misguided about what love really meant. As a couple, we desired very much to rid ourselves of our childhood troubles so we could establish the best possible future. I was ready to become a mother even though we hadn't married yet. My biological ticker was immeasurably loud, so we had lots of spur-of-the-moment opportunities. Because we never went to bed angry, I thought we were the strongest couple; but I was wrong.

I'm not sure if hormones or heat were the initiating factors, but shortly after we moved into an apartment on the south side of Calgary, Tory and I had a huge blowout. Sure, we didn't always mesh on everything, but this fight went on and on for two miserable hours. It just didn't end until Tory turned his back and walked out. I was furious that he would be so insensitive. He was still outraged that I had changed our plans about going back east.

When he didn't return that evening, I was devastated. Unfortunately, neither of us knew that I had conceived.

As the weeks rolled on, I didn't know where Tory was staying and he didn't call. I was burning the midnight oil waiting for his return. I told myself to let him go and move on, but I was exhausted and it was hard to go to work. Tory had done what was best for him, so I had to do what was best for me. I cried every day. I cried about everything and it was ridiculous that I was so miserable. I didn't understand why I was so emotional and tired.

71: Elias and Tory

I called my old boyfriend Elias for advice and told him that I had fallen for someone else. It was hard to talk to him about another man, but he listened. I told him everything about the trip back east with Tory and the terrible fight that had split us up. The whole time my stomach was circling around like a giant hula-hoop, but it just didn't register that I was expecting. Chewable antacids didn't do much for my bouts of indigestion or the numerous flare-ups of heartburn. I thought that it was nerves at the time.

"Do you love him?" Elias had asked the unavoidable.

"Yes, but Tory doesn't love me. I thought he wanted to marry me and have a family but that has all changed now."

At first, Elias was unresponsive, but he still loved me and I was shocked. It was hard to fathom that he had so much as a hint of feeling for me after all I had told him. He asked me to put aside the past so we could see if there was any chance that I might feel the same for him.

I couldn't see why he would care anymore. His love was so unconditional and I struggled to understand. I expected him to be cruel and shred me into pieces with names or walk away, but he didn't.

One morning, I woke up and fled to the bathroom. I can't use the term "queasiness" lightly, because it felt like a tidal wave was crashing inside my abdomen. No matter what I ate, it came back with a gut-wrenching vengeance. A twenty-four-hour flu would have been a walk in the park. I went to a drop-in pregnancy clinic. The nurse did a urine test while I waited. That was the longest five minutes of my life.

"Your test shows that you are positive."

"I'm... pregnant?" I was trying to hide the shock. No wonder I felt so lousy.

"Yes. How do you feel about that?" The nurse looked down at my fidgety hands in my lap. No point in trying to hide my bare ring finger.

"I'm not sure." My head was spinning with confusion as my thoughts went from how beautiful to how terrifying. Where the hell is Tory? I knew without any doubt that I would love my baby, yet I was suddenly second-guessing the big picture. My throat was getting tight and I really needed air. Am I too stupid to get anything right in this life?

"It's going to be okay. You have options. We provide an abortion service. It is safe and confidential.

"No, I don't want that." I couldn't look at her.

"If you are feeling overwhelmed and decide that you are not ready to take on such a big commitment there is the choice of private adoption. You still have time to think about it." The nurse's compassion and speech seemed so well rehearsed. I wondered how many girls she had counselled in the same situation.

"I can't do that either," I broke in. A tiny life had begun to develop and for me that meant no one in this world had the right to tear us apart and leave us forever unknown to each other. It would be unforgivable and nothing short of irresponsible for me to assume that my baby's future would be safe in the hands of social services. Upon leaving the clinic, I thought about Tory. Could he handle such a big responsibility? Would he come back if he knew? Would he love or want our baby? How on earth would I explain this to Elias? Countless questions whirled around in my head and it was making me crazy.

So, there I was, trying to sort myself out by discussing things with Elias again, but he was staring as though I had lost my mind. When I told him I was pregnant, I was sure there would be no forgiveness.

"You don't have to go through with this," he said. "It's not a baby yet; it's not even a fetus."

I understood what he meant, but abortion was out of the question. It didn't make any sense to him that I wouldn't consider any alternative. I told him that Tory and I had planned it.

He was angry and upset. He had little to say and I really felt like a bad person. Elias sought the advice of a co-worker and she helped him comprehend from a woman's point of view.

"Don't make her do something that she will regret for life. It's her choice, not yours." The co-worker's outlook helped Elias understand the situation from a different angle. Although I never met the woman, I was grateful that she didn't judge me or denounce my choice.

When Elias offered to fill Tory's shoes, I found it emotionally moving. But even though I loved Elias, I didn't expect him to step in for Tory.

Because I hadn't heard from Tory, I began to think that he had skipped town and moved to Montreal. Maybe he had made it big and was strutting through the fashion world. I asked around and tried to reach him at his work, but I had no success.

One night when I got to work, Tory was waiting to see me. I nearly fell over when I saw him standing there watching me come through the doors. I had been up all night hugging the puke bowl, so I knew that I looked a little beat up. The puking was out of control but I did my best to hide it, because I loved selling flowers and making people happy.

177

Obviously, I was there to work, so he asked if we could meet and talk at a more suitable time. The sooner the better I thought, so we met when I got back from my last round of clubs. At 2:00 a.m., I came right out and told him that I was pregnant. I don't know why he looked so surprised, as we had never used birth control. I told Tory what Elias was willing to do.

Tory seemed to be lost in a train of thought and I wondered if he thought I was trying to crack the whip on him. I let him know that I wasn't trying to chain him down. He was free to go, but if he committed I didn't want him to back down. Tory told me that he loved me and promised to do everything he could to prove it. We were going to be a family and I was so happy, but I was sad too, because I didn't want to hurt Elias again.

Elias was a sure thing whereas Tory came with no guarantee. In my heart I didn't want to let go of Elias, because I loved him; but I loved Tory so much more.

"Elias," I said, as my throat tightened with emotion, "I don't know how I could have managed without you. Please believe that I do love you very much. If I hadn't met Tory, it would have…."

"Don't… don't say anymore," Elias broke in. His voice was powerfully soft, yet it was painful to hear it. We were over. I threw my arms around his neck and cried.

"I'm sorry, Elias." My tears soaked into his shirt and I couldn't get a hold of myself. I never knew that love could be so difficult.

72: Tory

As Tory and I began to rebuild our relationship, there was a notable difference. He seemed to have transcended from being a boy to being a responsible man. It felt so believable, so right.

We moved into an old mansion sitting on a hill in the southeast end of Calgary. The house had so much character. French doors and a large mahogany stairway mounted to the bedrooms on the second level. Our apartment was a one-bedroom suite that overlooked the driveway. The ninety-year-old owner had been born in the very same room that he slept in. The house was extravagant in beauty and we loved the retro look with rounded archways and early nineteenth-century furnishings.

The outside of the house was surrounded by a wide veranda and stone pillars. The thick green hedges dropped a few leaves before transitioning into the deep rich colours of autumn. Dark skeletal trees stood off in the background as reminders that old man winter was on his way back.

Every night after closing, Tory would come by cab to take me home. I didn't mind taking a taxi by myself, but he insisted that it would be safer if we went home together.

Once in a while, he would stay at my work and have a few drinks. That wasn't a problem until he showed up drunk. At first, I didn't notice, until Tory came in with an attitude. He looked across the room and saw me searching under the table for a missing earring. The bartender, Laurence, came over and tried to help me find the tiny red pearl. When Laurence placed the earring in my hand, Tory was watching and assumed that something else was going on, so he made his way over.

"We have to go right now," he said rudely and I could smell the alcohol on his breath. I grabbed my purse and followed Tory, but as we reached the stairs to the door, he whirled around and blocked me. I tried to pass but he wouldn't get out of my way.

"What are you doing?" I asked, but Tory didn't answer me. His eyes filled with anger and before I had a chance to pick up on his mood, he grabbed the chain around my neck and twisted it over his fist. All the seconds while Tory was choking the air out of me, I was madder than hell that I'd taken him back. I was shocked at his brutality. I never knew he had it in him.

"You are mine. Do you understand?" he said through slurred words and puffy red eyes. "Don't you ever look at another man or I'll kill you!"

How many times had I heard that before? I knew the alcohol was doing all the stupid talking and acting for Tory. As he released the chain, I pushed him against the wall, ran upstairs to the exit, and out to the street.

"Eugenea!" He yelled as he tottered behind.

Outside, the cabs were lined up along the curb so I got into the closest one. Sure enough, Tory blundered his way into the back seat.

"Get out!" I was furious, but Tory ignored me and told the driver to get a move on. When we arrived at the house, Tory pulled out his cash and paid. I wanted to grab the money from his hand and throw it in his face, but that could have been to my detriment. I had plenty to say, but at 3:00 a.m., a mean drunk only gets meaner.

When Tory woke up the next morning, he didn't remember what happened and couldn't understand why I was so cold to him. He had done some awful things in the past, but physical abuse was not one of them. He cried when he heard those words come out of my mouth. Through muffled sobs, he asked me not to leave. He promised that he would never be abusive again and I believed him.

"We need to go home, back to Vancouver," Tory said and I knew he was trying to find a way into my heart. "We could be home for Christmas," he said as he stroked my arm. I looked into his swollen eyes and wanted the same. It had been five months since leaving Vancouver and I was homesick. Winter in Alberta never worked for me. It was a downer.

The next night I stormed into work with the intent to reprimand my co-workers who had seen what happened but hadn't lifted a finger to help me.

"I was about to call the bouncer, but I saw that you had it under control," my boss said.

"Why didn't anyone help me?"

"Your co-workers didn't want to get involved," he said defensively.

"Gee, I'll remember to thank them for their support and maybe I can do the same for them someday," I said sarcastically.

At closing time, I put in my resignation and told my boss that I was moving. He promised that I had a job if I changed my mind and honoured me with a silver rose pin. He was a good boss.

73: Tory and Carla and their Parents

By the time I had gotten back to the apartment, Tory had found a way to get us to Vancouver. We would not be going alone, because Tory's sister was our transportation. Carla was going through a rough transition because of marital abuse; she never knew when her husband would come out swinging. She tried on her own to flee from him, but she needed our support. She drove from Kamloops to Calgary to get us and from there we headed for Vancouver.

Halfway back to Vancouver, Carla wanted to go back to her house in Kamloops, many miles out of our way. She needed to get the rest of her belongings, but undoubtedly that would be a disaster if her husband caught us. As we drove around the corner on her street, Carla saw her husband's car in the driveway. Since it wasn't too late, she anticipated that her husband would go out for the night. So we waited in the car with the motor off. It was prickly cold while we waited, but none of us wanted to face the hard edge of a baseball bat or any other type of weapon.

It was no more than fifteen minutes when the car in the driveway backed out and drove away. We went around the house, but the doors were locked, so Tory climbed through a window. He let us in and we ransacked the rooms from top to bottom. I was sweating bullets at the thought that Carla's husband might come back. While Tory stood watch, Carla and I stuffed all her valuables into garbage bags.

"Let's go," Tory yelled. Twenty minutes had already slipped by; he was getting edgy. He wanted to stop playing the bodyguard and get out of there. We were totally paranoid that Carla's husband was hiding out and waiting to shoot us. Nobody felt safe until we got in the car and doubled back on the road out of town.

After my high-powered adrenaline settled down, I spread out on the back seat and slept most of the way. Not exactly fun: it would have been handy to have a few of those air sickness bags.

However, when we arrived in Vancouver we were in great spirits. Our days of running like a freight train were over. We were back. I rolled down the window and sucked in the cold air. Life was good. As we drove along the wet streets of Vancouver, the city lights dazzled through the sheets of rain.

The three of us were antsy to get out of the stuffy car so we could feel the splash on our faces. We parked right outside a café and went in with enough "chump change" to buy a newspaper and a round of coffees. We looked in the newspaper's classifieds for somewhere to stay, but didn't find anything affordable except an attic loft on Denman Street. Of course, we found this to be a tad tight for three people, so Tory was the scout for something more practical.

A week had barely escaped when Tory found a bigger place. We got the down payment and moved in right away. The move was almost effortless, because we only had a bed and a suitcase. With the exception of the loft, any apartment looks big when it's bare. But it didn't seem to matter, because I would wake up and see Tory's wonderful smile and I knew we would be okay.

The word was that Carla and Tory only spoke with their parents on rare occasions because there was so much bad blood. Their parents were harsh critics. So how does one tell estranged parents that one's girlfriend is pregnant? A girl they had never met! Neither of us knew what kind of reaction we might receive.

Well, we got up our courage anyway and made a phone call. After all was said and done, we both had a lump in our throats when his parents talked to me as though I was the new daughter in the family. We had tears in our eyes when they invited us to come to One Hundred Mile in the Cariboo for Christmas; to make it possible they sent us two bus tickets. The six-hour trip was going to be a reunion for Tory, his sister, and their parents.

Christmas Eve was about the dinner preparations, but the baby ranked pretty high with the soon-to-be grandparents. There was lots of love and laughter the night we arrived. Tory's two half-sisters wrapped a few more gifts and pushed them under the tree. In the morning, everyone dressed up and moved into the living room as a family. The smell of turkey wafted through the kitchen as the family talked and laughed about old times.

I was delighted to fit in with Tory's family but without even knowing it at the time, this was when the trouble started. Tory's parents had reacted with so much joy about the grandparent thing that I didn't sense any problems. But these people were completely unpredictable. The novelty wore off like a dirty diaper. Something snapped and it all went to hell.

On Christmas morning, a comfort dish of cheese and meats and a bowl of pretzels were set out for munching. But we weren't allowed to touch them until Tory's Mom could open with her "Value of Life" talk. Save the speech, lady! It was all about the horrible children she had mistakenly brought into the world. We got sucked in. It was too awful. Too bad the parents couldn't leave the past in the past.

Tory's mom switched from a likeable woman into a bi-polar nightmare. The family stories had switched from adoring baby moments to a Mom shrieking like a stick of dynamite was under her seat. No wonder Tory and Carla had run away and never gone back. With the snow falling and all the bus depots shut for the day, there was no way to escape the yelling and fighting. Every mistake that Tory and his sister had ever made was on the table. I wanted to say, "Hey people, let's put the turkey on the table, instead. Christmas should be a day to make memories for us to talk about with our kids someday."

They were furious that Carla had run off at fourteen and eloped without their permission. After she'd married, her husband had forced her into prostitution. It got heated up and nasty, when they were yelling in Carla's face that she had brought it on herself and she was to blame for her husband's monstrous abuse. At first, Carla put up a fight; she wouldn't go down easy. But she broke into tears when she couldn't handle her mother calling her "a whore and a tramp." She leaped off the couch and screamed that she had been a child at the time and her parents had abandoned her. They were disgusted with Carla. Nor was there an inkling of support in Tory's future to be a Dad. Pretty soon, Tory's Mom was lashing out at all of us. Christmas was over before it had begun.

When it was Tory's turn he wouldn't look at his parents, but that didn't stop the show. I wished for his sake that we had avoided all this trouble. When they dragged my name into the mess, I thought for sure Tory was going to start a tussle with his step-dad. They were choked that I was pregnant. I knew that was coming and I also knew we would be out of there in the morning.

The painful truth hit Tory like a bullet between the eyes. He was deadpan for the rest of the day. We ate dinner in silence. Even dessert couldn't lift the heavy mood and the gift opening wasn't much of an improvement. The day dragged on in melancholy bleakness. Carla got in her car and left without saying goodbye. I was anxious to speed things along so we could get out of there too.

By Boxing Day, Tory hadn't spoken a word to his parents except to ask them for a ride to the bus station. I wanted so much to wait in the nice warm car, but Tory would rather take the chance of getting hypothermia as opposed to putting up with his parents a moment longer. As for me I was dreaming that one of those big heroic Saint Bernard dogs would come bounding toward us with a brandy barrel around its neck. I just needed a swig to heat my extremities.

Our bus to Vancouver was an hour late due to a bad snowstorm, so maybe it was a stupid idea to wear my knee-length skirt and high-top boots. My cherry-coloured knees were stinging so badly they felt like a little elf had come along and got his kicks by snapping tiny elastic bands to torture my knees.

Six hours later, the bus dropped us at the Vancouver Bus Depot and from there we took a cab along Denman Street to our apartment. As we sat in the back seat feeling sleepy from our travel, I noticed a woman working on the corner. It was dark, but under the lamppost it was clear as day that it was Carla. I looked over at Tory and he was watching too. It was no secret, but to see her soliciting was another thing altogether.

Shortly after Christmas, I got a gift that topped any present I had ever received. It didn't come from a store; it came from my unborn baby. Deep inside my belly, I got a jolt. The baby was stirring for the first time and it knew how to pack a punch. At first, it was a nudge and then I got a lively kick to say hello.

My parents were so relieved to know that I was back in Vancouver even though it took some time before Louis forgave me. He was upset that I had given up a stable life and job. Because I was twenty years old and I was still in the early stages of getting to know my family, I hadn't thought how it might affect them.

74: The Beggar, the Modelling Agency, and the Ultrasound

Tory got a job as a chef and bartender at the Cloud 9 Revolving Restaurant and Lounge. The lucky boy had the best of the best. It fitted his lifestyle because he loved the city at night. I found myself alone most evenings and I couldn't bring myself to relax until he stepped in the door. Everything about our life together seemed perfect and I didn't want to mess with karma. As long as he loved me, it was all worth it. We still had a few wrinkles to iron out but we were working on them.

Although Tory had suffered in life, he did not have his eyes open to the suffering of others. Possibly, he didn't want to deal with situations that reminded him of his past experiences. I found myself stuck in the middle more than once. Like the time Tory got his first paycheque. He came home and twirled me in his arms and promised to take his queen out for dinner. But first he showered me with gifts. It was a special occasion that called for dressing up, so he wore his second-hand crème suit and I could hardly take my eyes off him. I put on a little black dress and it worked like magic. No one could see that I had a baby bump, because the dress fit so nicely and it looked so elegant with the tiger's eye necklace and earrings that Tory had bought me.

As we walked toward the restaurant I could see how beautiful it was inside. The windows were so big that I couldn't miss the striking red and black panelled walls. Tory had reserved the best seat in the house. Our table was draped in white linen and I couldn't see my shoes under the cloth when I sat down. Tory winked at me and took my hand to his lips.

My eyes were so busy taking in the décor that I was feeling giddy. The hors d'oeuvres and sparkling water were quite surreal and I was overwhelmed with Tory's romantic mood. The windows went from floor to ceiling, yet I had barely noticed there was an old man watching from outside. Our waitress came with a basket of buns and placed one on each plate. Before I could reach for the butter, I was interrupted.

"Excuse me, miss. Do you think I could have your bun?"

I looked up and saw a wrinkled old man with long white hair and a tattered full-length coat. His matted beard lay on his collar and his hands were swollen red and cracked. As I opened my mouth to speak, Tory startled me when he pushed himself away from the table and bounced to his feet.

"How dare you!" Tory shrilled at the beggar.

I sat astounded and I could feel my cheeks flaming in humility. Underneath his heavily matted eyebrows, the man's powder-blue eyes twinkled. I wished I could crawl under the table and vanish.

"Get away from us or I'll call the manager," Tory fired off, nearly knocking over a fluted glass. I was horrified. Then he ordered the man to leave at once, like he was the owner. I knew our food was pricey, but who cares about a crusty bun? Before I had a chance to right the wrong, the man was gone. What a way to spoil a romantic mood.

"You of all people; I don't believe it." I said as the waitress brought out our entrees. She placed my dish in front of me. I stared at my juicy steak and seasoned vegetables. It looked and smelled wonderful, but I had lost my appetite.

I should have run after the man and given him all the food on my plate. I didn't need Tory to dictate what was right. The poor old man was probably sleeping in an alley box and starving. Unforgivable!

I thought that maybe Tory was trying to protect me by making sure I had enough food for the baby. But when we went to prenatal classes, I could tell that he was put off. He sat on the sidelines and hummed and hawed in boredom. It made me worry that I would end up giving birth alone.

I thought it might be a good idea to look into something that Tory would find more interesting. I called one of Vancouver's modelling agencies and set up an appointment for us. A smartly dressed woman escorted Tory and me into an enormous office.

She told us that she owned the business so I knew we were in the best of hands. In that sort of profession, there are a few stiff-nosed types who look down at you if they don't like your shoes. But this woman spent a lot of time with us; we didn't feel silly around her. My wrap-around dress was very flattering, but it was not high-end. I should have picked something more designer-like, so she could see my fashion side.

Everywhere we looked, giant pictures were mounted on the walls and along the corridors. I was hypnotized by the scene. Black-and-white stills and colourful life-sized prints seemed to never end. I felt a fizz of excitement just to be there. Tory and I answered a lot of questions and I sure hoped we would say all the right things.

"Okay, let's have a quick look at your chart." She smiled as I put down the pen and passed her my general information such as birth, weight, height, etc. Everything was going well until then. Wait a minute! Did I hear what she just said?

"You are not tall enough to be a model."

Well she might as well have thumped me on the head with a fish. Goodbye to Tory's dream ideals... again.

But it wasn't all bad news! She believed I had potential to be an actress, so that was pretty cool. I was still disappointed, but then she told me to come back after the baby was born. She would train me so I would be able to get an agent. So my future modelling plans were flattened, but I had something far more exciting ahead.

My doctor booked me for an ultrasound. I couldn't believe it, but I was actually going to see my baby months before it would be born. What will technology come out with next? The tricky part was I first had to drink a ridiculous amount of water. Four glassfuls and hold the pee! Not at all easy when there's a baby hogging all the room and kicking my bladder like a little billy goat. Tory was so fascinated by the ultrasound equipment that I wasn't sure he would connect to the actual reason why we were there. Thankfully his curiosity increased as the technician glided the wand across my belly. He took my hand and together we stared at the screen. In the first few seconds, I could only see something that resembled a curled up frog and lots of murky waves.

Then, I saw a very blurry baby-like shape floating in a haze of fluid.

"That's our baby," I squealed as I squeezed Tory's hand.

"Oh my gosh, it's moving!" Tory was crying and the tech was smiling. I'm sure her job elated her. Everything looked good so the tech gave me a sonogram picture to keep. Thank goodness she pointed out the baby! Quite honestly, the picture was so hazy that I couldn't tell the difference between the head and the body.

My ultrasound was followed up with an obstetrics appointment. During my check up, Doctor Lees asked me the basic health questions as he checked my vitals. I was a little concerned why the baby hadn't moved in the last two days. He assured that all was fine, but just to make sure he pressed his fetal stethoscope to my belly and heard lots of sloshing around and a good strong heartbeat.

Tory was off to the side trying to stay out of the way, but the OB doctor would have none of that. He called Tory over and let him try the stethoscope. I could tell by the look on Tory's face that he heard the pitter-pattering of our baby's heart. I listened too. The precious rhythmic beats made my hormones go all awry. My eyes got misty and Tory… well, let's just go along with "men don't cry."

Then the nurse took a blood sample and I fainted right on the spot. Tory carried me to a small orange couch and opened the window. As I was coming to, I heard him softly assuring me that I was all right. My stomach was so woozy and I was dizzy for a while, but Tory soothed my face with a wet cloth. His eyes were damp and it was the first time I had ever seen him really scared. He held me in his arms and the baby was making quirky little movements. Hiccups! It was hilarious. We walked back from the doctor's office as the sun shone brightly. I thought we were the happiest parents in the world.

75: Damien

We had two months to go before our little newcomer would be in our loving arms. Tory quit his night job and went into framing and construction, so we would have more time together and more cash for our baby's needs. At the time it seemed like a good idea, but then he met Damien somewhere along the road. I don't like to blow my own trumpet as a psychic, but I knew this guy was bad news.

Damien had no family or friends. When he was five years old, his mother had wrapped her arms around him and they went to sleep in her bed. In the morning, Damien woke up to a lifeless body. His mom had committed suicide with him in her arms. He was an only child and his father was a mean drunk. I felt badly for Damien, but I didn't like him.

His energy level was demanding and obnoxious. He was habitually popping by at all hours without calling first. Tory didn't seem to care that Damien was so intrusive. I hoped the friendship was just a passing phase. But Damien became more and more involved in Tory's every move. I was afraid I had met my match.

I told Tory that Damien needed to back off; he was pulling us apart. That's when Tory and I hit a gridlock. Suddenly nothing seemed to be going right. Tory didn't want to hear any reason why he couldn't hang out with Damien. Then I learned that he felt a brotherly love for this guy.

To my shock, Tory told me that he was born to be wild and I was holding him down. What a lot of bull! He was just making excuses. He wanted to party.

Whenever Tory didn't come home I knew he had gone to the clubs with Damien. He didn't like my interrogations, but I was keenly aware that he wouldn't come within kissing distance of me without a shower first.

One morning, I woke up to find Tory's side of the bed unmade. It was his second day to miss work and I knew that he was on the edge of losing his job. It was mid-May and I was in my eighth month and I still had difficulty eating without throwing up. All I wanted to do was sleep, but I got up and set out to find Tory.

I was sure that he was at Damien's apartment, so I hobbled my way over. There was no answer when I rang the buzzer outside, so I waited until someone came out of the apartment block's front door. With nerves on edge, I walked so briskly through the hall, I was almost at a run. I got to Damien's door and knocked as hard as I could. There was no answer, but I heard shuffling, so I knocked again.

"Who's there?" Damien mumbled. I would know that voice anywhere, I thought to myself.

"It's me, Eugenea. I need to talk to Tory."

From where I stood in the hall, I heard low mumbling and then it went dead quiet. Maybe if Tory and Damien ignored me long enough, I would go away. I continued to knock. I hated to make waves, but I was feeling frantic that I was losing Tory.

"I'm trying to sleep. Can't this wait until later?" Tory hollered out with anger.

"Not until you answer the door," I said, stalling for time.

"Get out of here. Go home."

That was the clincher. Poking my eyes out would have been less painful.

"What do you want?" Tory finally opened the door. He stood there with his bare chest heaving and I was eye-level with his shoddy tattoo. His low-rider jeans were crumpled and he looked a mess. It's almost funny the way he was bolted to the floor like I might turn into a linebacker and gatecrash him.

"Where were you last night?" I asked haughtily.

"I don't want to talk right now."

"Oh good, that's nice. I came all the way over here for nothing," I said. "Forgive me, Tory, what was I thinking?" My eyes were desperately trying to see around him. But there was nothing to see: no girls or bottles lying around. All I saw was Damien acting like he was dead asleep on the pullout couch. The sheet was pulled back, so I knew Tory slept there as well.

That was the second when my thoughts took a wild leap into uncharted territories. I had a horrid image of Damien and Tory together in my head. Maybe there was more to this relationship than friendship.

"Go home," Tory said, as though he was reading my mind. His hand pushed against the door and nearly shut me out.

"What's going on?" I asked, as I pushed back really gently yet firmly enough to get my meaning across. "I don't understand why are you doing this? We need to talk."

"Not now."

"When? You're never home so when?" I asked. Tory had no comment; he just stood there staring at me. Suddenly, it was clear as a bell that he had nothing to offer anymore.

"I don't want you here. Go home." He wasn't asking.

For a long moment we stood in silence. No point in fighting the obvious. Why couldn't Tory see that I would move heaven and earth for him?

76: Moving away from Heroin

It was over, over, over! I was back at the apartment and my heart was crumbling. It was a horrible reality that I was never going to be with Tory again. The apartment had to go. I couldn't afford to live there alone with our baby.

The next morning as I sat on the sofa, I tried to focus on what to do when I was suddenly overrun with tears. Mom, bless her heart, was my saving grace. She left Calgary and moved to Burnaby, a suburb of Vancouver. She came over to help me with the packing. When she saw the condition I was in, she rushed over to the couch. She rocked me and I cried so much that I thought I would never recover. No one had ever sat with me that long, but I guess she knew that I couldn't see past the pain.

I didn't need the extra torture, but Tory showed up after Mom went home. I already felt so round and ugly that I was not surprised he found me unattractive and wanted to run off. But there was more agony, because he insisted on holding me. He got me at "I still love you!" Ugh! Why couldn't he just leave it alone? We stood in the middle of our boxed-up living room when he pulled me into the warmth of his arms.

The scent of his skin was off that day. My high senses picked up on something foreign. I had a nose like a beagle, so I knew right off the bat if he was drunk or high. When he let go, I saw a bruise on the inner part of his arm. Up close, it was easy to spot the trail of blue marks that ran from shoulder to wrist. He pulled away and tried to cover it up, but it was too late. I knew his love was for the drug—not me. It all made sense why he wasn't around for days on end.

Tory was not stupid and he knew that drugs were a train ride to death. I told him that he could die and then our baby would grow up and never know him. Tory was unmoved, except to pick up his shaving kit. Why couldn't he stop this insanity?

On June 1, I got assistance from welfare and relocated to a one-bedroom basement suite with a separate entry around the back. It wasn't much of a home, not airy or fresh, just an old basement with low lighting and little warmth at night. It was a bit damp and drab so I always fell short when it came to getting a good night's sleep. No matter how late I went to bed, I got only four hours at the most. It made the days between sleeps feel endless. My due date felt like it was a world away. I couldn't get Tory out of my mind, but I found comfort in knowing I would soon have my baby to love.

With the support of some of my family and friends, I was able to buy the baby's necessities. Every day, I was cleaning and reorganizing what was already organized. My restlessness was causing me to behave like an obsessive-compulsive freak. I wanted everything to be baby-perfect.

I went back to the beach where Tory and I had first met and tried to find peace, but I was really lost. The sand felt so therapeutic, so I just sat in thought while the boats drifted on the ocean.

"Are you alright?" A young man interrupted.

He was genuinely concerned and I felt a bit confused. Did it look that obvious? I smiled and he added that he was a bit worried.

"Oh, I was just enjoying the beautiful weather." I stretched out my hand and he shook it. "Marcel? Nice name, if I have a boy I think that would be cool to call him that," I said and Marcel smiled. His name suited his good looks, but I didn't tell him that. He was there with a couple of other guys who were just as nice. We sat on a big old log and talked, and when it got too hot we all went to the English Bay Café.

Marcel had soul and I liked his countenance. I liked the way he listened. There was an unusual chemistry that we both felt. He was quite shy, but he still commented on our chemistry. There was something in the air or maybe we had too much sun, but I felt it too. I wanted to buy my own dinner, but he picked up the tab before I could hail the waitress. Later, when I got back to my place around midnight, I felt pretty for the first time in weeks. My new friendship made me realize that some people cared and I wasn't alone. He felt like a big brother to me.

I had not been to the doctor for some time so I didn't want to put it off any longer. But it wasn't an easy trip, as I had to wait for two bus rides in the boiling sun and my feet were swollen to the point that I could only wear flip-flops.

I lay motionless on the examination table as Dr. Lees listened to the baby's heart rate. I expected to roll off the table and retrace my steps to home; Dr. Lees had other plans for me.

"You are sick and you need bed rest, so I am going to have you admitted."

"What? No!" I didn't want to be stuck in the hospital. Except for the dark circles under my eyes, I could manage. I promised to go right home and rest. But that wasn't enough for him. My doctor asked me why I was so stressed and what had happened since my last visit. It was hard to talk about it, so I just told him that Tory and I were no longer together. I shrugged it off in hopes that my face was not an open book.

It wasn't my face that was telling the facts—it was my blood pressure. The doctor told me that my heart rate was soaring. My body wasn't gaining weight, yet I had a lot of swelling in my ankles. He used medical terms like "toxemia" and "preeclampsia" to describe my condition. He didn't want to scare me, but the situation was life and death. When he said my baby could die, that was all I needed to hear.

"Die?" I was flummoxed. How did it get to this? Untreated, toxemia is a silent killer. So an hour later, I was in bed wearing a shameless tent-sized gown that didn't cover my backside properly. Under the scrutiny of my doctor and the watchful eyes of the nurses, I ate salt-free meals and stayed in bed.

77: Two Mr. Hotshots

I don't like hospitals, but it felt as though I had taken a vacation and gotten a break from my ridiculous life. I was connected to an intravenous drip and there was a big horse-sized belt around my belly to monitor the baby. I looked like a sea turtle in a harness. Three weeks went by and I was still in a hospital bed, but I had to get out for a day so I could pay the rent. My doctor told me he would only give me a day pass, so I had to be back in bed when visiting hours were over.

The bus ride across town was stuffy and hot, and my baby wasn't too happy when I sat in a cramped little space near the back. As I rubbed my tummy, I got another jab in the ribs. I was quite happy to know that my feisty little one was ready to bust out.

I met with the landlord, paid the rent, and picked up the mail. In that same hour, one of Tory's friends came by and told me that Tory had got a job in a strip club. He had signed up to do his first solo that night.

"You need to talk him out of it."

Tory's friend was on my side. I agreed that I must get out there and stop Tory somehow. There was plenty of time to be back in my hospital bed by eight, but unfortunately it was a tedious undertaking to get to the strip club. I took the wrong bus, so I had to backtrack. Plus, it was miles away, so I did not get there until it was too late to dissuade Tory. He was already backstage waiting for his cue.

I was in the midst of girls going wild, when the emcee announced into his mike that a guest was making his first appearance. At the mere mention of Tory's name, I could feel my skin tensing up. All eyes swept to the middle of the stage where Tory was dancing like Mr. Hotshot. He was in the same three-piece suit that he wore on our dinner date. That's okay! No one could miss the red block letters that squeezed across my chest and read:

BABY UNDER CONSTRUCTION

No pressure... except for the bright neon arrow pointing downward to my bump that had been Tory's idea. He bought his first gift for baby and me from a designer printing shop in Calgary.

The women moved out of the way as I pushed toward the centre aisle so I could have front-row seating. That way, Tory could see me dead square in the middle, baby bump and all. I wanted him to feel so uncomfortable that he would jam out.

What a dummy I was! Sure it was awkward for Tory to see me there, but he knew how to shake a leg. His sultry moves seemed to entice the ladies to cheer him on but he wasn't getting applause from my end. Even while shaking my head in disgust and cursing like my mouth had a mind of its own, he dropped his clothes one piece at a time.

What had possessed me to go there? I must have been crazy to try and make a last-ditch effort to talk Tory out of such a bad decision. In some ways, I hoped that it might help me to divide and conquer any feelings if I saw him at his worst. I wanted to get over him ASAP, I told myself, as I brushed back a tear and edged my way back through a mob of screamers.

When I got out onto the street the last bus went flying by. So I could stand around and wait until 5:00 a.m. or I could hitch. I didn't have thirty dollars to take a cab. It was dark and cold, so I zipped up my pale-blue hoodie. I loved that jacket. It was the only item that made me look un-pregnant for moments like that. If I looked like my waters were going to break, I wouldn't get a ride. I had a sudden flash in my head of me screaming and pushing in the back of someone's old beetle.

"Where are you going?" The driver looked to be about thirty or more.

"Downtown."

"No problem. That's where I'm heading," he said.

"That's great." I opened the door and popped in on the passenger side. When the car was well out of the area, the driver shot me a look that made me feel uneasy. Had I just entered into some kind of impending doom?

I tried to distract the driver with my casual chitchat, but he cut me off to say that he missed the pleasures of his girlfriend who was out of town. Right! What the heck is that supposed to mean? Well, he's not going to spread the love with me. There was a short period of silence and I was grasping at straws on what to say. Think! Think! Think!

I was trying to keep it cool, but then he got intimate and talked about his sexual urges. Out of the corner of my eye, I double-checked to see what he was doing. I was afraid that he might reach over and physically attack me. It was such a relief to see both of his hands still resting on the wheel. The guy was a total pig. He was anxious to share the details of his personal needs. I was mortified, but I pretended to be sympathetic while my mind was formulating how to stay alive. Don't panic and don't show the slightest tinge of fear.

After what seemed like the longest marathon of green lights in history, he was forced to stop at a red. With my heart beating wildly, I pushed down on the door handle and leaped out of the car. The second my foot met the ground I dashed into the street. I didn't look back until I made it across the road.

"Please come back. I'm sorry," he called out of the open door and he didn't move even when the light turned green. He was holding up the cars behind him so the drivers got angry and blasted their car horns. I rushed to the sidewalk with my hands cuddled under my belly. I had scarcely got my bearings when I saw the car had gone around the block. Three times he drove around and every time, he was yelling out apologies. I flipped him the bird and crossed onto a road that he couldn't access; I disappeared like a ghost. I told myself, "Don't ever do that again." But all the scolding in the world might not prevent me from... myself.

78: Toxic

Shortly after 11:00 p.m. I was back in my hospital room. So much had happened in one day that my head was spinning and I just wanted to collapse and fall asleep. But first, the nurse was ordered to take my vitals again. My blood pressure was completely out of control. In the morning, I was aching from head to toe. I looked down and saw my stubby ankles had morphed into fleshy ham hocks. It was no wonder that I felt so lousy. My blood pressure levels were dangerously high and Dr. Lees insisted the baby be induced the next day.

I thought I was going to have a cardiac arrest when Tory entered the room. The sight of him most likely sent my blood levels through the roof. I wanted to slap his face. How could he have been so shameless and egotistical?

"Tory, what is wrong with you? How could you do that?" I asked as soon as no one was in hearing distance. It was certainly not the warmest welcome he had ever received.

"I needed the money. What do you think?" he said and his face turned sour.

"What will you do next? Sell your body, too?" I added sarcastically.

"It wouldn't be the first time," he said, without shame. At that moment, I wanted to bury my head in the pillow and scream until I passed out. How had I not seen the truth that was right there in front of me?

"I guess there is a lot about you that I don't know."

"You seem to forget that we are not together anymore. This is my life, not yours, and I don't have to explain myself to you."

"Yeah, Tory, just do whatever you want. That's what you do best," I replied in malice and turned my face from his view. I was grateful it had never happened while we were together. Or had it?

"I wish I could do what you want. I don't know where I'm going with my life and now I'm about to become a father. I feel trapped and it's not your fault. I'm not trying to blame you. I planned this too, because I thought I wanted to be a Dad, but I'm not ready yet."

What a blow! My chest felt like a hot air balloon was stuck in my windpipe. Well, that's just great. A fine time for Tory to come out with it. What am I supposed to do? Wait for Peter Pan? What would happen in the days, months, and years ahead? I wondered.

Just then, Mom entered the room with a handful of daisies.

"I should let you rest. Big day tomorrow so I will go catch up on some sleep too." Tory yawned and I thought he was faking so he could go party somewhere. His talk was cheap so I didn't believe a word he said. He chatted a bit with Mom and they were super excited about the baby's coming arrival. It was only hours away and yet I already knew Tory would not be there.

"Sweet dreams." Tory leaned over the bed, kissed my lips, and hugged Mom on his way out. "How are things between you two?" Mom frowned as the night nurse came in and did her rounds.

"Not good." I said. I waited until the nurse was gone and then I told Mom about everything that had happened the night before. She was baffled. I knew it hurt her to hear it.

79: Dr. Lees and Holly

Early the next morning, I was strapped into the heart monitor and prepped for an IV drip to induce my labour. My friend Lori dropped by for a visit and she gave me a beauty makeover right there. Even when I was in labour, she was making sure that I didn't miss out. She gave me the latest tips on how to make my skin glow. But I wasn't the least bit interested. Lori was so nice to everyone. She respected boundaries. She didn't spin webs about her friends and she was always supportive. I just wished that Tory could have tried to make an effort. He was so unsupportive I could cry. In fact, I was feeling pretty sad, so I told Lori that I needed to be alone. She seemed a little disheartened, but she stuffed her beauty products in her sack and was gone.

"Why do you look so sad?" Dr. Lees had slipped in and took my hand in his.

"Can you fix a bleeding heart?" I wanted to ask him but I didn't. That's it! I refused to be sad another second. Even if I was alone with no one to share in the victory, I was going to be celebrating.

Okay, not right away. I still had to get past the pain. Oh, why didn't I get a C-section like the girl down the hall? She slept through the whole birth. Every vice-gripping contraction made me more jealous. Whoever said that having a baby was the most painful thing to endure was so right! "Ouch!" doesn't cut it. Back pain, hot flashes, and cold sweats made my legs feel rubbery. A few times, I had to throw up, so I was exhausted. My mouth was about as dry as a Texas desert so when I tried to deep breathe I was sucking dead air and coughing. I told myself to concentrate. Go slower. Okay, baby, let's get this over with!

"When do I get an epidermal?" I asked and the nurses laughed.

"You mean an epidural?"

"Yes, please." Well, I asked for it and I got it. That little needle poke took me on a trip. Wow! Suddenly I was sailing on a yacht in paradise and all I wanted to do was go "bon voyage." Just let me dream. I was passing out between cramps. My waters broke and bam ... the contractions were a minute apart.

"Okay, I want you to push. Push! Push! Push!" The voices were swirling around my head. I squeezed my face real tight and push down so hard that I was sure the baby was going to fly out and hit someone.

"Again! One more. You can do it," my doctor praised from the opposite end of the delivery table. What...? I can't believe the baby's still in there. By that time the room contained an entourage of interns and nurses, and I didn't care if the entire medical staff came in.

"Good job. Look! You have a baby girl." My Doctor held up a baby with wet, curled-up legs and I was utterly bewildered by it all. My hormones were deranged.

"It's a girl. I have a baby girl! No, I don't believe you," I squealed in delight. I knew I sounded ridiculous.

"She must be yours, because she's is still attached. We haven't cut the cord yet," the doctor laughed. I held out my arms. I was deliriously happy and all I wanted was to hold her for the first time. For nine months, I had been secretly hoping for a girl, but I was so sure that I was carrying a boy.

The nurses swaddled my baby in a towel and placed her in my waiting arms. Before I changed my mind, I named her Holly, because I always knew it would be my favourite choice for my first-born girl. But the name really should have been Angel. Her eyes shone like jewels and I couldn't help but cry. She was so perfect. So beautiful! I knew my family would be so proud.

My brother Josh was an uncle. Hopefully I would find him soon so he could see his niece. He should be here and part of the excitement. He was a man now and wouldn't need his father's approval. As I looked at my first-born child, I thought of Mom and I knew I had to find her son.

80: Tory and Holly

The next morning, the nurse came by with a tray of sloppy eggs and some other mushy stuff. It was pretty blah, but I was famished so I stuffed it down. A few sharp bursts of pain let me know that I qualified to produce milk for Holly. I wanted to breastfeed her, but it didn't come easily. She fussed and the nurse came round and tugged at me like I was part of a dairy farm. Eventually, we got it under control, but the nurse had already fed her a bottle by then. Whenever I put Holly in the crib, I took her back out. I wanted to hold her forever. I couldn't close my eyes, because I might have missed a second of looking at her.

Just as I expected, Tory was back. His face lit up and I saw a sparkle in his eyes. He was mesmerized. His eyes welled up and I could not tell if he was happy or scared, but I could see that he wanted to do better for his little princess. He just didn't know how or where to begin. Truthfully, there would have to be a lot of big changes if he wanted to make it work. I loved him, but he didn't have much to offer.

"Do you want to hold her?"

"I will try," he said, sounding unsure of himself. I passed the baby to him.

"This is your Daddy," I smiled as Tory held her like a china doll. He looked uncomfortable with a baby in the fold of his arms, but after a while, I saw his confidence grow. He paced the room and stopped at the window.

"This is your world, Honey." He looked into Holly's cupid face and promised to try and make a better planet for her. Tory stayed all day and he was there long after my family had come and gone. Of course, his parents didn't come and I don't think he even mentioned our daughter's birth to Carla.

The nurses were so amazing. I honestly don't know how women can do without them. In the morning, my nurse took the baby to the nursery, so I could have some "me" time. I sauntered down the hall to find the showers, but first I made a quick stop in the bathroom. In the stall next to me, I heard a woman shuffle in and shut the door. Within seconds, she was sobbing hysterically and it was terrifying.

Not wanting to embarrass or alarm her, I was in there for a good fifteen minutes. Finally she blew her nose, washed up, and left. As I stayed behind, I was stumped at what could have caused her to be so pitifully distressed. It was eating away at my thoughts when I overheard the nurses talking about a newborn who had died just minutes earlier. The bliss of life had been shattered. Right away my heart was in mourning for her. Back in the nursery, Holly released a muffled sigh and I held her tightly to my chest as I thanked God for every breath that filled her lungs.

I had been in the hospital for almost a month before saying goodbye to the wonderful doctors and staff whom I had come to admire and respect. I could hardly wait to go home; I had to keep my eye on Tory. I caught him more than once doing stupid things like balancing Holly along the length of his arm. He cradled her head in his palm but her body was teetering on the bridge of his forearm like she was on a tight rope.

"You can't do that! That's not how you carry a baby, so stop it! You could drop her so easily."

"Nah... she's strong like her Daddy," Tory boasted as I snatched her away from him. Then, Tory did it again for all his lame friends to see and I was furious. I was so tired of his crap. After all Tory had put me through, I was really on fire when he was yapping that he would never let a boy touch his kid until he broke her in first.

"Over my dead body, Mister!" I yelled and he shut up with all his stupid man talk.

Too late! I made a decision right there that I was going to be a single parent.

I called my Mom and she came with a truck and we moved everything to a bigger house. I suspected Tory would split and I was right. But I was glad, because I didn't care. He was a threat to my child.

81: Showbiz with Holly and Penny

That summer, I took Holly to Alberta so I could show off my sweet pea to friends and family. It was great to spend time with my foster sister Charlene, but I was shocked to learn that her mother Wilma had put in a missing persons report to the police when she heard I had hitchhiked to Winnipeg with Tory. The minute I was in Wilma's presence I was to trying to please her again. It was ludicrous, but I was always forgiving her. It had been torture growing up in Wilma's house and yet I was back. I couldn't shake her off. I could not stay mad at her for all the vicious things that she had done in the past because I was still trying to be that perfect girl. Why was I putty in her hands?   While   I was in Alberta, I saw friends whom I hadn't seen since I lived at Wilma's, like my friend Penny who lived two blocks away. She wasn't a fan of babies, but she was still excited to see Holly and me. As a matter of fact, it went better than I had expected. She called me at Wilma's and asked me to come over.

"Guess what? We are going to be in a movie."

"What?" I stared in disbelief.

"There's a movie set hiring extras so I thought we could go together."

"That's so cool. How did you find out about it?"

"I saw it in the paper. The filming is at the new airport," Penny beamed.

"Wouldn't it be something if we got discovered and became movie stars," I gleamed in excitement.

"Who knows? Anything's possible. We might become rich and famous too," she giggled. Her eyes widened. The next morning, we arrived in casual wear as requested, but we wanted to look the movie part. Holly was going to be there all day with us so I was not sure if I would be allowed to sign up. We decided to "go glam or go home," so we did our hair and put on our best movie-star look for the camera. We really had no idea how sensational it would be. The camera crews were vigorously prepping the scene as Peggy, Holly, and I entered.

The extras were lining up so I pressed my friend to hurry. I wanted to get signed in before we were turned away. We got our contract agreements and rushed right in. It was five minutes to show time, so Penny and I checked each other over just to make sure our hair was perfect. Our eyes met and there was no way to mask that we were both ready to take it by storm.

As we moved along I was drawn to the scene of costumes and props. From every angle, I could see spotlights and endless wire cables for the sound equipment. In the dead centre, there was a director's chair, but I didn't see the stars. The producers were exchanging information with a group of people. I couldn't believe how much time it takes to make a flick.

The tiny one-room airport had been supersized into the city's navigational core. I could hardly recognize it as the same terminal where I had met my mother. The weather was typically hot for August, but Holly didn't seem to mind. She slept through the entire eight hours of taping. As the filming proceeded, we played along. All we had to do was follow the two main actors along the tarmac.

At lunch, the catering mobiles served every kind of cultural dish imaginable. I was starving so I wolfed down a slice of pizza, a steak, and a burger. Most people would think I would pass up the dessert, but I saw three desirable choices, so I took one of each.

During the break, I suggested to Penny that we snoop around and search for the private trailer for the actor Dennis Weaver. There were rows of identical trailers, but the second to last had different lettering on the side.

"This has to be it. Why don't you knock and see if he's there?" Penny urged.

"What if he gets mad? Maybe he's taking a nap."

"Just do it," Penny insisted. I tried to tap, but I was so giddy that I rapped like a woodpecker.

"Who is it?" I heard a grunt from the man inside.

"I don't mean to bother you, but I'm a big fan and I was hoping to get a picture with you," I said nervously. No answer came back so I was about to leave when the door opened. Unbelievable! It was Dennis Weaver in the flesh and blood and I could hardly breathe. He was a movie legend for decades, plus he starred on a regular Western series, Gunsmoke . He wasn't too thrilled, but who could resist such glowing admiration? After a muffled snort, Mr. Weaver stepped down from his trailer and put his arm over my shoulder.

"Get closer," Penny said, as we posed together and she snapped her camera. The Polaroid picture automatically rolled out and the three of us stared at the photo. It was a perfect shot! The background was a bit dark, but my grin stood out like a Cheshire cat. I had Holly bundled in my arms, but Dennis stole the show with his dazzling smile.

Pretty impressive! But then I found out that he wasn't the only star getting attention. The other female extras were lined up in front of the bathroom mirror doing their hair and makeup so they could impress a new icon that I'd never heard of. I had spent half the day following the famous Weaver and hadn't even noticed his talented sidekick, Kurt Russell. I couldn't believe that I didn't know he was a big silver screen actor and I had missed out. Whenever I look back at that photo with Weaver, I can't help but wish that I had gotten a memorable trophy shot of Kurt too.

While I was in Alberta, I went to visit with Gabriella and Howie. They had moved to another ranch near Medicine Hat. When I got out of Charlene's car,

I knew we were at the right place because I saw Howie making his way across the yard to greet us.

"Is that really you?" Howie pretended not to know me.

"It is." I smiled at his teasing. He threw his arms around me and Holly, and it felt so good. It warmed my heart.

"Well, look who's here!" Gabriella said with a smile as she approached from behind. She's so sweet and pleasant that I wondered why I'd ever left.

"Hi Mom," I said as Gabriella glanced from me to the baby and back to me. Suddenly a weird sense of guilt made me wish that I had been the good girl they had tried to teach me to be. I always wanted to be in Gabriella's good graces. I was trying to find a place where I belonged and now I belonged to Holly.

"Let me have a look at my beautiful grandchild."

Holly was getting fussy, but that was okay, because Gabriella was an old pro with babies. I turned to Charlene and we hugged. I didn't know when I would see her beautiful face again, so I told her I loved her. After Charlene drove away, we went into the farmhouse for supper. I had missed the "good ole days" on the ranch, and Gabriella's home-cooked meal was still as wonderful as ever. So many things were different now they were living in Medicine Hat, and it didn't feel like home to me. A couple of days into my visit, I suggested I go back to town, but that was out of the question. There was a lot to catch up on, so I stayed for another two days.

All good things must come to an end. It was time to go back to Vancouver where I had a big awakening to the reality of single parenting. It was often lonely and I couldn't afford to go anywhere because I had to budget my living expenses down to the penny. It was tough, and sometimes I felt like a total failure, especially when Holly wailed in fits. At times, it was a difficult challenge when nothing I did seemed to work. But then, Holly would become submissive to my soothing words and settle into my cradling arms. I would drift off to sleep with her little body next to mine. She was my angel, my light of hope.

82: Mike, Don, and Tim

In the fall, I didn't see Holly for days. Louis had gotten married and his new wife Eva loved babies. She wanted to take Holly. At first it was great, but after a few days I missed my baby. I was disappointed and angry with myself, but I couldn't turn down the offer for a much-needed break. It made me so excited to know she would soon be home and I couldn't wait for when she returned.

In the meantime, my neighbours upstairs were having an open house and I was invited. Mike, Don, and Tim were hosting their party on a Friday and Holly wasn't due to return until Sunday.

The guys asked me to help and I told them I could. I put together some appetizers and spiked the punch bowl with a little fizz. Then I rifled through a stack of records and picked the best party hits for the night. I was not a social drinker but I nursed two beers until the party got going, and they made me loopy. Tim suggested that instead of missing out on the party, I take a short nap in a back room until the guests arrived.

I was out like a light, but not for long. It was pitch black when I was awakened by the sounds of smashing glass and blood-curdling screams. My head was trying to get out of a dream. Suddenly, the bedroom door was pushed open and the hallway light blinded me. It took a blink or two for my eyes to adjust to a backlit silhouette. Although I was still coming out of my drowsiness, I could tell there was a man standing in the door without moving. Both his arms dangled at his sides, but his left arm looked almost a foot longer than the right. Then he shifted just enough so I could tell that he was black and his left arm wasn't longer; he was holding something.

The light caught a glint of something silver. To my horror, I could see the reflective edge of a knife. When I saw the glistening point on the end, I was so scared I couldn't move. The man stared at me with death-craving eyes and I realized I had no way of getting out of the room without being attacked.

"Please… somebody help me," I tried to scream, but my voice came out as a whimper.

He was coming in to rape or kill me and I had no way to fight him off. I didn't know what to do.

"Don't you come anywhere near me. Go away!" I screamed, but with such an uproar, who would hear me?

Mike? I saw Mike! One of my hosts! He was in the doorway.

"She is not hurting anyone," Mike said. He told the man to go away and leave me alone. The man pointed the weapon at Mike's belly and I gasped.

"Stop it," I screamed. I was at the peak of hysteria.

"We don't want any trouble. It's a party. We're supposed to be having a good time." Mike spoke really softly, like he was calming a baby. He was so brave. The man released his grip and the butcher knife clattered to the floor. Mike booted the knife and it disappeared from sight. The man didn't stick around for a beating.

Outside the room there was mass destruction. The scene was changing from one second to the next. It looked like a prison riot. Everywhere I looked, I saw bodies lying on the blood-soaked floor. Smeared walls and shards of glass were everywhere. Cupboard doors hung off their hinges. Over in the corner, Tim was huddled in the fetal position and babbling nonsense like a patient in a psych ward. Clearly, his nose was broken and he was cradling a fractured arm.

It turned out that a gang of bikers from organized crime had targeted the party for the stereo. All they had to do was kick the door in and make a grab.

When Mike tried to stop the bikers, they threw him down the stairs, knocking him unconscious. One by one, the leather-clad bikers paraded shamelessly out of the house, taking anything of value. It was frightening to look down and see Mike lying on the landing. As each gang member passed by, they kicked him senseless with their Dayton boots. I was screaming at them to stop when a redheaded biker kid jumped on Don's back and got him in a headlock. Even in a headlock, Don was whacking the biker in the face.

The scrawny little biker kid didn't have a prayer, so he bit down on Don's ear and ripped it off. Don's a big man and he could have pummeled that kid so easily, but he was too shocked to react. Blood was running down his neck and staining his shirt. Don just stood there, speechless, in a trance, while his attacker bolted for the door. I was scared to death, but I managed to run to the window.

The streetlight shone on some of the bastards throwing bottles and running into the alley. When they got to the end of the street, they hopped on their hogs and gunned it. They were hooting and shouting as they did burnouts like they were on a drag strip. It was so hellacious that I was certain the whole neighbourhood would freak out, but at least the bikers were gone.

I heard sirens wailing and in a matter of minutes. The house was occupied with all the good guys. The paramedics quickly went to work. Then the police came in and looked around like they had seen this before. I watched them move from room to room. Their boots were making fresh tracks in the blood.

The worst part of it all was the police ruled out that there was anything they could do. Home invasions had been an on-going problem for most of the year. It was madness that the losers could get away with nearly killing people over a stereo system. Thank God that Holly was still away; I would have been terrified if the bikers had broken into my place.

83: Holly, Tiana, and Jonathon

The best I could do was move away from the crumbling neighbourhood. It took no time at all to find another house, but it wasn't cheap. So I checked out the newspaper want ads and found the perfect roomie. No more riff-raff, no violence, because I got the best life ever. My roomie Tiana was a single mother of her three-year-old son, Jonathon.

Overall, it was better financially for both of us. We could save a few bucks and have classy parties without the biker bandits. We could throw on some paint and in no time our place would be fit for the Queen... well, maybe the band members of Queen.

In our case, two young moms in the same kitchen was a recipe for disaster. We both had our own way of doing things. Six months later, our fun ideas had soured to an unsalvageable end. I should have got out right then, but I hung in for another month and the conflicts turned into a hand-to-hand war zone.

One morning, I had put Holly in her walker so she could push her legs to get around. At the time, baby walkers were not stationary so she was scooting around the main floor with nothing to stop her. She rode that thing like she was in a bumper car at the town fair. She would jet from one end of the house to the other and keep right on going. It's a good thing I kept my eye on her, because she zoomed after anything that caught her interest.

One time as she sped around the kitchen corner, I had a forewarning that something bad was about to happen, so I went after her. As I came around the bend, I was horrified! Tiana had made fries earlier and had left the cord from the electric frying pan dangling over the side of the counter. There was Holly with her little hand reaching to grab it. Another second would have been the death of my child. If the electric fryer hadn't killed her, the oil would have done so for sure.

Honestly, I wanted to put the gloves on and cream that woman. As it turned out, Tiana had left the house, so by the time she came back, I had calmed down even though I was at the end of my rope. I didn't say anything until she started razzing her son. I asked her not to yell, as Holly had just gone down for a nap. Tiana was in a foul mood so she went off and slammed her door so hard that Holly was shaken out of her sleep anyway; she cried hysterically. Well, that blew the roof off and we were in an all-out war, as both of us were screaming at each other. Tiana was shouting from her room, so I went and slammed her door and the knob fell off.

Well, she couldn't get out until I was ready to put the knob back in. Hah! I took my dear sweet time and let her stew in her own juice until she calmed down. As soon as she was quiet, I put the knob back in. Then I walked to the bathroom so I could plug in the curling iron. As I began to roll my hair, Tiana quietly opened the door and snuck behind me with her fist raised high. Luckily for me, I saw her in the mirror. I swung around and smacked her over the head with the curling iron. She was screaming mad, but I threatened to hit her again if she came anywhere near me.

84: Holly, Lori, and Drew

Holly didn't deserve to live in the House of Armageddon, so I gave my notice and moved into Lori's apartment in Burnaby. Originally, it was Lori's idea and I liked it, because we had had a wonderful friendship from day one. In no time,

Lori had become like a surrogate mother to Holly. There were no arguments or bad tempers, and she didn't care if a screaming toddler dropped food on the floor.

Holly's little toothless grin brought me to a total different meaning of the word "love." When she laughed, I laughed, but when she cried, it shattered me. Holly was a bit of a mischief-maker, but I didn't mind because she was so cute.

My new boyfriend Drew didn't find her amusing though; he would stare at Holly with indifference. In the beginning, I didn't let it bother me but then I noticed he was just putting up with Holly because of me. Okay, so he wasn't doing the jig every time he saw Holly, but did he have to stare at her like she was an alien? I didn't want to pressure Drew because I thought he might come around to liking her on his own. But six months later, he was completely unresponsive.

When Christmas came, Drew told me that he was going to pop the question soon. During the holidays, we were inseparable and we shared some warm and fuzzy feelings, but I didn't carry a torch for him. Ring or not, love was not flowing through my veins. Our relationship was so random and flat. I was looking for Mr. True Love not Dr. Feel Good. I was really burned when Drew said he would like to adopt a needy child after we got married. Really? Drew could barely look at Holly unless he was annoyed with her. What the heck did he mean?

Drew's the guy who always had a bag of weed. Although we went to many parties, it was boring to be with Drew, because he was tuned out on rock music and off in space. It was annoying when he heckled me in front of our friends if I didn't smoke. In the beginning, I gave in, but the more I "used," the more paranoid I became. Pot totally clashed with my personality. Plus, I hated waiting for the never-ending results to wear off. More importantly, I didn't want to be a parent with an addiction. It was so much harder to be jovial and happy after the short-term effects wore off.

When I was using pot, I had horrific nightmares. It was chilling to the bone to wake up screaming; I often dreamed that someone I loved had drowned in a tub. The next dream would be of someone falling off a cliff and dying. It got to the point that I was afraid to go to sleep, because every dream was about a friend or a family member who was killed or murdered. Then one night, I had the most horrible dream a mother could ever have. In the nightmare, I was strangling my baby with my own hands. I woke up terrified and in tears. The next day I called my Dad and he suggested I do a little research on dreams at the library.

85: Holly, Lori, and Russell

Lori took care of Holly so that I could hitch a ride to the local library. While waiting on the curb with my thumb out, a sporty little hatchback shouldered up to the sidewalk and stopped.

"Hi. I'm going to the library. It's about a mile up the road. Are you going that far?" I asked.

"I'm going right past it, so I can take you to the front entrance." The driver smiled as I went around to the other side. "My name is Russell. What's yours?" he persisted lightly.

"Eugenea," I said with resolution, but he didn't seem to notice. Over the short drive, we talked like we had known each other for years and I couldn't help but feel a warm glow inside. I tried to suppress any obvious signs of interest, but his eyes filled with approval whenever he looked at me. As the car approached the library, I was oddly disappointed that I was at my destination already. I felt reluctant to get out and it was so weird to feel that way. I knew that Drew and I had never sparked that kind of energy.

"Goodbye. Thanks for the ride."

"Maybe we will meet again some day. I enjoyed talking to you." He swiveled around to look closer at me and I felt the pinging excitement of an undeniable chemistry between us.

The library was deader than ever, so I ventured about freely. I sat down with a pile of books, but it was hard to focus on the reading material and not think of Russell's insatiable smile. As I read over the pages, I found that both my dreams had the same meaning: I was doing things with my life that did not make me happy. It was a sore reality check, so I went home and meditated on the matter. I had lied repeatedly to the woman in the mirror and thus I was denying my own soul its search for truth. I accepted that my subconscious had not yet learned to deal with the past, so I promised to give up the self-medicating and get into reality.

The death dreams ended. I could sleep without waking up in a total panic. I still had weird dreams of my body spinning out of control. In the dream, I tried to grab the walls or anything that could stop me but nothing was reachable. I knew the spinning symbolized the years of revolving doors of moving from one foster home to the next.

The second dream was more frequent. It always began with a house that I didn't recognize even though I felt I had been there before. I would enter from the front door to find a staircase that went on and on coming out of the ceiling but never reaching the bottom. There was also a long hallway that twisted into a labyrinth, which I would follow along until I was lost. On occasion, I would find an exit, but I could never leave where I had entered. Both dreams had a similar message: my problems were not over. I was still searching for balance and security in my life.

A month went by and I had already noticed Russell in my neighbourhood again, but he didn't see me. I was looking out of my window and nearly fell over when his car pulled up to the front of my apartment. My heart felt like it was popping out of my chest as Russell got out and walked to an adjoining complex.

"Lori, come here. Quick," I shouted. "Look, that's the guy I told you about. That's the man who gave me a ride to the library."

She followed my eyes and came around to get a closer look. "Ask him if he's got an older brother." Lori smiled at her own rebuttal as her brow gave an impressive lift.

As luck would have it, I practically ran into Russell a week later and of course I looked ridiculous. I was walking along the path from the apartment laundry room carrying a basket of clothes with Holly plopped on top. Her little head of tussled curls was blocking my view. By the time I spotted Russell, it was too late to find a bush and hide.

"Hello! What a surprise to see you! I guess you live here. Is this your little girl?" He stopped dead in front of me and I wished that I hadn't worn my ugly, round-about-the-house pants.

"Uh… yes, to both," I said, feeling the weight in my arms and wondering if he would cringe at the sight of my unruly hair and naked eyes.

"Here. Let me help." He picked up Holly and she went straight into his arms. What a traitor, I couldn't believe that she too was swooned by his grace. We walked up two flights of stairs trying to carry on a conversation, but I couldn't get my tongue unglued. In front of my apartment, my fingers fumbled as I twisted the key in the lock. Still holding Holly, Russell pushed the door open and gestured for me to pass.

"Thank you so much. That was so nice of you to stop and help," I said. I put the laundry down and took Holly out of his arms.

"Oh. No problem. Just happy to help," he said without looking rushed and for a split second I wondered if he had a motive. "So this is where you live."

"What about you? Do you live close by?"

"No. I came to see my friend and he's waiting, so I should probably go now," he said, as though he had pegged my thoughts. "What is your daughter's name?"

"Holly," I said.

"She looks like you," Russell said as I pulled Holly to my side. He looked me in the eye and I blushed.

"It was so nice to see you again."

"You, too." I couldn't look at him too long without blushing again. Then we said our goodbyes and he was gone, but I couldn't wait to see him again.

86: Holly, Russell, Steve and Annette

Whether I was heading off to work or going out for an evening, I often found myself running into Russell. His best friend Steve lived in the building next to mine, so it was no surprise. One evening, Steve came by my apartment to invite me to meet his wife Annette. Obviously, I knew that Russell would be there, so the situation was very appealing.

What a night! I really didn't know what to make of it. Most of the evening, I sat on the sofa alone. Russell couldn't bring himself to talk, so he sat on the carpet and focused his attention on Steve's pile of records. It felt like a blind date set up without a plan; it was awkward. Our first-time interaction was a flop. By the end of the evening, I didn't think we would be a good fit.

"I'm sorry about tonight," Russell said as we walked back to my apartment and he explained that he had just been through a breakup. "Why don't we go to a nice lounge and talk over wine and music?" he suggested as we shuffled along the pathway toward my apartment. "It will just be the two of us."

"Okay." I felt a little ruffled that he would ask me out, but I thought I should at least give it another go. It wasn't like there were a lot of life-enhancing improvements coming from my relationship with Drew. So the next night Russell and I went to a lounge and sat in a cozy corner where we could talk. He had grown up on the coast with his mother and sisters. He worked as a glazier. He was not into hobbies or sports at the time.

It was so nice to sit across from each other and have an adult conversation. Under the candle light, we glowed with exuberance and the added sensation of wine stirred our desires to be a little flirtatious. The radiance of our mood was irrepressible. We hit it off so well that I knew we belonged together.

In a matter of days Russell and I embodied an irresistible bliss-like love. I knew that one day, he would be the father of our children. He was the man who would love my baby girl. Not just with words, but with actions. It came so naturally for Russell to protect Holly. It was as though he had been there since she was born. I watched a chain of events as a father and daughter bond began to grow. My baby had become his baby too. Together, we read her stories and tucked her into bed, and we held her tight when she had a bad dream or when she was afraid of the bogeyman.

Right from the beginning of our relationship, Russell insisted that he chauffeur me to work so I wouldn't hitch.

"Promise me that you will never hitch again," he chimed over and over until I finally caved in.

"Okay, I promise. But if I get in a bind, then what?"

"Call me and I'll come and get you."

"Okay, that's great," I said, but a few weeks later, I was in a bind when I had missed my bus. It had been a rough day at work as I had not made my leather-wear sales quota and I was already an hour late to pick up Holly from the sitter.

As I searched for a pay phone to call Russell, the rain came down hard and heavy. I had forgotten to bring my umbrella. Water was pooling with every step and I knew I would be a soppy rag before the next bus arrived. Everywhere I looked, people kept dry in the dome of their umbrellas. I had to get out of the rain. I hated to break a promise to Russell, but in my frustration, I wondered what I should do. I decided it was better that I get home to my child and I hitched.

"Get in," the man behind the wheel yelled out the window. It was easy pick-ings. The driver showed no inclinations of any bad intentions. He simply saw the conditions and pulled over to help a dame in distress. I couldn't wait to get out of the rain, but I had barely shut the door when the driver decided to put on a show. As I was trying to buckle my seatbelt, he floored the accelerator pedal and caused me to slam against the seat. Then, he sped into the traffic like a daredevil.

"Watch out!" I screamed at the driver as he weaved in and out like he was playing chicken. The tires were screeching and other motorists were blasting their horns as he cut them off. For a second, I thought he had forgotten that I was in the seat next to him. But then he whipped around to look me in the eye. His wicked stare told me that I would not survive. I knew that if I got out in one piece, I would never again ride with a stranger.

For some bizarre reason, he howled in laughter like some wacko and I nearly jumped out of the seat. No doubt, he wanted to terrorize me so I tried to remain calm, which was impossible when he jammed his foot on the brake and hurled me into the dashboard. His laugh increased as I scrambled to get my bearings. All the while, we were approaching a large double-lane bridge.

"Let me out," I screamed at the lunatic as he swung so close to the rails that I could see right over the bridge. The black water below swirled with fury. One thing was for sure: I wasn't going to die on that bridge.

Suddenly, the driver slammed his vehicle to a stop and I was tossed like a salad.

"Get out!" he screamed in my face.

I don't know how I managed to get out so fast, but I would have crawled out on my kneecaps if I had had to. Seconds later, I was in the middle of the bridge drenched to the skin and trying to run in stilettos. Those shoes would be the death of me.

I stumbled forward and almost hit the concrete. The ground was rushing up at me, but I was damned if I was going to let myself fall. As the driver sped away, I ran through the rain like a fugitive. The whole time I kept thinking of Holly and how I could have been killed.

I got across the bridge and found a pay phone to call a cab. Regardless of the inconvenience, I vowed to my own heart that I would never hitch again. I was tearfully happy to reach the sitter so I could kiss and hold my tired baby. I carried Holly home and put her to bed, but I never told Russell. I was just too ashamed.

87: Russell, Holly, and Lance

After two months, Russell had become a familiar figure in Holly's life, so he was part of my family package. We were always together, so he asked me to move in with him. The apartment was in his mother's name, so she had the first say in most situations. As the days turned into weeks and the weeks turned to months, I felt isolated from friends. Russell was a great guy, but he could be a hothead. He never seemed to need a break from us and I couldn't quite understand that. But despite all my misgivings, Russell loved Holly and that made me love him more.

In the fall, I was pregnant, so Russell was about to become a family man in every sense of the word. We talked about our options and I told him that abortion was not something I would ever consider. Even though we were in love, neither of us wanted to rush into a wedding. However, I secretly hoped that he would ask me. Even so, a day or two before Christmas Eve, Russell told me that I was getting a ring. He just couldn't wait to show me and I thought I might pass out.

Deep breath! Deep breath!

I stared in shock. Inside a small heart-shaped box was a cluster of flickering diamonds. Right in the centre of the crest was a fiery red gemstone.

"Oh, it's so beautiful." I threw my arms around his neck and pulled him into a kiss.

We decided to keep it a secret until Christmas Eve. We had our first turkey dinner and Russell's family was all around. They got teary eyed when they saw the ring on my finger. Russell's mom and sisters spoiled Holly rotten. But the best gift was the love they gave my sweet little Holly. She had two doting new aunties and Russell's mom was a wonderful grandmother. But Holly made a gift that was more precious than any trinket or tie. She re-named Russell to "Daddy."

In the spring, we rented a third-floor suite and set up a nursery in Holly's room. Shortly after the move, Russell was laid off from work and that was hard on us. The baby didn't come on the due date. As a matter of fact, the baby had no plans of coming out for another sixteen days. That's an extra half a month of wearing the ugly, stretchy, pregnancy panel jeans and not being able to see my feet.

This baby was up to no good. Then, just like that, the baby was pushing to get out and the contractions were merciless. Immediately, I had to call Russell's sister to take Holly, and then we had to rush for the hospital. Nothing out of the ordinary here… except we hit a snowstorm on the way! I was truly shocked.

Russell promised to get us there in time. The wipers were swishing on high-speed because he could barely see the road. The blizzard never let up but we made it to the hospital. I was wheeled into delivery, but by then I was so exhausted I didn't want to be there for the duration. By midnight, I just wanted to sleep.

Shortly after 1:00 a.m., I held my little boy. I looked into his starry-blue eyes and glowed with love. My sweet baby Lance was born the same month and day as his Uncle Josh. I kissed my son and wondered if Josh would ever know that he had a nephew born twenty-five years to the day after him. Three weeks later, Steve and Annette had a baby girl and they called her Christina.

By the time Lance was four months old, Russell and I decided to make it official and get married. We couldn't afford a big gala; it was even quite a stretch for us to afford a simple wedding. I didn't have enough money for a real wedding dress, so I bought a grad dress instead.

Two days before the big day, my fiancé and I got into a tiff. It was a harmless disagreement and I thought nothing of it until he seized my wrist. Before I could pull away, Russell swung me to the couch and I landed hard on the sofa. I was completely stunned by his roughness even though I wasn't physically hurt.

"Screw you!" I jumped up and snapped at him. I couldn't believe my husband-to-be had just manhandled me. "I don't want to marry you."

"You can't be serious. You don't think I was actually trying to hurt you?" Russell had suddenly changed his tune from angry to defensive.

"You will have to call everyone and cancel, because I'm not marrying you," I spit out bravely. Russell reminded me that the wedding was in two days and his mother had already paid for it.

He apologized for his behaviour and two days later we married. Of course, it crossed my mind that he might manhandle me again and I could be making the biggest mistake of my life, but I wanted to believe him. I didn't want this to be a shotgun wedding like my parents' wedding had been; it felt wrong and right at the same time. Love is so blind.

The next day, the elders in my Mormon church baptized Russell, Steve, and

Annette. None of us had been churchgoers since our teens, but we all believed in the same God. For a while, there was this kind of sweet bliss as we juggled with the wedding, baptisms, and the newborns. But baby Christina was showing signs that something was wrong. She cried a lot and there were visible indications that she was not gaining weight so Annette and Steve took her to the doctor.

Although Christina was still an infant, she had to go in for heart surgery. It was a lengthy operation, creating insufferable waiting for everyone. We were so relieved when she was moved into recovery. But a few hours later, it seemed to go terribly wrong as Christina had unexpected bleeding and complications. As a result, the infant girl never recovered. Even though it was an unbearable situation, Annette and I had each other's backs and our friendship grew stronger by the day.

88: Russell, Holly and Lance, Nadia and Shawn

When I started my first job after Holly was born—selling leatherwear—I had to find a babysitter. Like most mothers, I was as scared as hell to trust anyone with my baby. Social services referred Nadia, but I had to test her out before I was confident that she would be okay. Although Nadia was married and had a baby son, her husband wasn't around much, so she had learned to manage on her own. Nadia was a gem; I was really lucky to find such a great sitter. She treated Holly like a daughter and I quickly knew that I could trust her with anything. Nadia was just a year older than me so we had a lot in common. She was fun and I liked her outgoing enthusiasm.

When things became a bit rough between Russell and me, I would sometimes show up unannounced at Nadia's place with my eyes red. She didn't pry, even though it was obvious that Russell and I were fighting. She offered to let me sleep on her couch any time. I never accepted her offer, but it was a comfort to know I could.

Nadia and I would alternate with babysitting and it worked out well because we had the same rules, such as no leaving the table until the food was gone. Sometimes though, this kind of thing backfires, like the time I insisted that her son Shawn finish his soup before he could play. Holly and Lance were done, so Shawn sat alone with his bowl. He stared at the soup with a kind of disgust but he grudgingly got to the end and slid down from the table.

As he went off to play, I picked up his bowl and turned around to see soup jetting across the hallway. Honestly, it was worse than an exorcism. Shawn was spewing a stream of puke like a fire hose. If I had not witnessed that scene with my own eyes, I wouldn't have believed it. I was up to my wrists scrubbing vomit out of the carpet as fumes wafted to my nose. There I was, hunched over on sore knees, looking like I was finger-painting soup into the rug. Long after the cleaning rags were rinsed and dried, I could still see a chalky yellow stain shaped like the map of Cuba. I was mad at myself for not having learned to be more flexible.

So, maybe babysitting wasn't the most fabulous profession, but I was blessed with other as-yet-undiscovered talents. As a parent, I wanted so much to give our kids a great Christmas, but I didn't have two cents to my name. Russell was still out of work so I got this crazy idea that I should make gifts for everyone. I borrowed a sewing machine and went to work on doll clothes and pillows and anything that would be a remarkable gift.

At first, there were lots of crooked stitching and imperfections because I didn't know how to sew. But I figured it out. For weeks, I was pinching pennies and sewing up a storm so I could get my projects finished for the big night. On Christmas Eve, I worried that my homemade presents would not be appreciated. But on Christmas Day, my kids were jumping around and having a ball, so I knew theirs were a success. Then I worried what the adults thought of my frilly heart-shaped pillows, until I got a really nice thank you call from my sister-in-law. She told me that no one had ever made her a present before and I could hear her crying. It got me thinking that I should make more things. I dove right in and started making all kinds of stuff. A couple of months later, I was building a clientele for women's and children's clothes.

It was a busy time with sewing and family but it was also a sad time. My sister Chloe had a baby boy and she was too young to give him the care he needed. When the baby turned two, social services took him away and his father's grandparents adopted him. Chloe was never the same after that. I had lost my nephew and Mom had lost her grandchild. It was devastating.

89: Two Families Side by Side

With my growing talent in sewing and the kids getting bigger, Russell and I decided to move. Steve and Annette were moving to a duplex and the suite next to theirs was empty, so we took it. It was an ideal situation for all of us because we wanted our families to grow up together.

Our husbands had been best friends for years, so that was great, but they both had a terrible spending habit that seemed to fuel the need for computer-like gadgets. Basically, we couldn't afford to spend that kind of coin without it compromising our bank account. Before I could put a plan into action, our credit line was maxed out. And there was no magic wand to make our skyrocketing debts disappear.

On top of all that, we had no caller display back then, so the creditors were calling and they were down our throats for payments. I was on pins and needles. I loved my husband, but it was terrible when he got carried away with his big-boy toys. I could live with the problem, but I couldn't stand his rough side. On occasion when he didn't agree with something I said, he would turn into a bully.

I didn't obsess about it, because he always apologized and gave me the same old singsong that he would never do it again. One night after the kids had gone to bed, we had the worst fight of our marriage. Before I could run out the door, I got a blow to the stomach. I slid down the wall and cried so hard that my kids woke up. Russell was so upset that he grabbed a kitchen knife and dropped to his knees. He pointed the knife to his stomach and threatened to harm himself. Holly and Lance were crying and pleading for him to stop. How had it escalated to this?

I knew the man I married wanted so badly to be a good husband and father. I loved him and he loved me. So why couldn't we get it right? Russell was torn down emotionally. He was so upset that he went outside in his robe and sat on the swing like he was in mourning. I kept looking out the back-door window to see if he was okay. Long after the house was calm, Russell came in, but we didn't talk about it.

I kept wondering how to prevent such abuse from happening again. I was really lost and so was Russell. We couldn't be together another day without some kind of intervention. I called my sister Sheila and asked for her help. She came right away, I wrote a letter for Russell, and she took me and the children to my friend's farm outside Langley. I knew that Russell would have found my letter and would be worried out of his mind if I didn't call. It was very hard to wait it out yet I didn't want him to panic. I called three days later and he asked me to meet him. At first, I refused, but he kept asking so I agreed on the condition that it was in a public place without the kids. I didn't want Holly and Lance to be in the middle of adult issues, especially if Russell was going through any anger.

My husband and I cried when we came together. Three days was an eternity for both of us. He was truly sorry about the way things had gotten so out of control and he promised that if I returned, he would be a changed man. He had my sympathies before I had any time to think it over. He wanted to work it out and so did I. I wanted to go to marriage counselling, but Russell really felt we didn't need to.

It was so easy to brush marital difficulties under the carpet and hope they will magically dissolve and never rear their ugly heads again. It was so easy to get caught up in the moment and never resolve the underlying issues. A third-party listener with the professional training could have helped our marriage. It wasn't about hanging out our dirty laundry; it was the dirty laundry that's holding back the progression.

Russell suggested we try for another baby. Well, those words were the trigger for me to run right home with him. I didn't realize it at the time, but that is an easy mistake with adults who have been in foster care. Speaking personally, I knew the desperation of wanting a family I could call my own. I don't regret having any of my children, but most adults who were raised in care end up with their children in care as well, because they have many painful issues to work on that they do not address while they're growing up or in their adult lives.

90: Our Babies

Our first breakup was over; Russell and I were pretty lovey-dovey. Two months later, I was glowing with elation that I was pregnant and Annette was pregnant too. We planned it together so our babies would be born at the same time. In the coming months, Russell and I had our fair share of problems, but he was a better husband and no matter how upset he got, he never hit or hurt anyone.

In the last month of our pregnancies, Annette and I couldn't see down to our feet or tie our own shoes. Our beach-ball tummies forced us to waddle like ducks. Regardless of the swelling ankles and mood swings, I loved how we shared a kind of euphoric sisterhood. I could see that our husbands were living in a similar bliss as they assembled cribs and painted the baby rooms.

Our nursery was completely finished but our little bundle of joy wasn't ready. Again, it was obvious that baby number three would be late like its older siblings.

On a Sunday afternoon, we were eating dinner with our friends, Sheldon and Kathy, and their two little boys. After, as we chatted in the living room, I had the odd contraction. I wasn't alarmed until they jumped to one every minute. Russell grabbed the phone and immediately called his sister to look after the kids. Luckily for us, she was home and able to save us some time by meeting us at the hospital. From there, she could take the kids back to her place. Russell loaded the car and we were out of there, but it wasn't quick enough. I felt a burst like a bubble popping.

"Oh no! We have to stop the car; my water just broke," I yelled as fluid gushed out and soaked my pants. Sheldon and Kathy had followed behind our vehicle and pulled up behind us. I felt embarrassed when I saw Sheldon get out of his car and run over.

"What's wrong?" Sheldon asked as Russell pushed the automatic button and rolled the window down.

"Eugenea's water broke and the seat is all wet." Russell's voice came out a bit ruffled and that's all it took to bring on my tears. "Sweetheart, what's wrong?" Russell looked more flustered than ever.

"Your car! I have ruined your car!" I blubbered as Sheldon ran back to his vehicle.

"Don't worry, it's just a stupid car. I'll clean it later. Besides, it doesn't matter. That baby wants out, so we'd better get you to the hospital," Russell teased and we hugged. Poor Sheldon had taken my tears much too seriously. He came round to my side of the car and yanked the door open.

"Don't move. Let me help you," Sheldon said and I saw that he had come back with a towel. I tried to assure him that I was okay but he was determined to help. He busily stuffed the towel between my legs and around my belly, as though to stop the baby from coming out.

"What are you doing?" I asked, staring incredulously at him. As he considered my question, he mulled over it just long enough to realize how funny it must have looked. That's when he stopped and we all pealed with laughter. The kids sat in the back looking scared, so we got back on the road.

"Hang in there, Honey. We're almost there." Russell said as he rubbed my hand. Contractions were now every thirty seconds and the pain was off the Richter scale. We actually made it to the hospital without having to make a delivery pit stop. Again, Sheldon leaped from his vehicle and ran off in all directions in search of a wheelchair and I couldn't believe how funny he looked.

I had barely got in the wheelchair when I was whisked away with a fan club of family behind me. I had no clue who was pushing the chair as the wheels glided through the automatic doors. Russell's sister had already arrived. She looked tired, but I could tell by her face that she was thrilled to be part of the excitement.

"You're going to be an Auntie again," I said, wishing it was over already. I felt like a corkscrew was coiling into the walls of my uterus. I could already feel the urge to push against the spasms as they grew tighter and tighter. After we signed the admission forms, a nurse slapped a plastic bracelet on my wrist, and it was time for the dreaded goodbyes.

"Is Mommy going to be okay?" Holly asked, biting her lip and holding back tears. She was only eight years old, so she was very concerned. I looked at my five-year-old son Lance staring back with a similar look of concern.

"Of course I'll be okay," I promised and I was grateful that Auntie quickly moved in to assure them. We hugged and I blew them a kiss as Russell wheeled me toward the elevator. The doors opened to a matte grey corridor droning loudly with tube lighting. I hadn't seen any mothers-to-be, but I heard a moaning sound and I felt a grip of panic. Sure, I had done it twice before, but it's kind of like the anxiety of a needle prick. Except a hundred times worse!

I decided that I would endure the rising pain by using my coping skills. Right! I was so pathetic. After lots of juvenile cursing, it was blatantly obvious that I still had not mastered the Lamaze techniques. There must have been ten or more nurses around the bed, but I was too exhausted to care.

Yippee, the hard part was over! We had a baby girl and she was a beautiful little thing. My heart thrummed with emotion when I saw her. I looked at my husband and he was blooming. Before we had a chance to count her fingers and toes, our nurse insisted that I rest. She whisked our baby over to an examining table. The nurses huddled around and the doctor was actively going over the baby. From the delivery table, I could tell something was wrong, though I couldn't see what.

"What's wrong with her?" I called out. I wished I could jump down and assess what was going on.

"She's not ready to breathe on her own. But don't worry, we are setting up a respirator right away," the nurse calmly informed me. I was very worried. The longer they took, the more uneasy I became. It was almost an hour before we got a good look at our little girl.

We didn't see anything abnormal about her, but the next morning the doctor had our daughter x-rayed long before I was awake. When I rolled my eyes in the direction of the bassinet, she was gone. The nurse had taken her during the night.

That morning our doctor looked troubled, as though he was searching for a way to say something. He asked me and my husband to meet him in the x-ray lab.

I didn't want to read any charts or see any tests. "Just tell me in general terms that my baby's healthy." The doctor was straightforward as he explained that our baby had a lesion in a heart valve. He had posted two x-rays against a light for us to see. The first x-ray showed an image of a healthy infant—not ours. Then he pointed to the next picture. The second baby had a massive heart; the organ filled the chest cavity.

"This is your baby's x-ray," the Doctor pointed again and he assured us that her heart was far from normal. I couldn't believe what he was saying, yet it was right in front of us as clear facts on the x-ray. I caught his eye and that's when it all started to come into focus. My heart sank. I looked down at my child as she slept peacefully in my arms. For a moment, my mind recalled the frustrations and tears that Annette had suffered over the loss of her child.

As he continued to talk, I could feel my glowing sheen of motherhood sinking like mud under my feet. I wanted to reach over and tear the x-ray into pieces. At the same time, my thoughts were fighting an unbearable reality. Let me out of here, I thought. If I would have been nearer the door, I would have run out.

But I stood silently as the blood drained from my face. The air had been sucked out of me; I was at the brink of collapsing.

After I regained some presence of mind, we left the x-ray room. I was so torn with emotion that I was afraid I might drop my baby, so we walked back to the nursery rather than my room. The nurse took our little angel for more tests. She was only a few hours old. What were they doing to her? How could I help her? When we got back to my room, family and friends were waiting to hear the news.

They knew something was wrong from the looks on our faces. I could hardly speak without tears so Russell filled them in and they reached out with empathy and love. I told Annette that I felt like God was forcing me to walk in her shoes.

"You are not going to lose your child, too. You must believe that God will take care of her. I promise," she assured and I saw the power of faith in her eyes. Her kindred spirit was all I needed. I no longer believed it was a cruel parody from God.

Sheldon approached me as I sat on the bed. He had prayed for our baby and he had a testimony that our daughter Caitlin would grow up to be a healthy adult. Later, when everyone had gone home, I prayed for a miracle.

That same day the doctor came again. He had new results to show Russell and me. To our shock and relief, there was a big oversight on the x-ray. It wasn't an oversized heart after all. It was nothing more than a blurred vision of a large thymus gland overlapping the heart.

Our baby was not completely out of the woods though. She had tracheomalacia, which meant that the cartilage in her windpipe was underdeveloped. It was weak and floppy, so it blocked air going to her lungs. Whenever she cried, she would start to suffocate. It was quite scary, because I could hear the despairing pitch in her cries. Plus, she still had the hole in her heart valve.

"She can't get the oxygen in when she cries, so you have to pick her up. Don't let her struggle to breathe. Give her a pacifier to keep her calm so she can suck and that should strengthen the muscles in her throat."

Those were the doctor's orders and we followed them to the letter. We would do whatever it took to avoid the option of a tracheotomy. This was a problem that would go on for over next 12 years.

My children were thrilled when they saw their baby sister. It was instant sibling rivalry on who should hold the baby first. I couldn't wait to go home. Over time, the novelty of a new baby wore off for our children; they became more relaxed around Caitlin. As for Russell and me, the nights ahead were quite exhausting. When Caitlin let out the slightest peep, we bounded out of bed like a couple of dogs. She was fine, but we still wouldn't leave any room for risk.

Six days after I gave birth, Annette was in labour. She had a baby girl, too, so it was a very exciting time between our duplexes.

216

91: Nadia and Calvin

Meanwhile, Nadia was on a new path to find her own happiness. She was busy with school, work, and her child, so I didn't see her often, but I missed her a lot. Although her marriage had ended after years of problems, she was still young. With her bubbly effervescence and good looks, it wasn't long until she met her future man, Calvin. How thrilled I was when she asked me to be her Matron of Honour.

In the months leading up to the event, we poured over bridal magazines and scoured through countless patterns. Since I knew we both loved the same things, I had a good idea of what she wanted. In the fabric stores, we gasped excitedly as we eyed the rows of lace. Nadia wanted a truly unique princess-style gown, so she sewed her own design.

I sewed the bridesmaids' dresses. Nadia and I never left each other out on any of the details. Even when she was at work, I would be working tirelessly at the sewing machine. I loved Nadia's dress; it had a real Cinderella edge.

On the big day, my best friend looked gorgeous and I was already tearing up before the ceremony had started. The wedding began on cue and the brides-maids walked in perfect rhythm with the music; I nervously rushed along the grass like a schoolgirl on a first date. I doubt anyone noticed though, as Nadia followed and she was such a graceful bride. With bouquet in hand, she walked right up to the man of her dreams. The nuptials proceeded and I knew her Calvin was definitely the one.

Time flew! Nearly a year later, I was at the hospital videoing Nadia and Calvin with their new baby boy.

92: Russell, Holly, Lance, Caitlin, and Mom

It was a beautiful experience but the year itself had had a lot of ups and downs. Russell got a job working odd hours with late nights and irregular shifts. But there seemed to be no wage. He got special benefits such as stereo equipment in exchange for cash. It made me want to pull my hair out, because it did not make sense when we had bills to pay. I wanted advice, so I confided in Nadia but that was difficult because she and Calvin had moved to Vancouver Island, which was a ferry ride away.

Then, if things weren't already hard enough, our landlord sold both duplexes and we had to move. Our new rental was so much smaller: it only had three bedrooms so the kids had to share. The new place didn't feel like home to us. We no longer lived next door to Annette and Steve. They'd been our neighbours for five years. We were sad without them and we rarely saw them.

School let out for summer, and the kids were very excited to go for their annual two-week vacation with Grandma Karina. My mom had moved to the Sunshine Coast—a ferry ride away from Vancouver—and she liked to take the kids camping every year.

For the first time, I was planning to tag along so I could chill out and de-stress from both sewing and my struggling marriage. My mind was in a complete daze when I thought about my husband. I was always coming up with new ways to stimulate our marriage, but falling flat and getting nowhere. Mom's advice often helped me to get better clarity on the situation, but it would be difficult to talk with little ears around.

As we boarded the ferry to Mom's new home, the kids turned and waved to Russell and he waved back. I was losing him to something else and it made me feel like an empty shell. It wasn't another woman. I was just no longer important in his life. I looked over the rail of the ferry to the water below. The sand sparkled like diamonds as the sun gleamed on the water. As soon as the ferry docked, the kids rushed ahead of me. Mom was waiting with open arms. She had planned our camping excursion.

The next morning we packed all the food and gear into the car and drove to the campground. Mom was in her element. She loved camping and cooking over a fire. It's not my thing, but Mom and the kids loved it.

Later, when I put supper on the picnic table, we had two unexpected visitors: Uncle Gary and my cousin Dave showed up. They lived together near Mom so they knew where she would be. Uncle Gary brought along a tent, groceries, and booze. I knew that my mom loved her brother and would never turn him away. But I wasn't thrilled with the drop-in visit; I didn't want a drunk around the kids.

Mom and I were just getting ready to clean the table when I heard a gurgling sound coming from the tent where Caitlin had been napping. I turned to see her looking through the tent screen. She wasn't fussing, but I sensed some urgency so I unzipped the tent. Within seconds, her rosy cheeks turned purple and her lips turned blue. Her glassy eyes rolled back in her head and she was gasping for air.

"She's not breathing!" I shouted. Without a moment to spare, I snatched her in my arms and clapped her on the back. I was getting nowhere, so my mother pulled Caitlin out of my hold, flipped her over, and patted her so hard I got scared.

"Give her to me."

Uncle Gary grabbed her and repeated the same actions as my Mom and me. He somehow seemed to believe that he could do the same thing better. Losing seconds, the three of us were madly scrambling to save her. In the panic and mayhem, Caitlin was flipped around like a Raggedy Anne.

We were too far away from civilization for medical help and without phone access there was no way we could call 911. The only option was to scream for help, so Holly ran up the path screaming for a doctor.

Luckily, there was a doctor and he came out of his tent just as Holly rushed toward him. Meanwhile, I was so panicked to save my baby that I plunged my fingers down her throat and probed around until I found something lodged in her airway. I finally tweezed it out with my fingers. Mushy bits of food had caught in her airway, Seconds later, Caitlin was breathing again.

I did not want this to happen again—not to me nor to anyone else. My daughter had nearly died. She had teeth and knew how to chew, but her throat had seized up. I insisted we take Caitlin to the nearest hospital immediately. I had to keep her safe.

After what seemed like ages, a doctor in emergency examined Caitlin thoroughly. He saw no reason for her to be admitted, but told me that her trachea should not be exposed to campfire smoke. For the rest of our visit, the kids and I stayed at Mom's place. They spent a lot of time shopping in the small town of Gibsons and going to the beach with Grandma. Time passed quickly and I was unable to get into any deep discussions with Mom.

93: Russell, Holly, Lance, Caitlin

Back home, I knew that wishful thinking couldn't change my husband. I had trouble falling asleep and when I did, my sleep was often broken up by more nightmares. One night, I actually awoke from a dream to find myself atop my husband. I had his big head in my hands and I was slamming it up and down on the pillow. I wasn't awake, but as he opened his eyes, I was looking right at him.

"What are you doing?" His deep, agitated voice brought me to consciousness. We stared at each other for a second or two before I slid off and turned over. He didn't say another word; my thoughts were going a mile a minute. I didn't shift a muscle in hopes that he would drift off.

The next morning, I had forgotten all about it as I scooted around the kitchen making school lunches. I got the kids out the door and I was washing up the dishes when I heard Russell shuffling around in the bedroom. He came into the kitchen wearing his robe and I noticed dark circle under his eyes. He didn't talk for a while, so I just passed it off, knowing he wasn't a morning person.

Then he grumbled something about a pain in his neck and that's when I remembered. I started laughing and Russell stared at me baffled, so I couldn't hold back. I told him what had happened in the night.

"I remember that! I thought it was a dream," he said in surprise, but then his eyes narrowed and his tune changed. "So, you really are trying to kill me," he teased and I laughed even more.

He readily admitted he hadn't suffered from his night of shaken-baby syndrome. Russell told that story over and over to our friends. Each time, he stretched it a little bigger. At first, it was funny, but the more he bragged, the more I started to wonder what my actions really meant.

I had dreams about Josh too and I would wake up sad. I knew Josh wasn't dead, but he was a ghost to me. The years were piling up and Josh's whereabouts were a mystery that I wanted to solve. His years of absence had become my mission to bring him home.

As a wife and mother, it was easy to get sidetracked. Whenever I was not in searching mode, I suffered a nagging ache for my brother. Ever since Josh and I had been pulled apart, my worth had diminished. I didn't feel deserving of him. I condemned myself whenever his name was mentioned. At times, I wished I could jump into the past and see him again. Finding Josh was my ultimate dream, but my inner child had rejection issues and they held me back from what should have been one of my greatest passions.

Finally, I couldn't stand by and do nothing. Both my parents had given me documents and government letters, so I began to concentrate like never before. I used the letters to backtrack and ask questions. It was crucial that I push my parents to talk about the past to unearth clues. I went over every issue so Mom and Dad could tell me their sides of the story. I began to dig deep and sought through page after page, listing after listing in the telephone directories, but there were no matches to Josh's biological or adoptive name.

Mom had too many doubts. Whenever we talked about Josh, she got upset. However painful though, it was worth it, because the facts brought me a step closer to Josh. I would mull over the details and then call her back. I really think she hated exposing the guilt in her heart.

That summer, I was pregnant again, but that didn't discourage me from planning another trip to see Mom. I couldn't wait to tell her the baby news and get a little more info out of her. Before I had a chance to call her, Mom called me and I was shaken right to my soul by what she had to say.

"It's me, Mom."

"Hi, Mom," I said. I had no idea what was going on for her.

"Something terrible has happened and I…" She stopped. Her voice was filled with dread.

94: Mom and David

"Mom, what's wrong?" I heard sobbing. "Is it Josh?" I dared to ask.

"No. It's David… he's dead." Mom sobbed loudly. She was so frantic and hysterical that it was hard to make out what she said.

"David? My cousin? Are you talking about Uncle Gary's son?" I was feeling panicky.

"Yes. David."

"Oh, Mom." It was hard to talk. "What happened to him?"

"I can't talk on the phone. I need to see you without the kids. Can you come here right away?"

"Yes." By then, I was crying too, so I didn't push her for any more details. I promised to make arrangements as quickly as possible.

When I got off the ferry, Mom was a complete mess. She couldn't get a word out without falling apart. She looked ten years older. Her puffy eyes drew me into her sadness. We held each other so tightly that I could feel the darkness of her pain. I was torn to see her this way. Eventually, she drove us to her trailer, while I was trying to figure out what to say and how to ask.

"We don't realize how precious life is until something awful happens. I can't understand it. Why would my beautiful nephew take his own life?" Mom asked, but she didn't look in my direction; she just stared numbly at the road ahead. Her hands shook so badly that she had to pull over.

"Suicide?" I gasped. Why would he do that? I was mortified. Uncle Gary had adopted Dave when he was a little boy and he had always struggled to fit in.

Mom's trailer was dead quiet that night except for the endless ticking of a clock. It was enough to make me feel crazy. From my bedroom, I could hear Mom in the master suite.

"Mom, please don't cry," I said softly. I felt around for her hand. She was feverishly hot and sweaty with the shakes. I knew my voice would bring her little comfort. It was a sleepless night. In the morning, I made her breakfast but the food never touched her lips.

"I see Dave every time I close my eyes. I don't want to sleep but I am so tired. I see his face in my mind and that's all I can think about," she said in a low voice, her chin quivering as she summoned every ounce of courage to say more. Each waking moment teetered her on the edge of torture and I didn't have the remotest idea of what to say.

"He was too young to die… I had no idea he was so unhappy," she said, shaking her head. "Yet, it was right in front of my face. I was the last person to see him alive. If only I had known, I could have stopped him… it's my fault. I should have seen this coming." Mom was on a roll and the tears welled up as I rushed back to her side.

"No, Mom, you can't blame yourself," I quickly pointed out. "How would you know? Dave was a very private person."

Then she fell quiet and it was a while before she continued.

"He was always on the outside looking in for a place to be loved," Mom said and that hurt so much that we sat there crying with our hands knotted together. "I saw him at the mall. He was leaving the bakery and I remember thinking how odd it was to see Dave holding pies instead of a girl's hand. I should have known right there and then that something must be wrong," Mom admitted tearfully. She recounted that Dave had accepted her offer of a ride home and he was unusually talkative as she drove. "I wish I could go back to that moment," Mom added. "I would change things."

When they got out of the car, Dave asked Mom to come over to his place for pie. It wasn't like Dave to invite people over and Mom was so glad, because she didn't want him to go back to his place alone. Uncle Gary was away for the weekend so Mom decided her dinner could wait.

Dave cut the string from the pie boxes and took out the pies. The dessert was almost as sweet as the moment. They laughed at funny memories and Mom couldn't help but want to do something nice for Dave. She wanted to make him happy, so she asked him out for dinner.

Mom always insisted on paying, but that time, Dave stood his ground. He couldn't afford to pay, but he refused to be a tightwad. He insisted. After the second piece of pie, they decided to meet for dinner the following night. With a carefree hug, Mom patted him goodbye and strode away to her trailer.

It had been a lengthy afternoon so Mom was ready to flop on the couch and simply dismiss the world for a while. For her, eating pie with her nephew was a perfect ending to a not-so-perfect day. Just as she settled for the evening, there was a loud crack outside. She strained to see out the window but there was no movement. She thought it could have been a branch, but it wasn't natural.

She waited to hear more, but all was quiet. The noise made her feel strangely uncomfortable. She rolled that around in her mind and brushed it off. It must be the neighbourhood kids playing in the street. With that, she went to bed, drifted off, and slept easily. In the wake of a new day, she got up to see the sun rise. With a smoke in one hand and the coffee brewing, she read the paper. The fact that there was no milk was a small matter, but it was the very thing that would alter her day—perhaps even change her life.

She decided to borrow some milk from Dave. She made her way across the road and onto the green of Dave's lot. Her feet padded up the steps leading to his trailer. She recounted to me how the front door felt against her knuckles as she knocked. When there was no answer, she went around to the back. Patient, but unwilling to give up, she pounded on the front door again.

Figuring that it was too early for Dave to be out, she didn't want to startle him if he was still asleep. She could slip in quietly and borrow a cup of milk. As her hand turned the knob, she felt a flutter in her stomach that made the hair on her neck stand up. An inner voice warned her to flee, but the door opened and it was too late. She did not fully enter the room before she saw Dave sitting lifeless in his father's armchair. Her eyes widened in horror as the scene unfolded.

"Dave?" Mom heard herself quiver his name, yet the sound was shockingly scary to her ears. The only other sound in the room was the deafening beat of her heart. She saw a rifle straddled underneath her nephew's chin. His arms hung loosely around the barrel as it glinted against his naked chest. Mom couldn't move. The underworld of a vile death had entrapped her soul.

Dave was still wearing the same tightly fitted jeans from the night before. The dark blue denim was stained to a wine red. She saw the pool of blood swill around his bare feet where the rifle butt was still anchored to the floor. Frozen with shock, Mom knew he was dead but she desperately ached to resuscitate him. It was a nightmare that could not be true, but there he was, his face drooping like melted wax.

Mom couldn't scream. Waves of shock had parched her mouth to ash. She could barely breathe. She needed something to hold onto but blood was splattered everywhere. It had trickled like wine in a glass into veins down the walls. Her eyes raced upward to a spackled ceiling of red globs and cone-shaped spears. She felt imprisoned as her hands clasped her mouth.

Mom couldn't bear another second; she stepped back awkwardly. In an attempt to get out of the room, she lost her footing and stumbled down the steps. Her screams cut the air and catapulted across the trailer court. In every direction, neighbours heard her ear-splitting shrieks. They left whatever they were doing and rushed to my mother's side.

Baffled by Mom's hysteria, the neighbours questioned her, but she couldn't talk. Blinded by hot salty tears, all she could do was cry as she wildly pointed her finger. Instinctively, their eyes followed her sign and they bolted the stairs, mobbing the doorway, totally unprepared.

It only took a moment for their human curiosity to lure them inside the gloomy darkness. The realization of David's self-annihilation stopped them dead in their tracks. Their senses were no match for the stinging odour of raw flesh. Just like that, they saw the horror scene. Then, in panic, they nearly knocked each other over in a race to get out, pallid white and emotionally gutted.

From then on, they could only gasp and cry in shock. There were no more questions, just words of comfort with tears and compassion for my mother. She described to me their soothing voices as she cried and jabbered nonsense. She wailed and begged for someone to get her nephew a doctor. Then out of nowhere, the old man from the corner lot put his arms around her shoulders.

"Karina, I'm sorry. But there is nothing we can do," he said. He tried to comfort her, but Mom desperately fought the inevitable truth that Dave was dead and had been since the night before.

Help was on the way. She heard sirens wailing in the distance and seconds later she saw the neon lights flashing. While some of the police went inside to investigate the scene, other officers whisked Mom away. They took her to a quiet place and asked her endless questions. They had to cross-examine her testimony, but she couldn't deliver it without distressing herself.

It was a tailspin of words played on words so Mom was put went through the wringer. To re-live every second through every word caused such her so much trauma. If she could have chosen to die during that inquiry she would have taken it. Eventually, the police concluded by written evidence that it was suicide.

Mom didn't know what was worse: the sweating nightmares or the sleep-deprived fatigue. She desperately wanted to escape the insane head games that left her struggling with her own suicidal thoughts. She heard voices and saw constant replays as her mind played tricks.

I stayed for as long as I could with Mom but after I went home it got worse for her.

Uncle Gary didn't know about his son when he got back from Vancouver, so Mom had to tell him. Subsequently, Mom had to go back to the police station to make yet another statement.

When she left the station, she was not empty-handed. For the life of me, I will never understand how the gun ended up in my Mom's car when she left. The hard-core metal mirrored in her eyes and despite her inner hysteria, she drove anyway. That gun had taken her nephew's life and here it was again. Mom told me that Satan was having a real heyday with her mind. This was a call for a professional counsellor; it was just too big for both of us. She made the right choice and got help.

I shall never forget how the demons clung to Mom during her dark days, but I also remember how she began to rebuild and heal. In the beginning, every issue—big or small—was a setback. But gradually, she took baby steps and slowly moved onward. Whenever she disagreed on anything with her kids, she assumed the worst. She was on the edge of her seat in fear that an argument would cause them to end their lives. On behalf of her kids, she fought harder than at any other time. She changed her course and became a better person. It was so moving to see her build and strengthen the love in our family. It changed our lives.

During that time, I kept thinking back to my childhood memories of Josh. I wanted to find that boy and bring him back to his mother.

95: Russell, Nadia, and Payton

With three kids and a baby on the way, I had a busy household. At six months, I was tired and my cheeks didn't have the prenatal glow anymore. I went for a routine ultrasound and I loved the experience. Of course, I knew what to expect, but this was different from the other three. Not only did I hear the beautiful thrumming of my baby's heart, but I also saw the screen up close. As the technician slid the computer-like mouse across my tummy, there was a perfect image of a tiny head and body curled in the fetal position. Since space was limited, there wasn't a lot of action. Then out of the blue, he moved—and yes, I said, "He."

"It's a boy." I openly delighted in the knowledge. I couldn't help but smile.

"Not necessarily," the technician quickly pointed out. She said I could have mistaken it for the umbilical cord.

"Hmmm?" I personally thought that seemed a bit weird. She explained that some things look quite different on a sonogram. Funny way to put it, but she could not convince me that I had it wrong. Of course the due date came and went right out the window. The days carried on and my belly stretched like a balloon.

Fortunately, Nadia was there to lighten my load. She planned to visit me for two weeks. This girl knew the real meaning of fun, maybe too much fun, but she was no slacker. She came prepared to do whatever was needed. She had her one-year-old boy and a bag of stuff to tide them over. In life I have found people who are replaceable, but not her. She will always be my best friend.

She understands me; she really gets me and I get her. Through each other, we actually find a part of ourselves.

She is gifted with an open mind and she knows how to bring out the good in people. The world could collapse and fall into the toilet but that girl is a troubleshooter. She has a way of pulling us both out of the flush. Together, we laugh in the face of hurdles. She says something silly and then I add something sillier, and we giggle like teens.

We loved it when people mistook us for sisters. Sure we were different but our personalities and ideals seemed to come from the same mould. We felt like twins from a past life or two spirits who had separated from birth. Odd as this may sound, together we became a whole person. We were amused to see the way people stared at us. We could feel them looking in and wanting to be a part of our high-on-life goofy enthusiasm. It was contagious. We boosted each other's strengths and always found humour in our imperfections. I often would start a conversation with her ending it or vice-versa. Our bond was similar to being inside a protective bubble where we treasured whatever time we had together.

In the long wait for my labour, she became a personal housekeeper and nanny. She pulled up her sleeves and rolled out a carpet of duties. She worked impressively hard, but when two weeks was down to one day, and the baby had not surrendered the womb, my doctor recommended another ultrasound. So Nadia and I went to the hospital.

We had to go through the city during a Friday rush hour and we ended up taking a wrong turn. She reached over to get a map out of the glove compartment. When Nadia slowed the car and glanced down at her map, she smacked right into the driver ahead of us. Our mouths hung open in shock as we watched the aggravated driver get out of her car to look at her fender.

"You're in labour," Nadia eyed me and I knew what she meant. Then she leaped out of the car and rushed to the woman.

"I'm so sorry. I didn't mean to hit you. I am trying to get to the hospital. My best friend is having a baby." Nadia turned and pointed to me. I could hardly believe it. She even cried—such an actress. She should have won an Oscar.

Oh, no! I felt their eyes move in my direction and I wanted so much to slide out of view, but there was no way I could slide out of sight. With a belly expanded beyond my knees I wasn't going anywhere. I tried to keep a poker face, but I could feel a mounting flush of guilt riding up my neck. Then there was that awkward moment of what to do.

"Don't worry about the car. I know where the hospital is. If you follow me I can get you there faster," the woman said. She was so caught up in Nadia's performance that she actually got in her car and escorted us to the hospital. Then she drove off and we never saw her again. Nadia claimed her emotional shock was the reason she had overreacted.

Right, I thought. It was just hilarious how she had pulled the other woman into her drama.

When the ultrasound was finished, the doctor said I would probably be in labour by Monday or so. At thirteen days overdue, this baby was already building a reputation for lateness. Nadia was leaving the next morning. That hardly seemed fair. After all, she had come to see the baby too. Nadia was annoyed and insisted that I should be admitted and induced. Monday was too far off and it was absurd to have to go through another blistering weekend in full term. With a little persistence I got the doctor's approval. Satisfied, Nadia left to take care of the kids and Russell came to be with me.

I was anxious to get it over with. As soon as I was induced, labour kicked in full force. I concentrated through the contractions. Suddenly, I felt the rush, the intensity to push with every fibre. One more push and it would be over, so I clamped down.

"Stop! Stop pushing!" I heard the nurse shout, but for me, it was full steam ahead. Talk about willpower. How was I supposed to abandon such a force? Kind of like trying to go backwards when you're running at full speed.

The baby was in trouble: he was caught in the passage with the cord around his neck. His heartbeat was barely on the monitor; it had dropped to twenty-five counts per minute.

The nurses told my husband that he would have to leave. That was upsetting and frightening, but they needed to act quickly. Should anything get worse, the nurses didn't want a panicky spouse to make it harder. It was quite a scare but thanks to a combination of careful hands and a scalpel, our baby took his first breath.

Shortly after my baby's arrival, I got what I had waited nine months to do; I got to hold him. As I did, we shared a tender moment of one-on-one. He opened his blue eyes and looked about, and I was pleasantly surprised. I had never seen a newborn take such notice of his surroundings.

Then the nurse took him away for observation. Meanwhile, another nurse stepped in and sat down. With her most gentle approach she talked about the dangers of oxygen loss. Russell and I heard shocking talk of possible brain damage. It didn't matter; Russell and I knew better. Our baby had come into the world with his eyes wide open as though he might have already missed something. We named him Payton and before he turned a year old, he was walking and chatting easily.

Generally speaking, most gloating parents might believe that such a handsome little tyke would only strengthen the bond between his parents. Not so. That sweet toothless smile could never be the bonding plaster that filled the cracks in our hearts.

Judging by Russell's lack of concern, he seemed to exempt himself from the critical state of our marriage. Talking had no merits, so I tried to say it on paper. I wrote how much I loved and needed him. It was crucial that he pay attention to the approaching disaster of our relationship. He folded the letter, passed it back, and set the record straight. In his most vulgar wording, he told me that he wasn't going to change and, if I didn't like it, then I should leave. That couldn't have been clearer, except for one thing. He was leaving—not me. Enough was enough!

I wanted companionship and romance but I wasn't ready to uproot myself. I decided to cut our relationship short and things got nasty. That left me feeling even farther away from happiness. Why did I keep making the wrong choices? Why did I enter bad relationships? I decided to take that experience, run, and not look back.

96: Holly, Lance, Caitlin, and Payton

I took back my life and moved on. I just wanted to put it all behind me.

It wasn't easy at all, especially when my home was broken into. Thankfully, there was little damage. However, it seemed to start a chain of events that wasn't about to cut any slack for a while. Other than a broken window, the only thing missing was my dog's pedigree papers and my marriage certificate. Of course, I didn't know that until Teddy, my golden lab, was stolen and I had no papers to show the police. Even worse, without a marriage licence, the divorce delayed another six months.

So Russell was stuck with me for a little longer.

My son Lance missed his dog Teddy. Brimming with hope, he tirelessly rode his bike searching alleys and roads for his dog. Then Lance's bike was stolen and the police assumed it was all connected, but they had no proof of anything. It certainly seemed like the floodgates had opened and whatever could go wrong seemed to be doing just that. Even the sanctity of my own space wasn't safe.

Talk about fear. I don't think my kids will ever forget the night we sat on the bed. In the middle of reading our nightly story, we heard the smashing of glass. We ran to see what had happened and found a huge rock had been hurled through the front window. There were a lot of lights on in the house, making it easy for someone to see in. So we ducked down and scrambled under the kitchen table where I held the kids until they settled down. I didn't want them to see my fear, but we were under attack and I didn't know who or why.

I wanted to believe that everything would be fine but the broken window made me innately aware that it wasn't. Just days after I had the window replaced, someone was outside with a BB gun and popped a bullet through the same glass. If I had taken one more step forward, the pellet would have hit me. The police came and looked at the hole but I didn't feel much protection from them.

Through the course of these ongoing events, Holly was acting out and she was about to show how tough she was. Like most teenagers, she wanted to be with her friends, while I was overly protective and strict.

On this one occasion, I didn't want her to hang out at the mall. In the past, she had suffered at the hands of mall bullies, so that only enforced my concerns. Even though I was stern, I gave in to Holly when she promised to be back in an hour. After all, what harm could happen in an hour? But again this proved to be a huge error.

The hours passed and, when I didn't hear from Holly, all trust was gone. I was ready to ground her the moment she came home. But she didn't come home at all; by late evening, my anger had turned to gut-sick worry. Every time the phone rang, I lunged forward and snatched the receiver, but it wasn't her. I called her friends but they hadn't seen her. I kept telling myself not to panic: she is just late. But it's quite a stretch to think positively when the night drags into morning. For a mother, it's a long terrifying ride when your child is missing. My body and mind were terribly restless, yet I was exhausted as though I had aged twenty years.

For all I knew, she could already be in another city, another province, or even another country. Or, what if she was close by but held against her will? I never dreamed I would see the day where I would have to call a missing person's report and give the police a description of my girl. But I did.

Until that day, I had never really understood my mother's sense of loss or the countless pain of emotions my mother must have felt when she discovered her children had been taken away. I cried for her, I cried for me and I cried so much for Holly.

Not knowing how my daughter had vanished and not knowing if she was alive felt as though a knife was twisting inside my heart. I needed a shoulder to scream and cry on, but it was too painful to open up about it. I had three others who needed me and I couldn't fall apart in front of them. Only in the dark of night did I allow the tears to roll onto my pillow.

On the third day, I finally got a lead from an anonymous tip. Holly had been spotted outside a nearby restaurant. I grabbed my keys and ran to the car. It wasn't far, but time was against me, and this was my only chance to get her back in my arms. As I drove around the back street, I saw Holly standing at a pay phone with her back to me. There was a boy with her and his arm was wrapped around her waist. I left the car running and ran toward her.

"Holly," I called out. My head was buzzing with thoughts about what I should do or say. Turning slowly, her cheeks flamed and she looked mortified. Right then, I was sure my heart would crack in half. She was alive and so beautiful and I just wanted to throw myself at her feet. I tried to hug her but she was as stiff as a pillar. I was afraid to let go, especially when she didn't engage with me. Choking back the tears, I pleaded Holly to come home with me. If only it could be that easy. My intention was to resolve whatever was upsetting her once I got her home, but Holly didn't want that.

Refusing to get in my car, Holly pushed away from me. I tried to bring her back but her skinny little boyfriend was acting like Mr. Bodyguard. I went home and got the police involved. Holly was only fifteen, so I wanted them to force her to return home. She was my responsibility and I didn't know what else to do. I was in over my head.

When she returned home, I couldn't promise her that everything would be okay. We had so much to work on in our relationship, but the more I tried to keep Holly, the harder she pulled away. She kept running off with new kids and, for days at a time, I wouldn't see her. I had told her that I didn't want to be with Russell and the trauma of my failed marriage was hitting her hard and I should not have dragged her into that. She deserved to have her parents' love and support no matter what was going on between Russell and me.

She started hanging out with a boy with whom she really seemed to connect, but he was a bigger control freak than I was. I was worried that Holly would endure a lot of hurt from Raji. Shortly after they got involved, she was pregnant and he was a permanent part of her life. She had settled down so I went to her old school to enroll her, but I was turned down. Regular schools would not allow pregnant students to attend. It was frustrating, but they gave me an alternative school where she would also be able to bring her baby later.

Holly fit in quickly. She buckled down, studied hard, and that made her family and teachers proud. Given her age, it was no shock that adoption was once again brought to our attention. I didn't want to lose my future grandchild, but Holly's walk in life was not for me to choose. Obviously adoption was a sensitive subject, so I had to brace myself for whatever she chose. I decided that I would offer to take the baby if she didn't feel ready to be a parent.

In the back of my mind, I always worried about social services, especially when my sister Iona was a single mom struggling with four boys. Her "old man" was stealing her welfare money and buying drugs. Social services came and took her kids away. A family adopted her first two boys but where the other two went was a mystery. The youngest child Desmond was three when he died in foster care. He was riding his bike and fell over a cliff to his death. Iona was not told until six months later, so she couldn't even go to the funeral or know where her baby was buried.

I was losing more family all the time and that pushed me harder in wanting to find Josh. I made contact with the Alberta Post Adoption Registry, a provincial-government-run agency. The registry sent me a list of my foster family names so I finally had the right name of the family where Josh and I had been fostered together. I tracked down a long list of families under the name of Ross, circled the possibilities, and made the calls.

But I still came up with nothing.

When Sheila and I were little, we had the same doctor. Our two sets of foster parents took every precaution to make sure our appointments were not on the same day. So there was the strong possibility that Josh had gone to that same doctor. I got my medical records out and found the doctor's name and wrote him a letter. The doctor replied that he remembered Sheila and me, but he had never met Josh.

97: Holly, Raji and Baby Ashley

In the months that followed, I found a wonderful friend in Jack. At first glance, I didn't think anything about my neighbour. He was just the boy next door. Jack didn't have any kids or a wife, so I just assumed that wasn't part of his life plan. Plus, I had six years on him.

Over time, I began to really like this guy and I found my guard slipping because I couldn't stop thinking about him. I didn't want it to happen, but trying to stop Cupid is like trying to stop Christmas from coming. Jack is the kind of person I had always dreamed of. Yet, it was hard to be in love, because I wasn't sure if my children's hearts were open to see me take another shot at romance.

In the midst of all this, Holly's due date came exactly when the doctor predicted. After a restless night, Holly was bug-eyed with exhaustion. Raji wasn't much better; his anxiety was written all over his face. Holly needed to get to the hospital so I helped her into the car and away we went.

It was tough to watch my young daughter go through the damp sweats of labour. She was barely sixteen and already bringing a life into the world, prematurely leaving her childhood behind to raise her baby. Raji was tired and being a wise guy. Holly was in pain and he was annoyed with her outbursts.

Russell came in and stayed at the head of the bed so he could support Holly. I told Raji to get rid of the attitude and stop being mouthy. He settled down and soothed Holly's face with a cool cloth. The three of us were coaching Holly and then a glorious everyday miracle happened.

Now, don't get me wrong—this wasn't just any miracle. This was exceptional, because as a prejudiced new grandmother, there are special bragging rights. If I had had it my way, my granddaughter Ashley would have been listed in the top ten babies of 1995. She was the most gorgeous baby on earth. Her beautiful mocha flesh and curly hair certainly was a credit to her father but the large lacey eyelashes and pudgy pink kisser came from her mother. Once I knew that mom and baby were resting, I went home. The kids couldn't wait to see the baby, so we dressed up and invited Jack to join us.

Through a windowpane of the nursery, we could see the rows of newborns. Right away, the kids guessed that the cocoa-skinned beauty was our little starlet.

That was a pivotal turning point in the way that Jack and I saw our future together. Our mutual feelings of love had grown to being very serious. As springtime came around, Jack and I shopped for a house. We found a cute little home in the suburbs, so we cut a deal with the realtor and closed the sale.

A month later, we got engaged and set a date for our wedding. Together, we shared the news with the kids and they were so excited. Three months later, Jack took possession of the house and moved in. The kids and I planned to move in after the wedding.

Like every bride, I wanted a flawless event. I had heard about weddings that looked like a three-ring circus. Right from the start, I said I wanted Jack to give me his input. Together, we picked out every detail right down to the toasting glasses.

Over the months, my mind was fully inspired with all kinds of designs for my gown and the bridesmaid dresses. I chose a natural silk. I loved the texture; it felt like the fabric had my name woven into it. It was soft like tissue, light as paper, and it inspired beauty. For the girls, I bought yards of blue-and-white striped gingham. The dresses were absolutely beautiful. Caitlin wore a miniature copy of my dress.

On the day of the wedding, we girls had a lot of fun. Right after we got our hair and makeup finished, we gathered up the dresses, crinolines, and whatever else was needed, and went to the hotel. My boys spent the night at the house so they could go with Jack to get their suits.

For the better part of the day, Mom travelled by ferry and fought the traffic to arrive. Sure enough, when I got to the hotel, she was waiting in the lobby. Underneath her big black-rimmed hat, I could see she was filled with thoughts of endearment. We were about to embark on one of the most beautiful moments ever shared between a mother and daughter.

I didn't want to cry on my wedding day. So I was grateful when the bellman interrupted. He took our bags and we followed him to the eighteenth floor. The photographer and video expert arrived at the same time, so they got shots of special moments, like when my Mom saw her granddaughters all dressed up. To make the most of every moment, Mom's job was to help me with my gown and veil. Of all her children I was the only one that Mom was able to see get married.

"I want to give you something special for your wedding day." She smiled as she presented a little box. She pulled out a silver chain. On the end was a heart-shaped locket. She popped it open and I saw a picture of Mom that was not much bigger than a kernel of popcorn. I could hardly believe that she had actually got a tiny headshot of herself inside that little space. Right then, I realized how hard she had tried to bridge our lives together since that day at the Lethbridge Airport. I told her how much I loved her and she hugged me the way moms do.

Downstairs in the hotel lobby, Mom helped me into the limo. The short drive took us close to the wharf. It was the best possible option given that we were having our reception on an old paddlewheeler. I followed the girls as we excitedly climbed the walkway. From the dock's edge, I saw the guests looking over the rail. They were cheering with excitement.

Well don't that beat all, I thought. I tried to find Jack but he was not in sight because he didn't want to see me until I was walking the aisle.

Caitlin had no problem taking the lead. Her curls bobbed as her dress swooshed with her every step. Holly and Nadia followed along in their beautiful floor-length gowns and white gloves. I greeted my handsome Dad with a hug and I knew he approved. As I cupped my arm into his waiting grip, he smiled and gave me the nod that my prince was waiting.

Jack knew how to make that tux and top hat work for him. I must say he looked really fine. His best man and my boys weren't too shabby either. My little guy, Payton, looked so cute in a tux and bow tie that he almost stole the show. Luckily, Jack and I had rehearsed the night before but I still cried anyway. After the exchange of vows and rings, we kissed and everyone went wild with excitement. It was time to get the party started. We took a short break for a photo shoot on the deck and, when we came back in, the food was hot and ready.

It all seemed to be flowing along quite nicely. Dinner transformed to toast time. Our emcee took the stand and did the honours. I felt radiantly happy until the emcee commented that someone was missing. He dabbed at his eyes as he talked about my unending search for Josh. For such a jolly moment, it was both a touchy and a touching subject, which lowered the mood of gaiety. The room fell quiet and it was uncomfortable to feel the eyes on my parents and me.

Obviously, nothing could have been more of a blessing than to have shared this experience with Josh. Deep down, I was hoping for a miracle, but this wasn't the Oprah show.

Nevertheless, our wedding felt magical. Jack and I couldn't believe that we were about to begin a new life. We would take each day with humour no matter what. Keep life simple and love each other.

At the end of the evening, we headed off to a waiting carriage. Just as the horse began to pull forward, my kids ran over and climbed in too. It was really cute, because we all squeezed together like a real family. Baby Ashley sat on her Mommy Holly's lap and she looked like a little dolly dressed in her layers of pink. She lifted her eyes to feel the delicate sprinkle of rain on her baby face and then she raised her palms.

"It's wet, Grammy." She beamed and we knew that the rain and the ride were the highlights of her night. I grabbed my lace parasol and popped it open as we all tried to fit under.

Part Five: Finding Josh

98: Jack, Holly, and Ashley

When Jack and I returned from our honeymoon, we packed up the kids and moved everything into the house. Ford hired Jack as a heavy-duty mechanic. I had a steady flow of customers asking me to design and sew whatever they needed. We added a master-bedroom extension so Holly and Ashley would have their own room and not have to share with Caitlin. Ashley was a good baby, but Holly was struggling with her overzealous Mom—me—and the need to be with her peers. I wanted her to be home on weekends but she was still young and that was tough on her. As hard as it was, it was time for me to accept that Holly and I had to call it quits.

I needed to back off so Holly could take care of her child without any power struggles from her Mom. I didn't want to be a monkey on her back with all my nagging. Holly and Ashley moved, but they were still within walking distance so it was hard for me not to want to watch them like a hawk. I am sure that she found me quite annoying, as I was always dropping in on her.

Although Holly was young, she was smart and determined to build a life for her child. I still fretted over her but in a short time she put herself through college. From there, she got an excellent job in Vancouver. Holly has built a very suitable home life for herself and her child. More importantly, it is wonderful that my grandchild is in the hands of a devoted mommy. I believed that if I gave Holly space she could do it. I am so proud of my girl. I knew that social services would never be pounding on Holly's door to take her child.

A year after our wedding, I opened an in-home daycare service so I could stay home with the kids. At the same time, I dug deep into my search for Josh. In the past, I had had setbacks and failures, but I didn't see them as a defeat anymore. They only made me more determined and strong because I was doing this out of love for my brother and my mother.

99: Government Bureaucrats and Mrs. Ross

The words of our emcee might have been untimely, but they empowered me to keep looking. I asked many agencies for help. I sent them my information so they could begin a search from their end.

Most of the agencies were affiliated with the Alberta Post Adoption Registry. They offer access to non-identifying information about adoptees and biological parents. However, both parties must register in order to create a connection, so a search can only move forward if the adoptee, sibling, or birthparent—everyone involved—registers. Otherwise, it could turn out to be just a long waiting game. With an agency, you have to pay a starting fee and then you may want to do most of the search yourself so you don't end up spending thousands of dollars. Searches are often lengthy and drawn out.

Once the starting fee is processed, the agency calls the Registry and the adoption is no longer sealed. When the name is uncovered, the agencies can run a name check through the Motor Vehicle Branch to find a match. If a parent requests a search after they give up their parental rights or after their child has been apprehended by social services, then disbursement fees are reasonably fair.

All the hype was dashed away when I realized that there was no material about my brother.

When social services enforce a split between siblings, it seems corrupt to expect the siblings or the adopted (and renamed) child to absorb the cost. After all, a child cannot order a removal or separation from his or her siblings. From experience, I believe it would be safe to say that the majority of fostered or adopted siblings would find their separations to be terrible calamities. Such separations should not be used as the foundation for a business venture. How can a government reel in payments from a misfortune of such magnitude? It was a tragedy—not a choice. The social system should not be allowed to prey on the vulnerabilities of sibling searchers by profiting from such decisions. No legislative ministry should have the authority to refuse the constitutional rights of siblings by sealing the birth records.

I understand that the government's argument is to consider an adoptee's right to privacy. However, if that were the real issue, why is the government eager to give the name to an agency only after a transaction of fees? I did not expect the government to search on my behalf; I could do that myself. But I needed my brother Josh's current name.

I have always advocated that every foster child and every adoptee at the age of majority should be entitled to right of access to their own information automatically, including their medical files, childhood background, foster placement, and origins.

I applied through Alberta's Freedom of Information and Protection of Privacy Act for my own information. A small fee of $50 covered the cost of paper and shipping; the information came in the mail.

To my shock and disappointment, bureaucrats had tampered with nearly every page of my personal data. What I had purchased was 180 sheets of whited-out paper. My ever-hopeful chance of gaining back crucial pieces of my life was gone. As I finished reading my data from cover to cover, I was totally shocked by how many times I saw the word, "Retarded."

No matter where the compass pointed, it was not in my direction. I really felt like I had nothing reliable to work with until I heard about a Native agency. This non-profit organization designed for the purpose of family reunification introduced me to a great coach, Mitchell—a guy who had real aspirations to help others.

No matter how much I tried to stay focused on finding Josh, something always seemed to be brewing to distract me. A sick child can be one of the scariest challenges in life. My daughter Holly was miserably sick with flu-like symptoms. For days, she retched in pain. She ended up in hospital where the doctors discovered a cluster of tumours inside her.

Luckily, her condition was operable, but when she returned home, the tumours grew back. Holly would look at me and I would put on a smile, but inside I wanted to scream. I kept begging God to let her get well or let me take her place. I felt guilty for all our arguments and the stupid things that I had done in the past.

It was pure agony to see my girl go through such a rough patch in that unforgettable summer. I couldn't even bring myself to say the C-word. I just prayed that God would extinguish her pain and let my girl recover. Eventually, my prayers were answered and Holly was back on her feet. She had a few glitches but, boy oh boy, that girl was a power tool. She had the strength of ten. Her determination to get strong was the best part of her courage.

When all had settled down again, I made contact with two political advocates. Both women had campaigned against the ministry in Alberta. These advocates agreed that it would be punitive to expect a profit when the Social Service Department was the one responsible for splitting up siblings. This knowledge did not resolve my situation, but it was a nice change to have compassionate council in my court for once.

My coach Mitchell, was on his toes. He advised me to request Josh's baptismal certificate from the Presbyterian congregation with whom Josh's family was affiliated. That might have been beneficial if I had known his adoptive name. In my situation, that idea failed, but for all those siblings out there searching, I would say to them, "Go for it." It certainly is worth a shot.

It was so amazing how quickly my advocates wrote Alberta's Ombudsman asking for help. Unfortunately, that office did not have the authority to investigate matters related to legislation. The most impartial office in government turned me away, which again was no surprise. However, as I look back on that idea, I feel that it might have been more successful if the media had been involved.

Well, life went on and so did my thinking cap. Could I match the names of the two sets of foster parents with one street name? Somebody on that street had to know something. I could not believe my luck when I found the Vancouver Adoption Registry had opened records for British Columbia. Throughout the decades, they had compiled a research library for all of Canada. Jack and I went to the downtown office and scoured through an extensive pile of books dating back past the 1960s. It was exactly what I was looking for. There was information on names, occupations, addresses, and phone numbers of every household.

All I had to do was go back to the 1963 records and match the two foster names to the same street. Bingo! I found it. History had repeated itself on paper and I finally got the break I needed. I stared down at the page and it was all there in black and white: "Mr. R. Brockton, Dairy delivery; Spouse, Eleanor; Henderson Street, Calgary," and they were on the same street as the Ross family!

I scribbled down a page of phone numbers and made my first call to Mrs. Ross. She did not remember me until I asked about Josh. After forty years, she was not expecting my call. She did not show an ounce of excitement and, after a brief chat, she had to go. I was miffed and I wanted to call her back. I waited a couple of days and that paid off. When I called back, she told me that her niece was having a baby so she had booked a flight to Vancouver. I asked her to meet with me for just an hour so I could find out what she knew about Josh. She hummed and hawed; she was tough, but I got her to commit.

We met and it was extraordinary for us to see each other after all those years. She was tense at first but, over lunch, she began to relax. I was glad because I did not want her to feel that I was starting a pow wow with her; I wanted her to be upfront with me. Our meeting was not about the past. It was about Josh. Regrettably, she did not know where he was. She had sent him back to social services three years after I had moved away.

"Why did you keep Josh and send me to the Brocktons?" I asked.

"I was going to the hospital and I couldn't care for two children," she said.

I never let on that I knew she was the one who had started the accusations of my being mentally retarded.

"I saw Josh after he left our house. He was pushing his mother in a wheelchair and I do remember that he came to see me on his bike. It was a long way, so I drove him home after, but I never saw him again."

Then Mrs. Ross mentioned that she had fostered another little girl after Josh had left. She claimed there was a history of mental issues, so she had her locked up in an institute. A sick feeling rose in my stomach as I wondered whatever became of that girl. It was scary to think that I could easily have been that girl in a room with bars on a window.

Oddly, Mrs. Ross never showed any emotion as I related the abuse that went on at the Brocktons. During the luncheon, her sister-in-law was sitting with us; she was emotionally charged. Unlike Mrs. Ross, she openly voiced her desire to help.

The three of us talked for almost two hours and I did not want it to end. I was doing most of the talking because Mrs. Ross was not saying too much. Either way, I was bubbling with gratitude. The tiniest memory of Josh was a silver lining for me. Before saying goodbye, Mrs. Ross promised to send childhood photos of Josh.

That never happened.

100: The Brocktons

I began searching for the Brocktons; they no longer lived in Calgary. Using a search engine on the Internet, I found several listings. On my second try, I had the right number! It was Eleanor's husband Randall who answered the phone.

"Hello, may I please speak with Randall?"

"This is Randall."

My heart was kicking harder than a pony in a sideshow and I could barely breathe. I had to think quickly, but I was not sure what I should say next.

"Hi, Randall. My name is Eugenea, I am not sure if you remember me, because you have not seen me for almost forty years. At the time, I was small when I lived with your family for nearly a year back in 1963. Is there any chance you might remember me?" I blurted it all out so fast that I was actually feeling a bit winded.

There was nothing, not even a sigh, and I thought I had lost our phone connection. Then I heard him gasp and I knew I had the right house.

"Yes, I know who you are," Randall said at last. "You're the little blonde girl. Oh, my goodness." He broke off. "I cannot believe it. I always wondered what happened to you. You were so little when you came to us." There was joy and pain in his voice and it was obvious that there were times he had wondered. "How are you? What happened to you?"

He was full of questions so I gave him a brief update of my life and kept it light at the same time. He said that he had loved me and had wanted to give me a good home. He wished he could have kept me and was sad when I went away.

"I have never forgotten you and I can still picture your blonde hair as you rode your little red trike up and down our driveway."

Eventually, I asked to speak with Eleanor, but she was out and would not be back for another hour. Randall was very excited to tell his wife about my call, but I asked him to keep it a surprise. I had to know if she would be thrilled or indifferent.

An hour later, I got her on the phone and told her my name. It did not sink in right away, so I told her how we knew each other. I heard her gasp with shock as if someone had jolted her with a live wire. Then, she tried to cover it up by pretending that I had the wrong person. I kept pushing her buttons until she finally admitted that she did remember me.

What should have been an exciting conversation turned out to be tinged with fear. She was not overjoyed to hear my voice. No, it was a threat to her. She had long ago crushed my face out of her mind only to learn that I was an hour's drive away. Her breathing turned to a snort of disgust when I mentioned that I wanted to see her.

"No, I don't want you to come here. I don't want a visit, I'm not ready for that." Her voice rose to a pitch that was notably higher than before. She just wanted me to go away.

"I don't want to upset you or make you miserable. I am searching for my brother and I need your help. That's all," I said in my kindest voice, but she was not buying it. I finally let her go, but I continued to call. The following morning, Randall phoned. He did not carry the same enthusiasm as the night before.

"Do you have a good or bad memory of living in our house? Do you remember?"

"I think I know where you are going with this." I came right out and told Randall that Eleanor had not been a good mother to me. "I don't want to say this to hurt you, but I do remember the abuse and pain she caused." I spoke carefully. I did not want Randall to hang up on me. He explained that he was so exhilarated about my call that he had told his daughters. They responded, but not with gladness; they remembered how bad it had been.

"You don't know the half of it," his children had said and Randall was deeply troubled to know his wife had such a brutal side. I felt that he was scared of what I might do.

"I am not here to square things. I don't want to hurt Eleanor. I am looking for my brother and I am hoping that she can help."

Randall was surprised and relieved that I did not want revenge. On the contrary! However cruel Eleanor had been, she had taught me to watch my back and be strong to survive the oncoming years.

"I have to see her. It's important," I told Randall. I did not expect a truce; I just needed Randall to get me through the roadblocks. He agreed and, at some point, he managed to soften Eleanor's hostility. The thought of being in the same house with this hardened woman was scary.

When Jack and I entered the Brocktons' front door, Randall looked me over then hugged me without limitation. He invited Jack and me to come inside. I didn't see Eleanor.

"You are still the same little girl; you haven't changed, except that you are grown up." Randall was smitten.

"I remember you now," I smiled as I had forgotten what he looked like, but it all came back as if it were yesterday. "Is she here?" I asked.

"Yes, I am here." A timid voice echoed from upstairs. Eleanor was watching from an unseen corner. As I walked up the stairs to the main area, I saw that forty-something years had not changed Eleanor's face. Her scent clung in the room and it was hair-raising to recognize it after all this time. She looked older, but her hollow cheeks and angular jaw defined the same woman. I quickly dashed a flashback of memories from my mind.

The four of us sat in the living room. It was quite a challenge to initiate a conversation. I was dying to hear what they knew about Josh. First, we had to get past the anxiety so we could be reacquainted. Eleanor looked terribly uncomfortable; the strain was showing. I could feel my own struggle as the clock ticked back in time. I reminded myself that I was doing this for Josh, my parents, and myself.

Eventually, the conversation rolled around to the past. Eleanor told me that Mrs. Ross had come over once and, on that day, she had pleaded for them to take me. Eleanor had three little kids already, but for some unknown reason she agreed.

The two families agreed to keep Josh and me apart. Some years after I had moved away, Randall and his family had left the province, so they did not know what had happened to Josh. It seemed as though it had been a long evening but in actuality we had only used up two hours. By the end of the evening, Eleanor's fretful eyes relaxed and she had opened up considerably.

Never before would I have believed that I could ever reopen such wounded emotions. It was most gratifying to know that Eleanor had made a true sense of connection with me, even if it was only for a flickering moment. She was no longer a phantom shadow of my past. I hoped that we would remain friends and I can happily say that we stayed amicable. Randall called on occasion and I did visit Eleanor a second time.

Later that week, I called my coach and he assured me that I had somehow righted years of wrong, but I should not feel that I owed them anything. Before I knew it, Eleanor passed away and I realized that I had found closure but no assistance.

I went back to the Vancouver Adoption Registry and traced another ten families who had lived on Henderson Street in the 1960s. I called every parent and every grown child, but the result was the same. No one knew what had happened to Josh.

101: My Ancestors

In spite of the lack of real progress, I was going full steam ahead with online Internet search sites across Canada. Most of the search engines had free access so anyone could enter an adoptee's name and birthdate. A friend of mine moved to Calgary. We corresponded for a while and eventually lost touch. But I knew that my friend had gone around the city posting baby pictures of Josh with his birth name. On the bottom was a special message for Josh about how to make contact with me. Although there was only the slightest chance of his ever seeing the posted pictures, her generosity filled me with hope and optimism.

Josh had ridden his bike to visit the Ross family. So he must have lived within minutes of their home. That meant he probably was still in a school somewhere between the two houses. I bought a Calgary map. I really encourage searchers to do that. It really helped to narrow down the area where Josh would most likely have lived at the time. I crossed off any private schools and pinpointed the exact school within a five-mile radius. I had one particular area in mind, so I planned to go to Calgary and visit the schools in that area. Most schools have class photos for each year, so all I needed was a peek. I was so close and all I had to do was save some money and go there. In the meantime, I didn't want to leave any stone unturned. I scoped through microfilm, Vital Statistics, Labour Relations, elections, and hospital records. I put ads in the Calgary paper, and I still had no prospects.

I had learned that Josh's mother had died between the adoption and his eighteenth birthday. Knowing that she was in a wheelchair, I guessed that she had probably died from Multiple Sclerosis. I tried to trace her back through the MS Society, but I didn't find anything. From there, Jack and I went to the University of British Columbia and combed through sheets and sheets of microfiched obituaries dating back to the year of Josh's adoption. When that failed, I called the cemetery records, but there was still no match to his mother. I was so bummed.

Then my coach suggested I get involved in genealogy records, because a lot of families get connected that way. It felt like it was my last resource, so I gave it my all and went digging on the Internet once again.

An old friend from church had firsthand experience with that sort of thing. She found my family names, birth dates, marriages, and deaths all compiled online. It was surprising how fast the data came up on the screen. My mother's paternal lineage was right there for anyone to see: a long list of kings, queens, dukes, knights, lords, and noble aristocrats as far back as history goes. My forefathers bore the battle shields of Auchinbreck and Argyle in Scotland.

I sat in front of the computer as other genealogists stood around and we could not help but find it shocking. In many respects, the rare historical finding of lineal royalty was quite refreshing. It felt good to have such grand ancestry, even if it was unimportant to anyone else. But the kings of old were bequeathing nothing to my generation, so the archives of my ancestors couldn't produce anything beneficial to my search.

My Grandmother Elaine's indigenous mix of Métis, Blood Tribe, Cree, and other bloodlines had intermarried with Scottish and French. My aboriginal ancestors had been great leaders who fought in the Red River Rebellion in Manitoba and the Battle of Batoche in Saskatchewan. Some of these veterans were fur traders with the Hudson's Bay Company.

When the North-West Mounted Police were established, my ancestors joined the troops and a new era began. Over the centuries, they fought over land and their inheritance. There were many flaws, persecution, discrimination, and death. Facing countless hardships, they rolled with the punches.

I loved the stories of bygone eras and the picture postcards of my native kin. But, that aside, genealogy was not the answer for me to find Josh.

102: Nadia and Suzanne

Nadia and Cal decided to move to Edmonton, Alberta. On the outside, I was trying to be supportive. Underneath, I had a sinking feeling that our rock-solid friendship would ebb away. A thirteen-hour drive meant fewer visits. Time would gain on us and before we knew it, we would be old. I wanted Nadia to change her mind. She had touched my heart so much that it would be hard to let her go without a fight.

She suggested that I go to Edmonton to help her find a place to live. I felt reluctant to go because it ingrained the truth that she would be leaving and that was just too much. Finally, I realized that the miles would separate us physically, but not emotionally. I had to believe that nothing would ever replace our friendship.

While Nadia was putting her house on the market and getting ready to move, I was busy networking my search to talk shows such as Oprah, Leesa, and Morrey. I knew that could have big possibilities and I wanted to keep an open mind. Basically, I was down to the wire for ideas and getting nowhere until I met a reporter named Suzanne Fournier. Then, it was as if the stars had fallen into some kind of alignment or something, because my story became "newsworthy."

My journalist's life was similar to mine and our connection felt healing. She was strong and supportive, and a voice for so many others who had gone through painful childhoods. To me, Suzanne was an amazing and talented journalist who wanted to help me find my brother.

One early afternoon, she dropped by to get my story. Her photographer followed her into my living room and unstrapped his gear. He set up his camera and clicked for that perfect shot.

I will never forget that summer's day in 1999 as I unfolded the daily newspaper and opened to the second page. There was a picture of me on the couch holding up an old studio photo of Josh, Sheila, and me. Josh was in the middle with his arms around our shoulders and we were smiling contentedly.

Suzanne pointed out that while the government had the ability to pull siblings apart, it forbade any contact, and then expected to charge siblings for their reunification search. She wrote about foster-care abuse and negative labelling and how I had asked for government help but that, because Josh had had a name change, the government would not release any information. She noted how I had to pay the consequences of the government's actions and yet they still expected to be paid for a search.

She addressed Aboriginal groups and Alberta MLAs who were willing to advocate for me. Her article opened the eyes of readers to see the impact of the poor choices that siblings in care are left with. It was so informative and good that an Edmonton journalist read the story and called me for a phone interview. The result was a second story that came out a few days later. Surely, with all the feedback, some progress would come out of it.

103: Josh

On Sunday morning, the phone was ringing before Jack and I were out of bed. Jack rolled over and answered. After a pause, he put his hand over the speaker and turned his face to me.

"It's for you and I think it might be your brother." We stared at each other and then I grabbed the phone.

"Hello? Who is this?" I was wide awake.

"Hello, Eugenea. This is Josh, your brother."

I was speechless. It had worked. Josh had seen the story about him and here he was.

"I can't do this. I'm sorry. I'm just not ready for this," he said and, just like that, he was gone.

244

"Oh, no, he hung up. I can't believe it. I just talked to Josh." I sprung out of bed and dashed to the kitchen to check the call display. Both the number and name were blocked; there was no way to trace the call.

"What am I going to do?" I said loudly, fearing that a lifetime's work had already ended and we had not even met. I could not allow myself to believe that. He would call back—I knew he would. I just had to wait.

I was so pumped with excitement that I had to take a long hot shower to drown some energy. As the water caressed me, I felt quite overcome with emotion. I prayed for peace of mind and strength.

I didn't want to leave the house, but I had to go because I had church meetings for a big part of that day. Although my mind was anxious for the phone to ring, I still managed to dress calmly. Just as I reached out to grab my purse and leave, the phone rang again and it was Josh.

In the beginning, our conversation seemed suspended by the very fact that we had found each other. I was at a loss to put together what my heart needed to hear or say. My head was racing for words just to keep him on the line. I thought of so many questions, but I didn't want to scare him off. I needed to give him time to be ready. It felt like I was in a dream as Josh slowly opened up about his childhood adoption. He told me about his parents and we learned that our lives had followed such different trails.

His parents were well-known figures in their community. They had sheltered him so much that he did not remember what life was like before them. With amazing resilience, he didn't even remember me. Josh said he lived in Edmonton and I nearly dropped the phone. Was this providence? Nadia and I were flying there in four days to go house shopping for her.

"We could meet," I said excitedly. Why wouldn't we? I thought to myself.

"Possibly," Josh added, but I felt him distancing himself. I was afraid that he might bail on me again. "What do you want from me?" Josh asked bluntly.

"You called me," I reminded him, although I thought his question was awkward and demeaning. Then I had an epiphany as I thought about all the years of research I had invested into that day. "Actually, I do want something from you. I want my brother back in my life," I answered hoping to corral his fears.

"Okay. That I can do." He sounded relieved and I wished I could reach into the phone and hug him. We ended the conversation with my requesting for his contact information, but he declined and promised to call again. In contrast with all my unmanageable happiness, I wondered how much Josh was willing to put in. That night when I told the kids, they were significantly quiet and I could see they were shocked. It was like they had given up on the idea that Josh would ever surface.

Then, almost simultaneously, they plugged in with a load of questions. They wanted to know what he was like and when would they get to see their Uncle. I didn't have those answers, but later that week, Josh called back and I was grateful that he had kept his promise. Before he hung up, he gave me his cell number, and I knew we were making progress.

Nadia was so happy for me when I told her about finding Josh and she was even more excited to hear that he was living in Edmonton. Of course, she wasn't trying to dictate what I should do, but she was eager to get in the game if I would I let her. She had all sorts of plans popping into her head while I was juggling with the adventure of a proposed meeting.

Nadia and I were on a time crunch: we had four days to fly out, find a house, meet Josh, and fly back. How could we do all that? On the day of our flight, we opted to dress the same. We looked fashionably savvy in our pinstripe suits, heels, and simple jewels. Once the plane was off the ground, we could hardly contain our happiness as we revelled in the fluke that my long-lost brother lived in Edmonton and that was our destination.

An hour later, I stood at the baggage claim with Nadia and I had a feeling that Josh was there, watching. How would I know? With luggage in tow, we made our way to Calvin's van. I did not see anyone holding a newspaper and looking around for a photo match. Yet, somehow, I could not help wonder.

The next morning I called Josh on his cell, but he was too busy to see me. After thirty-seven years, it really hurt to hear that. It was a slap in the face, but Nadia and I used up the day in search of a home.

On the second day, Josh and I talked on the phone but the day passed by and our reunion was again on hold. When it came to day three, Nadia had secured the keys to her rental. She would be living just a few blocks from Josh. The house desperately needed cleaning and painting, so we had one day left to get it all in.

It was a good thing that I had a lot to do, because not meeting Josh had me tied up in knots. Why was he so afraid to see me? Then it occurred to me that perhaps he did not intend to meet me. I didn't know how I was going to go on living without a face to his voice. It had not crossed my mind that he wouldn't agree to meeting. I told myself that was crazy and went to clean the bedroom, when Nadia brought her cell to me.

"Hi. What are you doing?" Josh asked.

"I'm cleaning Nadia's new place. Can you come?"

"I can't make it today. How about tomorrow?"

"I leave tomorrow morning. Remember?" I said and I felt a crushing ache inside.

"I want to wait until tomorrow. Can't you stay an extra day?"

He was giving me nothing but lip service. He knew I could not delay my flight for an extra day. I already had commitments to a daycare job and my children needed their mother. Not knowing what else to do, I stood my ground and told Josh that if he did not see me now, it would have to wait until the next time I came out. He already had Nadia's address and all he had to do was come. As we talked, I noticed a white truck had passed by the house a few times.

"I'm here," he confessed from his cell. The truck stopped right in plain view where I could see him from the window of Nadia's living room.

"Don't go anywhere. I'll be right there," I promised and clicked off the phone. I was tripping out with the fact that Josh was right outside that door. Both Nadia and I were psyched as we tearfully hugged. Meanwhile, I was the one that had to go out the door and make my way across the driveway. My heart was beating so hard that, quite honestly, I thought it was going to bust.

As I stepped out and looked back for assurance, I could see the impact this was making on Nadia and Cal. Anticipation and curiosity were eating them alive. I went on and made it to the truck. What do I say? As I passed around the hood, I could see Josh through the windshield. He sat motionless under his seatbelt with one hand on the wheel. I worried that at any second, he might gun it to the floor and leave me in the street. I had to choose my words carefully. I didn't want to blow him off by saying the wrong thing. There was a lot to take in, like the fact that he was so shockingly different physically from what I had expected.

"Well, what do you think?" He took his chance at the question as the motor engine purred.

"I can't tell. You need to take off your cap," I said.

"I don't have much hair anymore," he blushed as he pulled off his cap.

"Please come out of the truck so I can take a look at you."

There was a frown of reluctance, but he opened the door, slid out, and pinned himself against the truck. It was an extraordinary and emotional moment, causing me to throw my arms around him and cry. Josh did not respond; his arms dangled lifeless and his form was stiffer than a mannequin.

"I have to go. I have to get home to my kids." He seemed overcome and anxious to flee. I stepped back and wiped my tears. I wanted Josh to say something that would connect us to our past. I suggested we go and talk somewhere quiet, like a small café. Nadia and Cal's timing was bang-on perfect: they came out and joined us. After the introductions and some easy chatting, Josh and I went to a nearby café.

"Do you remember the time when we laughingly rolled down the grassy hills together?" I asked as I sipped the whip off the top of my cocoa.

"No. I have no memory of us, because I blocked it out a long time ago." Josh looked sad. I sat stonewalled, but he was not interested in talking about our past. At times, the air was very thick between us. An hour later, he took me back to the house where I gave him a big hug. He did not reciprocate, but I knew that goodbye was not forever.

104: Josh, Fritz, and Marie

When I returned home to Vancouver, Josh called almost daily and I learned a lot about him. He talked loosely about his early marriage, his wife's abandoning him, and the strenuous years of child support. He never remarried, but he took another swing at parenting foster kids. With a trucking business and the foster twins, he needed a nanny. On top of that, he was paying for tutors and private schools. In all, it was not easy, because his twins suffered from fetal alcohol syndrome and Josh was on the road a lot.

I was surprised that social services allowed these children to live in a foster home with only one parent. Josh's adoptive parents were the backup he needed to secure his family. They had a lot of wealth. They owned oil wells, a TV station, and a hockey team, so there was no worry about a lack of funds.

Apart from my husband and kids, Josh was at the top of my priority list. Obviously, our next family vacation was set for Edmonton. A few weeks later, we landed at the airport and Josh was there to meet the kids and drive us to the hotel. Just for the record, we loved every second that he shared with us. I did not expect their feelings to soar to springboard heights, but the kids simply gravitated to their new Uncle. My brother seemed comfortable as he openly showed interest in their pursuits.

Although Josh talked about his home being like a king's empire, he was not inviting us to the family parlour. He was keeping his adoptive family in the dark about our connection. He said he felt that it was too much for his sick elderly mother to deal with emotionally. He also said his father had died several years ago.

This confused me and I wondered about the accuracy of the government record system. Such a big error did not make sense. My lawyer's letter had stated that it was the other way around: the mother had died, not the father. I was concerned about this, but I had kids to entertain so Jack and I focused on tours and shopping, and I wanted some time with my best friend Nadia.

Josh took us on a sightseeing tour of Edmonton. On the last stretch of our tour, he drove around the homes in Sherwood Park, one of the quieter neighbourhoods. As he drove us back to our hotel, he flaunted that we had actually passed his house. I felt like I was canoeing without a paddle. Nevertheless, it did not matter, because I had already figured out where he lived.

As our trip neared its end, Josh cut loose. His spirits were on the upswing and our relationship did not feel so alien. Gradually, he became curious enough to want to ask about his real family. On returning home, I called my parents. They couldn't wait to hear from their boy. Ultimately, Josh called our parents yet, as beautiful as it was, there was a problem. My parents wanted to see Josh, but he vetoed their request.

It was no secret that Josh craved approval. He felt the need to dazzle us with what we were realizing were little white lies. He made up stories of owning jets, homes, and fancy cars, and I overlooked it because of his childhood. It didn't sit well with me, but I would not let his fabrications put a gap between us. In the short time of knowing my brother, I was eager to accept him.

Late in November, Josh got in his truck and drove all the way from Edmonton to come and see me in Vancouver. He wanted to meet Sheila, so I let her know and she came with her husband, daughter, and granddaughter. It was so wonderful. I really believed that he loved his family and, given time, he would come around.

Josh explained that he didn't go by the name of Josh. His family and friends called him Fritz.

"Why Fritz?" I asked.

"That's been my legal name since I was adopted. I don't go by Josh anymore."

I felt an unspoken resentment. No darn wonder it took so long to find him.

Josh was a real whizz on computers. He wanted to have online contact with me but I didn't have a computer, so he bought me one. Shortly after my birthday, Josh had a computer delivered to me by one of his truck drivers. As they unloaded the computer from the truck and put it in my van, the driver said the weirdest thing to me.

"Fritz gets to play bachelor of the week while Marie's out of town."

"Who's Marie?" I asked him.

"That's his wife."

"Oh... He said he doesn't have a wife. Are we talking about the same man?"

"I would guess it's the same man who has said he's your brother. He's got foster twins. A girl and a boy."

Why would Josh lie to me? As the semi drove away, I thought about all the calls I had made to Josh and the many times he didn't pick up. Later that day Jack was hooking up the computer when Josh phoned to see if I got my present.

"Who is Marie?"

"Marie? I don't know any Marie."

"Really? Well, your driver says that is your wife."

"That's pretty funny considering I'm not married." Josh roared, but it was not a laughing matter and I was not asking. I knew he was lying.

105: Jack, Family, and Foster Families

The following summer, Mom was going to the southern part of Alberta to visit relatives and I was going to the north. Eventually, we would meet in Cardston where I invited Josh to meet with us. Josh had talked to Mom and Dad for two years already, but he was not willing to see them. This was painful payback for both my parents. Mom was very heavy hearted to be in the same province and not see her son.

On Canada Day, Jack and I, Lance, Caitlin, and Payton arrived, after an exhausting drive, at Howie and Gabriella's house. My kids had heard many wonderful things about them. This was the time for them to see how special Howie and Gabriella were to me. We took a drive to Waterton National Park, which is very similar to Banff. It was a sweet visit and I hated to say goodbye because I never knew when I would see them again.

We stopped in Calgary to visit Bruce and Ida. First, we went together to the Calgary Stampede and the next day we rode the elevator to the top of the Calgary Tower. In the middle of chatting with Ida in the backyard, my cell went off and it was Josh. He was on his way to see us.

Three hours later, he arrived at Bruce and Ida's door. The kids were excited to see their Uncle. Josh stayed for dinner and afterwards we looked at Ida's photo albums. She showed Josh the pictures of me so he could see what my life had been like when I had lived with them. The night rolled on and Josh had to make the trip home. It was always hard to let him go because I knew I would miss him so much.

It was unfortunate that Josh wasn't willing to stick around to see Mom; she was very upset. There were certainly moments when I thought Josh was so cold to his parents, but I guessed that was his way of dealing with his parents' failures.

By the end of our journey my kids had seen some of the places where I had lived and gone to school.

For my birthday, Jack and Lance bought me an air ticket to Edmonton. Of course, I would stay with my best friend Nadia, so Josh would not have to worry. I was there for five days, but I was not going to get much time with him. I decided to get to the bottom of where he lived. I could not find a listing for his estate on a city map. Nadia suggested we drive to the city hall and find a blueprint. There, we did not have to go inside, because the front window was covered from top to bottom with maps of every district. We drove out to the area where Josh lived and found the exact house, but we didn't see him. The lot was full of trucks. He had two large workshops next to his house.

Later that evening, Josh and I met for dinner. Actually, when I got there, he had already started dinner without me and was halfway through his meal.

"So what did you do today?" he asked as I squeezed into the bench to face him. I told him that Nadia and I had gone to visit an antique store.

"Which one?" he inquired.

"It's on Wyre Road across from the gas station."

"I live just around the corner from there," he said wittily.

"I know. You live in the grey house. I saw your name and address right outside the gate." I glanced over the table to look him in the eye. "Your little sister is smarter than you think but don't worry, I have no plans to drop in on you. Your secret is safe."

He was stunned that I knew where he lived.

106: Mom, Dad, Sheila, and Josh

After I flew home to British Columbia, I did another background check, just to make sure that I had done all my homework and had the right brother. All the information that Josh had related was correct yet I still sensed something was wrong.

Josh told me that during spring break, he and his kids had gone to Mexico to stay at their timeshare. This was a bit of an oversight on his part, because he had recently sent me a picture of the house he owned in Mexico. Why would anyone stay in a Mexican timeshare if they owned a house there?

An interesting pattern had begun to emerge as my family began to wonder if Josh was not really my brother.

Mom, Dad, and Sheila were having second thoughts about Josh's inconsistencies. What I found more disturbing was the possibility of danger. Uncle Don—Mom's older brother—insisted that I show him all the photos I had, so we met for coffee. I pulled out Josh's picture and handed it to him.

"Well, what do you think? Is he my brother? Do you think that is really Josh?" I asked.

"I don't think so. He doesn't look at all like him. I remember that little boy and this man is nothing like your brother from what I remember." He turned the picture so I could see it.

"He is bald like your grandpa, so I guess it's possible. But that's the only similarity there is."

If Josh were not my brother, why would he do this to our family?

In the fall, Mom came to visit me for two weeks so we went over all the details I had. She looked at Josh's picture and knew for certain he was her boy. Josh called me to say he was in Vancouver making a delivery and he wanted to see me. I told Josh that Mom was at my house and he decided it was the right time to meet.

I was so thrilled, but Mom was not. She suppressed her excitement, because she was sure that Josh would chicken out and not show up. Not even fifteen minutes before show time, she was back on the radar. She scooted around, tidying up, along with a quick redo of her hair and makeup.

The real panic came when Josh's semi pulled in front of the house. With the truck lights beaming like a landing aircraft, Mom went into the guestroom and stood in the dark, peeking through the curtains.

"It's too dark out. I wish I had my glasses so I could see him," she said as I put my arms around her waist and laid my head against her shoulder. Josh turned off the engine and sat in the dark. Mom and I couldn't see anything but the glow of his cigarette.

"Is our mother here?" Josh asked as his eyes circled the kitchen. Before I could answer, we heard the shuffle of footsteps and he turned to see Mom come out of hiding.

"I'm right here." Her voice had a tremor. She eyed Josh with such an ache that I felt her desperation to hold him. He stared back and there was no movement out of either of them. She didn't smile or cry; she just stood with her hands shaking at her side.

I wished for Mom that Josh would throw caution to the wind and melt into her waiting arms, but he didn't. I looked over to Mom and saw how that shook her more.

"Please come and sit at the table so we can talk," I quickly cut in and pulled a chair out. Mom blinked back the onset of tears as she sat next to me. Josh followed along and found his place on the other side of Mom. I had always imagined this day would be cause for a champagne toast and a grand welcome, but Josh had let it go far too long for such an honour.

"Take off your hat, Josh."

Mom was taking it all in. She noticed every movement of his body, but Josh was so unreadable, so placid.

"You won't like it; I'm as bald as a baby's bum."

He pulled off his cap and we couldn't help but laugh. His old marble gleamed and it was quite comical how we could count, on one hand, the frizzled hairs on his head.

We all welcomed the icebreaker and it was so good that it came from Josh. For our family, connection came through the bond of personal emotions, yet I didn't see the slightest blip in Josh's response. It was odd how nothing seemed to derail that poker face of his.

"You look like your dad," Mom said, as her eyes locked on his.

"Really? In what way?" Josh asked.

"Your eyes. You have eyes like your father," Mom said and that's when I thought for sure she would break down or get mushy. But she held a tight face. Gradually, she tried to explore Josh's life and he let her in. He told her about his flamboyant lifestyle, but I could see that his fortune did not amount to a hill of beans to her. She was only impressed that he had any time at all for her.

They had a lot of catching up to do but he was exhausted, so he bowed out early and went to sleep in his truck. Mom wanted to mother Josh with kindness, so the next morning she cooked. Josh got the continental five-star breakfast without the hotel. Unfortunately, he did not have much time to hang around.

When Josh waved from his fleeing rig, I could see how hard that was for Mom. Her mood shifted from exhilaration to an uncomfortable solitude. I tried to joke with her, but humour was an obvious distraction from her thoughts. The next day, she was so happy again and back to the old Mom I knew. We had a wonderful afternoon with my Dad. We met him in Langley and went for lunch at an all-you-can-eat fish 'n' chips restaurant.

Mom was dying to tell Dad that Josh was truly their son and she was one hundred percent positive. That was the opening show and eventually they talked about old stuff, like their high school dating and their short marriage with three babies. As the three of us talked, I felt a connection and I really knew that it was time we had fun as a family.

However, that night, Mom withdrew into a sullen mood and I could see that she wanted to go, home so Jack and I drove her to the ferry. We talked about Josh, and she told my husband that she was ninety-seven percent sure that Josh was her child. She wanted so much to believe, but already she was beginning to doubt. I was confused that she didn't know whether Josh was really her child. How could she not know?

Two days later, I came home from shopping to find Josh's truck parked on the other side of the road. Why was he back so soon? Did he miss his mother and want to make more time for her? I had a great visit with him and I wished he could stay forever. That night we went out for dinner and the next morning he left again.

Mom was so upset that Josh had returned when she wasn't there. She regretted her impulsive decision to return home, but she was glad that Josh had finally accepted her.

107: Marie and Fritz

Two weeks later out of the blue, I got a call that made sense out of everything.

"Hello?" I said as I picked up the line.

"Who is this?"

"Who is this?" I asked back.

"I want to know who this is, because your number keeps showing up on my cell bill." The woman on the other end was brash and I did not understand what was wrong with her. I thought maybe someone had been charging calls to this woman from our house. "My husband's cell phone bill lists your number. Why is he calling you? Do you know a man named Fritz?"

"Who are you and why should I tell you? I don't know you."

At first, I wondered if Fritz was in on this, but then the woman claimed to be his wife and her name was Marie. Fritz or Josh or whatever his name was said he had no wife.

"What's the story? Does he tell people that his wife is dead or what?" Marie was dying to know.

"No, he just says he's not married."

"You are not the first person he has lied to. Did he say he has children?"

"Yes, but I am really uncomfortable with this because I don't know who you are."

"I am his wife. Again, my name is Marie, and we were married January 11, 1992."

I asked her how many kids they had and she said two, naming them.

"Fritz was doing something on the Internet. Is that how he met you, through a chat line? That is how he met some girl in Australia. He was proposing to this poor girl and she was going to fly here," Marie explained.

She did fly here, I thought to myself. I remembered talking to that woman on Fritz's cell the night that he picked her up from the airport. I wondered what ever happened to that pretty young girl. Marie said that it wasn't the first time he had messed around.

"What does your husband do for a living?"

"He owns a trucking business."

"What else?" I asked.

"Nothing else."

"What's his last name?"

"Addard."

"Okay. How long has this been going on?" she asked.

"Three years."

"Three years?"

"What is your name?" she asked.

"First, I want to know about the new baby."

"What new baby?"

"The baby you and Fritz bought overseas."

"We are not getting a baby. We couldn't possibly take in a baby, because the twins already have special needs. Have you met Fritz?" she asked.

"Yes," I nodded, as if she could see me through the phone. "We've met a few times."

I could tell she was confused about our relationship, so I added that we should go back a bit. She should tell me about Fritz's parents.

"Is this a romantic relationship that you are having?" she asked.

"No," I said and there was no response from her. "Maybe now we can continue this conversation and you'll understand where I'm coming from. If you fill in the blanks properly, I will definitely tell you everything," I hinted.

"Does this have something to do with some people claiming to be his biological family?" Marie clicked in.

"Yes," I said.

"Oh! Okay!" Her voice warmed with relief. "Well, that's not true either. He was never adopted. If I had known that he was such a liar and how weird he was, I would not have married him."

"How do I know you're not some fake so I will believe Josh is not my real brother?" I interrupted her.

"You don't know, but I have no reason to make this up."

"Why do you stay with him?" I asked sympathetically.

"I can't leave him. What would happen to the kids? I know he is not much of a father, but he is the only father they know."

I felt sorry for Marie. She felt trapped, because she knew the government would take the kids away if she left her husband. She had no resources or funds because she had given him all her savings for their trucking business.

"How did you meet Fritz?" Marie asked and I told her everything, going back to the first day. When our conversation came to a close, we both knew that Fritz was a fraud. Unfortunately, the question of motive continued to pick at my brain. Fritz was also pretending to be an adopted son to the richest family in Edmonton and that came easily because he had the same last name.

If he were looking for a gold mine, he was at the wrong house. What did he have up his sleeve? I would never know and maybe not knowing was better. Not long after, Marie called again to say that she had not told her husband about our conversation. She warned me that Fritz had a shipment to deliver in Vancouver. I did not want to see him, but Marie pleaded with me to not let on that we had talked, because she needed time to sort things out.

"Fritz is a sociopath, not a psychopath. I will send you proof that he is a fraud, but I have to warn you that the police investigated him last year for putting bad porn on the Internet."

I wondered if it get any worse.

Later, Fritz called to tell me that he wanted to phone my dad and was planning to go visit him for the first time. Of course, I called and warned Dad that Fritz was on his way. I told him that Marie was afraid of Fritz and it may be better to say nothing at this point. He agreed and promised to call back after the visit.

I hoped that big fat liar of a so-called brother was not expecting to light up Dad's walkway with his deadpan personality. No matter, his lack of heart did not stop his neurotic soul from ringing the doorbell. Of course, Dad was not going to sink the man, but it didn't stop him from having a little fun. It would have been interesting to be a fly on the wall that day.

Dad stood in his doorway and talked about anything at all that would have bored the hell out of Fritz. He kept Fritz out on the porch for forty-five minutes. Fritz was so disgusted that he got in his truck and called me to complain. He couldn't believe that his so-called biological Dad didn't invite him in.

"I stood out in the freezing rain for almost an hour and I was soaking wet, but he wouldn't invite me in. He was dry in the nice warm entrance and talking my head off. He didn't even care that his own son that he had not seen for forty years was out in the pouring rain," Fritz announced grudgingly. He deserved what he got! What a lousy first-time reunion, I thought. No five stars there.

Unfortunately, Fritz knew where I lived and he could show up whenever he wanted. It was freaky and I worried about my kids. With the knowledge of his past, I wanted to seek police advice. I went to the authorities and they told me that it would be hard to press charges against such a bizarre case. After I finished my statement, I kept thinking that there had to be something else I could do. When I got home, I called Nadia and told her everything. I asked if she wanted to do some snooping around for me.

"Ooh! That sounds like fun. When can I start?" she piped in with excitement.

That's so Nadia, ready to plow right in and help, so I asked her to go to Marie's house and check things out. I suggested that she look for a wedding picture or photo albums. At least that way, I would know there had been an actual marriage. Nadia was the perfect spy. From her van, she could stake out the property without being seen. She saw the driveway was filled with trucks so she knew Fritz was home. Nadia called me from inside her van.

"I don't know what to do. I can see all the trucks and I don't want to go too close."

"No. I don't want Fritz to see you. Are you okay with talking to Marie?"

"Yes."

"Would you call her house and tell her that you are there on my behalf?"

"Okay," Nadia said and then we hung up. She called the house from her cell and Marie answered.

"Fritz is home. Why don't you come to the door and tell Fritz that you are dropping by to say hello?" Marie suggested.

"It's not a good idea because Fritz lied about having a wife. Plus, he might think you are involved and that could backfire." Nadia replied. That made sense, so they arranged to meet on Saturday morning when Fritz would be out of town.

By late Saturday morning, I was on the edge of my seat but I had to wait for Nadia's call. I feared that Fritz might show up and freak out. All these horrible thoughts ran through my head. When Nadia called, I knew that she had pulled it off. She made a spooky owlish noise and we laughed in sheer relief.

"So, what happened?" I practically begged.

"The first time I called, the kids answered and they yelled in the phone, 'Who are you? Who are you?' Then they hung up so I had to call back," Nadia laughed. "Marie said she was sick, but she still planned to see me. I got there and as I entered the house I couldn't believe how beautiful it was. It was decorated in white with oriental blue accents. Marie has beautiful Persian rugs and white leather couches and it's amazing that her house stays in one piece. The kids are absolute terrors, and they are such monsters. The little girl kicked me in the leg three times. The whole time, it went from one horrendous confrontation to the next."

With all the anxiety and stress, Nadia was still able to get a close-up peek of Fritz and Marie's framed wedding pictures. She saw the family album and baby Fritz was there with his family. It was unmistakable. From baby to adult, the pictures captured the real Fritz. It was proof that Fritz had not been adopted at the age of eleven. The kids stopped fighting momentarily to point out their Daddy in the album that Marie had laid out across her lap.

"I was so scared that Fritz was going to walk in that door any second. I could hardly wait to get out of there," Nadia said and I could hear the lingering paranoia in her voice.

"Wow, you did it. You did great," I jumped in. She really took the bull by the horns. I wish I could have been there too. It would have been the summit for both of us.

The police went to investigate Fritz, but he was not home so they questioned Marie instead. Since Fritz was out of town, they called his cell and got a statement over the phone. The only thing the police could do was put a restraining order against him. I don't know if there was any legal paper work or just a verbal warning but he was not allowed contact with my family or me.

Fritz knew the police had questioned his wife and he was furious. He called his house and threatened to deal with her, whatever that meant. He slammed the phone down and left Marie feeling terrified. Her husband was mentally and emotionally abusive, but never physically. She did not think he would rough her up, but he might smash all their stuff. It would not surprise Marie if Fritz were to take everything of value and leave her penniless. I guess she thought I was a real troublemaker because she called me right away.

"What have you done?" she snapped, as if it was my fault that her husband was such a sly man. "Why did you go to the police? Do you realize what you've done?" She was very angry.

"You forget that I have a family too," I defended myself, but she interrupted saying that Fritz had thrown a screaming tantrum. "Before you say any more I want you to know that I taped a conversation with Fritz and I'm taping our conversation as well. Would you like to hear what Fritz said?" I asked.

"I have to go. I hope you have a great life," she said and I was so glad that I didn't have to talk to her anymore. I did not want to be in the middle of a steamy war between Fritz and Marie.

It was only a day or two before Christmas when Fritz disobeyed the order and called again. "Hi. How are you?" he asked.

"I'm fine, how are you?" I answered coolly.

"I'm gonna take off for a bit," he said, using his pity-me voice.

"Oh yeah, you going somewhere?" I couldn't wait to hear. "Holidays?" I put in as an afterthought.

"Yeah, going south... Mexico. So, what goes with you? I thought I would give you a shout."

What was I supposed to say to him? I was so hurt that he turned out to be some creep and not my brother. I could hear the motor of his semi in the background and I knew he was on the road somewhere.

"Well, I've been told that you are not my brother and that you actually know that you are not my brother," I blurted out.

"I know that?" He pretended to be shocked.

"So, what I need from you is documentary proof; otherwise, we can't communicate. Okay? It's up to you so the ball is in your court. It's up to you! Prove to me that you were adopted." I said angrily.

"Who told you that?" As if he had no idea.

"If you can't prove to me that you are adopted, then I can't talk to you."

"Okay," he replied. "You have a good Christmas, alright?"

"Alright."

"Goodbye then."

"Bye," I said, but he didn't hang up right away, because I heard his tires screech in the background before the line went dead.

108: Alice

My brother-in-law Carlton—Sheila's husband—had passed away just after Christmas in 2002 and he was the only person who ever came close to being a brother to me. Carlton you were a good man! Also, I had lost a brother or really never found one in the first place when Fritz turned out to be phony. Because New Year's Day had significance as a disastrous day in my early childhood, I decided to make my New Year's Day resolution for 2003 to find Josh.

My work had sat idle for three years and my enthusiasm was not the same. I felt beaten down and discouraged. Luckily, I kept all my letters and files so I did not have to start at zero. I knew it would not take long to get to the top of my game again. The sooner I got on it, the better. Most of the material was still organized into labelled categories. The first section was called, "How to Search" and the second was "Documents and Letters." The next five sections were "Adoption Agencies," "Notes and Journal," "Directory Listings," and "Computer Data."

To begin once more, I decided that I would delete my name from all the search engines and do a more labour-intensive inquiry.

I asked Dad to participate. I needed another pair of eyes to search the files I had on Henderson Street and to seek out information at the University of British Columbia's Law Library. We planned to go to the Post Adoption Registry on the following Friday, since Fridays were the only days permitted for researchers. However, almost right at the start of the race, I was interrupted by a call from an unknown woman who referred to herself as Alice. Although she asked for me, I didn't recognize her voice.

"This is she," I spoke loosely, thinking the woman was possibly a forgotten acquaintance.

"You need to sit down, so find a seat. Are you sitting down?"

"Sure," I said, as I struggled one-handedly to grasp a chair.

"You are looking for someone. Maybe a brother?"

"Yes," I stopped moving. For a split second I didn't breathe as I nearly toppled the chair to the floor.

"Who is this?"

"Again, my name is Alice."

"Yes."

"Well, I believe you registered by computer with our company—Adoptees Canada—several years ago. We have a match and would like to know if you are still interested in a reunion?" Nothing on earth could have interrupted that moment. "Are you still there?" she asked.

"I can't believe it, are you sure?" My voice shrilled weirdly. Suddenly, I began to feel a surge of warmth as I tried to stay calm.

"Why don't I ask you some questions to make sure we have the right people?" Alice suggested. "How many siblings were there?"

"Three," I blurted out.

"Oh, you sure there weren't four?" She seemed confused.

"No, it's three," I confirmed.

"Maybe this isn't the right brother. He said there were definitely four. Three girls and himself," she recalled. Then it suddenly clicked in my mind that my brother was talking about Chloe, who had been only two months old at the time.

Excitedly, I sprang from the chair and yelled, "It's the baby; he's talking about the baby. Yes, my mother had a new baby and I didn't remember her. But my brother would have been old enough to know that."

"Okay," she sighed with relief. "I will call him and tell him that you are his real sister. Why don't you tell me a little about yourself so I have something to tell him? Let's start with… are you married?"

"Yes, I'm divorced and remarried. I have four kids and I live outside Vancouver."

"What do you do in your spare time?"

"Oh, lots of things like reading, sewing, crafts, the list goes on," I said quickly.

"I should tell you about Josh. He is separated, but he has someone in his life and he has a son.

"Where does he live?" I could hardly wait to hear.

"Calgary."

I knew it all along. All this time, it always seemed so right that Calgary was the place because that's where Josh had his roots. Why would he want to move away and lose that forever? Subconsciously, he may never have put a lot of thought into it, but logically it made the most sense.

"When would you like to talk to him?" she asked.

"Now!" That sounded so hasty but why not now? "How about in half an hour?"

"Okay," she said. "I'll see if that is alright and will call you back."

Alice didn't leave me hanging. She called back right away to say that Josh was very pleased to hear that I wanted to talk to him. I could feel my head and heart churning into a whirl of dance and drama. I was bubbling with excitement and nearly tearful and yet I felt held back by doubts.

Would I know this time if Josh is really my brother? Maybe this was a friend of Fritz's and it was a conspiracy. Paranoid? Definitely! But for obvious reasons.

109: Josh

Generally speaking, it is cold in January but I felt hot with nervousness. I prayed for that phone call and nearly jumped out of my skin when the phone rang.

"Hello?"

"Hello. May I speak to Eugenea?" a man asked and my heart was doing a backflip.

"This is Eugenea." I paced around the kitchen still attached to the phone's umbilical cord.

"Hi, I am Josh, your brother. I think you must be my sister."

"Oh... Wow! I don't know what to say... Umm, possibly," I said and I wondered how stupid that sounded.

"Do you remember me?" he asked. I was about to answer him when I saw the recorder button and I was so happy that I remembered to tape the call.

"I remember you. I do remember you," I said, thinking to myself, he has no idea!

"Well, we were together for a short bit at a foster home—the Rosses. Remember that?"

"I do remember that." I was flushed with emotion. His voice sounded just like Dad's. It was so remarkable.

"You had fairly light hair at the time, I think."

"Yeah, I did."

"You used to wear a small dress. Like, a sailor dress. Remember that?"

"Yes, I do," I answered. I couldn't believe he actually remembered my favourite dress.

"Yeah, I think we've got the right people here."

"I think so. You know, we both lived at the Rosses for a while. Do you remember what happened after that?"

"Yeah, you went to a house down the road and they wouldn't let me see you."

"Well, I was right across the street from your house."

"Was that where the two boys lived?"

"No. Did you know the Brocktons?"

"The postman?" he asked.

"The milkman." I answered.

"He lived across the street, right?"

"Right," I added.

"They were like real nice people."

"No," I said adamantly.

"No? We must have the wrong house." Josh was getting confused.

"We both lived on Henderson Street at the same time, except I lived across from you. I could see you from my house, but I wasn't allowed contact with you. I don't know why that happened," I explained.

"I wasn't allowed contact with you, either. I was told that the Rosses were pushing for one child, not two. That didn't work out, because after you left, I went crazy. I went nuts, doing all kinds of weird things and they locked me in the children's shelter and I never went back," Josh said, and I felt his isolation and pain.

"Do you remember being in the orphanage?" I asked.

"Are you talking about the farm? I remember being sent to a farm. You might have been too young to remember that." Josh was right; I didn't remember any farm except Grandma's place. "I think it was in the summer," he added.

"Holy! I don't recall any of that," I said, and wondered if by some chance Josh was confused with Grandma's farm before our time in care.

"Did you see a social worker for a number of years?" He changed the subject.

"Yes, you were adopted right?" I asked. I needed to hear it from Josh.

"Yes," he said and I told him that I had met Sheila again during our teenage years.

"Are you French, Scottish, Cree, and English?"

"Yes," I answered.

"So am I," he said.

"Really!" I laughed.

"I think we've got a match." He laughed too.

"So you just registered online last night?"

"Yeah. I never thought about putting my name on the net. I put my adopted name and that didn't work, so I entered my birth name, and came up with our surname all over Quebec. Shows how much French we do have."

"Your biological father lives out here."

"Oh, you know him? What does he do?"

"He's retired and doing okay for himself. He owns a few properties and he's kinda kicking back now."

"Did he have any other children besides the three of us?"

"Yes. You have many sisters to meet," I happily announced like I had delivered these girls myself.

"Wow! So you are in contact with him?"

"Yes, I just saw Dad on Sunday," I said and I really felt happy that Josh asked. Obviously we had a lot to talk about and we both had a lot of questions.

Eventually, we had to hang up. We could have talked all night.

Later, when I replayed our conversation, I heard a younger version of my father's voice. I cried as I went over the tape again. I am sure that my friends thought I was obsessed, because that was all I could talk about for days. I even talked to Alice from Adoptees Canada and I told her about my experience with Fritz. Alice kept strict confidence, so Josh didn't know anything about our family. Whatever he said came from his memory.

When my parents heard the tape of our phone conversation, they felt he was authentic. They believed the voice belonged to their son. Mom was just so happy, happier than I could ever remember, and Dad was... let's just say speechless.

110: Josh and Ronnie

In time, Josh sent emails and we exchanged our undesirable school pictures to see if our gene pool was an obvious match. Shockingly so, I could see myself in him and he too recognized the child in my photos. I believed that Josh was authentic. I didn't feel that he would turn out to be a case of mistaken identity.

I emailed the adoption registry to ask if identifying information can be exchanged when two siblings are matched. After all, Josh was entitled to a copy of his personal file. Somehow, Josh received a copy of my email and assumed that I thought he was a fraud.

At first, he was hurt until I explained to him that he would be getting a record of his childhood that he was rightfully entitled to have. Josh didn't want me to have any lingering doubts so he sent me a copy of his adoption. He offered to go for DNA testing but we both agreed it wasn't necessary.

The only way to stop the doubts was for me to grow a set of wings and fly to Calgary. It was obvious that I was bound to go ASAP because there was no way I would have the patience to wait for a summer trip. I wished my family could be there too, but that was not possible. There had to be a way to share such a beautiful moment, but how? I did not know. However, all things are possible so I believed that I had to put it into action quickly.

Then it clicked. What if I emailed a letter to the Calgary paper? I could start with an interest in the city events. I hoped they would suggest something fun and unique to entertain a brother I did not know. More importantly, I would share the news of a reunion and hope with all my heart that they would find it of interest.

Yes! Yes! Yes! A Calgary journalist would be there as Josh and I met. When I told Josh about the journalist, he was happy to share our story too. We both realized that it would be our way to inspire and bring hope to so many. On the plane, I forced myself to write a small entry of what I was feeling.

It was only a brief memory but I didn't want to forget a single moment of the anticipation. I wondered if Josh and I would instantly recognize each other. So much had come and gone. I had already been a mother, grandmother, divorced, remarried, and some of our family had already died.

The plane was off the runway and soaring. I looked out the oval window and saw a heavy mat of clouds below. The clouds gradually dissipated and I could see the city of Calgary. As wonderful as it was, I felt both exhilarated and euphoric, except I had a jittery stomach. The plane suddenly dropped because of bad weather, but I hardly noticed because it was only minutes from landing and my nerves were already frayed. How would I get off the plane and not become a wreck?

It was an easy terminal to get around, yet I was overwhelmed. I came to the end of the hallway and I knew Josh was just beyond the doors, so I ducked into the washroom. It was hard not to be completely rattled from head to toe. I leaned against the wall and it would have been so easy to stay there and hide out for a while. What if he changed his mind and didn't come? I wondered as I went to the sink and looked in the mirror.

What a mess. My eyes jutted out from two hollows. My crow's lines betrayed my concealer and right away I pulled the corners tightly. Will I still be the same little sister to him? I questioned myself as I tried to get my trembling hand to stencil a line around my lips.

All that was required was for me to let go of my inhibitions. Ready to take on the world or at least the airport, I made my way back to the corridor. I realized that I had spent far too much time in the bathroom. I was on my own looking for the way; there was no one in sight—not even a stewardess.

I got to the stairs and walked down the steps toward the sliding doors. As I reached the bottom, the automatic doors glided apart. Then I saw him, bigger than life, and for a second everything came to a stop. I stopped. It's him! It's really him! I knew that face. I knew the man holding a mixed bouquet and staring back.

"You must be Ronnie," Josh smiled and I remembered that was his nickname for me as a child. Josh held out a beautiful bouquet of flowers and I laughed because I had flowers for him too. I dropped my carry-on bag and threw my arms around him.

The tears came fast and uncontrollably as we held each other so tightly that our bodies shook. To this day, I am really amazed that we didn't collapse. Every second was dreamlike, yet I could hear myself whimpering from a place that came from deep within. It was a place that I didn't remember, because it had

"How does it feel to finally meet after forty years?" The man waited intently.

"There are no words to describe how we are feeling," I cried out with a glee that was contagious.

"It's so nice to know I have a family and it feels fantastic to finally have my sister back," Josh said. His smile illuminated his face every time he looked at me. I told the press that I felt like a rocket had gone off. It was the only thing close to describing the eruption of so many emotions.

We answered the media's questions as we talked about our apprehension, our abuse, and the scandalous Fritz. By that time, the crowd had really thickened and seemed to be fascinated. I could see the emotion written on their faces.

"I called her Ronnie. That's what I called my sister when she was little and I always will," Josh vowed and I was tickled pink to be so endeared. There we stood, filled with laughter, as our eyes sparkled with the happiest tears.

Josh and I meet at the Calgary Airport

"Excuse me, Miss. Did you forget to pick up your luggage?" A woman with greying hair wearing a security uniform tapped me on the shoulder.

"Oh, thank you. I completely forgot about my suitcase," I said as I eyed my bag in her hand.

"I knew it must be yours, because it's the only bag left going round and around the carousel unclaimed and you are the only person without a suitcase." She laughed and dropped it next to my feet.

"What are your plans for your weekend together?" The man from the media brought the conversation back to us.

"Well, we heard there is a city museum that has records of orphanages with pictures of kids and babies that boarded there. We want to see if there are any pictures of us and we want to see what it looks like now," Josh explained.

"We have a lot to talk about." Josh and I spouted in unison and we laughed together and I could see that everyone around could feel our happiness. What started out as mild curiosity for people passing by had turned into an engaged audience. As the excitement of our reunion came to a close, I noticed that Josh was wired. All that time, he was wearing a mike on the collar of his jacket.

We finished with the media and left. Once outside, I remembered how bitterly cold Alberta could be in the winter. We picked up speed and Josh put his arms around me. Mother Nature didn't care what our plight was. She was in a raging mood and pummeled our faces with splintered pricks of ice.

I tried to bury my head into my shawl as I thought about my yard back home. Already lush and green with tulips poking their heads out of the soil. Josh had come with his girlfriend Kelsey and she was just as excited as we were. I gravitated to her and I liked her from the very start and it was easy to see why Josh loved her. The city lights danced and sparkled over the glistening snow as we drove toward their house. We could hardly keep our eyes off each other without tearing up and grinning.

"I can't believe this is actually happening. I am on such a big high." I said to Josh and then his eyes filled again and I couldn't hold back. He pulled the car toward an embankment of hardened snow and turned off the car.

"Don't move," he pleaded. He leaped out, ran around to my side, and opened the door. He wanted everything to be perfect as he took my arm. It was so sweet—a moment that would last in our hearts forever.

Josh dragged in the suitcase as we made our way into the house. It was so relaxed and comfortable that it was easy to feel warm and fuzzy inside. That made it so much easier for Josh and me to talk.

We snuggled in on the couch to watch the six o'clock news and leaped with anticipation when our story hit the headline. No matter how unique the situation was, it was still weird to see it on TV. It was so touching and every time I see that clip, it's like I'm reliving all those emotions again. What a treasured memory!

After supper we drove to Josh's work and I met his co-workers. They had been a great support to my brother and were so thrilled to hear the story on the news. Josh's best friend Mario had worked a double shift so that we could spend more time together. Kelsey slept at her daughter's house so Josh and I spent our first night talking for hours.

Josh told me that he saw the movie Mary Poppins and thought that I had been taken away to become the little actress Jane. As a child we looked identical.

Even now we still have a similar look.

We listened to music and talked about how our lives had turned out. At 4:00 a.m., I finally went to bed. Josh gave up his room and slept on the couch. I tried to sleep but my mind was racing with mixed feelings. I dozed off, but was awakened by the sound of footsteps. Josh was going through similar emotions and I heard him walking back and forth across the creaky floor. I wanted him to hug me, but I was too shy to ask. By 6:00 a.m., we were both up for the day.

On Saturday, we bundled up and drove to the mall to do a bit of arm-in-arm shopping. Totally hungry, we made our way to a nice little restaurant. The waitress seated us as we continued to talk on and on. After finishing a delicious meal, the waitress told us the manager was treating us to lunch. He had seen our story in the newspaper and wanted to support our celebration.

The city was nothing like I remembered. We drove through Calgary looking for all the places that we could remember staying at when we were small. He began with the day we had arrived at the Palisade Hotel after the long train ride through the Rockies. We stared at the faded old station that was no longer in service. I wondered what he saw and I wished that memory would come more clearly to me. We took pictures and tried to find the shelters.

Most of the children's shelters and orphanages were gone, so there was not a lot of information we could dig up. We had been separated on the north side of the city, so we drove until we found the Ross and Brockton houses. With the correct addresses, we recognized the houses because there had been very little change over the years.

I could see the old window from where I had looked for the unreachable little boy playing in the snow. As Josh drove us back to his house, he cranked up the stereo and we sang to the tunes. We laughed as he tried to bellow out words he couldn't remember. What a great feeling! It was so fantastic to reconnect after all those years. I was so happy and he was so thrilled to see me. I wondered how he had managed so many years without having our real family.

When we got to the house, Kelsey had dinner ready and Mario was there to join us. He brought yellow roses and non-alcoholic champagne to celebrate. I also needed my best friend to be there and was so happy when Nadia called on her cell to say she was close by. Within minutes I heard the tires of her van as it crunched across the hard-packed snow. I barely knew Josh, Kelsey, or Mario, but when Nadia arrived, it was as if we had all known each other for years. Interestingly, some of us had. I spent the evening in the greatest ease as we all celebrated our reunion with much love and laughter. Nadia stayed overnight and we slept in Josh's room. I lay in bed talking to her and asked her what she thought of him.

"You can tell he is the real one. He is such a sweetie." It was so good to have my best friend right next to me. We joked around and got the giggles. No matter how old we got, we were always like college kids when we got together.

On my last day, at 2:00 p.m., two police officers arrived at Josh's house and we filed a complaint against Fritz. We were shocked to find that there was no way to lay charges against him, because he was not considered a threat. The police said Fritz has a right to legally impersonate anyone as long as he doesn't harm, steal, or threaten anyone. They couldn't arrest him for being crazy, but they would pursue a restraining order on him.

Nadia left the next day so it was just Josh and I. Our time together was coming to a close but we knew it was just the beginning. We had finally begun where we left off, yet it was a new life together. I wanted to be strong emotionally, but I would look at Josh and get choked up.

"Josh, you know I love you so much. It has always been and always will be that way. You are my brother. Nothing or no one can stop or change that." I said and promised to call when I returned home. After passing through the gate, I looked back. He smiled but his eyes showed that he was already missing me. As the plane topped over the black of the night, I clutched the flowers in my hands and thanked God that Josh was alive and found.

111: Josh and Mom

The response to the newspaper and the CBC coverage was more than I expected. We got calls from Canadian adoption sites; friends, family, foster parents, and foster siblings were calling and writing emails to congratulate us. The Calgary police spoke with the Crown Council and, to our dismay, the police stated that Fritz could continue his actions and nothing legal could be done about it. There would be no way to get back the family items such as pictures, the wedding video, or the bracelet that my mother had bought for her real son. It was very disturbing for my parents and family to not have any closure with Fritz. He had robbed so much more. He had stolen three years of our search.

I called Josh to let him know that I had arrived safely and I had shared all the wonderful moments with my family. During our conversation we were still very emotional. It would take some time to come down from such a high. Later that night, I phoned my parents and told them as much detail as I could and invited them to view the TV tape.

Mom made arrangements to fly to Calgary the day before Josh's birthday. The same journalists wanted a follow-up story with Mom and Josh. For the first time, she had a chance to tell her side of the story.

The journalists met Josh at the airport and they waited for the passengers to unload at arrival. Mom was so nervous she became confused and lost her way. Ten minutes passed before she realized that she had to go downstairs and exit through the sliding doors to get to the main arrival.

As she reached the bottom step, her heart began to pound so hard she could hear it. Suddenly, she was short of breath and thought she was suffocating. She was scared she would die right then but, as the doors opened, she saw Josh standing there waiting for her.

"Hi, Mom," he said as he smiled at her. With trembling hands, she reached out to her child who had grown into a good-looking man. After waiting four decades, a miracle had happened and now she was embracing her only son for the first time.

"Oh, my boy! My handsome boy! I love you, son."

Her voice quavered as she spoke the words.

"There wasn't a day in my life that I didn't think about my son," she told the reporter. Mom talked about what had happened on that New Year's Day back in 1963. Josh held his mother, giving her the reassurance that he was right by her side. The media asked Josh how he was doing during all the excitement.

"I always felt alone," he said, looking away as he thought back to his childhood. "To find out that I have family is terrific. A total surprise," he continued. "This is a great birthday present. I couldn't ask for more."

"Now I have my son back, my boy," Mom smiled as she looked over at Josh.

The four-day reunion would enable them to look through childhood photos of Josh that Mom had treasured for so many years. Kelsey had planned a surprise birthday party at a restaurant for the Saturday evening. At the party, Mom was introduced to some of Josh's co-workers and friends. To Josh's surprise, one of his long-time old friends Hugh was one of Mom's distant cousins by marriage. Hugh Dempsey had married Pauline, Senator James Gladstone's daughter. He wrote many books about our First Nation relatives and other aspects of Canadian history.

Mom's flight back to Vancouver came on a Tuesday. My husband and I met her at the airport. I spotted her standing near the baggage department. She glowed with incredible elation as she greeted me and swung her arms around my neck. She climbed into my van and talked endlessly about her historical visit with Josh. It was fun to have her stay overnight as she related every detail about the experience of their reunion.

I can honestly say that I had never seen her so deliriously happy. Her eyes beamed with pure joy as she continued on, reliving each moment.

"Thank you, Honey, for finding my son. I know you worked so hard and I will always treasure what you did."

As I looked into her face, I saw how much it meant to her—how all the years of sadness were gone and I was so happy too.

112: Our Family

In the beginning of July, Sheila and her daughter flew to Calgary to meet our brother. She stayed a few days as well and they enjoyed the summer days at the Calgary Stampede. I flew to Edmonton on July 11 to visit Nadia while her boys went camping for a week with their dad. It was so much fun to have the whole house to ourselves. After two days we took the three-hour drive to Calgary to visit my brother, Kelsey, and Mario. We arrived in time for Kelsey's wonderful barbeque of shish kebobs and Mario's delicious caramel apple pie with ice cream for dessert.

On Monday, Nadia and I went around the city to find the other shelters. We were successful in tracing the place where my sister had stayed, but were unsure of the other residences because so many had been restructured. On Tuesday, we took Josh to meet Ida. She told him about the time Fritz came to her home and ate dinner with everyone, the whole time pretending to be Josh. She looked closely at him and knew unmistakably that he was my real brother.

Tuesday morning, Nadia and I said goodbye to Josh, and then we went to Calgary City Hall and the library to examine all the references to the shelters. Over all, we had nine crazy days of window-shopping, painting, and garage hunting. For me, sharing time with Nadia is like being on a holiday. On our last day, we squeezed in more shopping, lunch, and laughter before I grabbed a hug and waved goodbye as she dashed for her van sitting in a no-parking zone. I marvelled at the very thought of our kindred spirits and how much she had meant to me all these years. Seasons had come and gone, and we continually grew closer together.

That summer, my husband and I worked hard to prepare the house for the month of August. Josh, Kelsey, and Mario had decided to use their vacation time to drive to the West Coast. An hour before their arrival, they made a brief stop in Mission to pick up Josh's son, Mervin. They had planned to stop at my Dad's house first but, at midafternoon, they pulled up to my house instead. Totally surprised, I ran out to greet them and gave Josh a huge bear hug. I finally pulled away and wrapped my arms around Mario and Kelsey. Josh introduced his boy, Mervin. He was already taller than Josh by several inches. I squeezed my new fifteen-year-old nephew and told him that he had many cousins to meet. After we unloaded the car, I phoned Dad, Grandma, and the kids to invite them over.

Within an hour and a half we had a houseful of family. It was a hot summer afternoon when Josh met each of my children, my granddaughter, and my husband. There were at least four cameras clicking as family members greeted Josh and Mervin.

I saw Dad walk through the front door and greet his son, and he sure looked shaken up with all the excitement. Grandma Norina was very happy too. I had waited so long for the day when my parents would recognize the face of their little boy who was now a forty-five-year-old man.

I loved every second of watching this moment come true. I wondered if all the excitement was overwhelming for Josh, who continually smiled through all the gaiety while everyone fussed over him. Or did he feel the same way I did? It was exuberating to see and know the love that had held out for him all those years. He was finally home with his family and we were all excited and having fun together again.

We were all in the doorway as talking and laughter echoed through the main foyer. At some point, we made it to the kitchen table, where we continued through dinner until night. Mom and our stepdad Bart brought their camper two days later. Sheila came over to our house to see Josh. Mom, Sheila, Josh, and I laughed, cried, and hugged as we came to realize that it was the first time we had all been together since New Year's Day 1963.

The fun escalated as they plotted, in secrecy, the events of my birthday. I was treated with lavish desserts and gifts, but the greatest gift of all was my brother, who stood in the kitchen with his arms wrapped around my shoulders. As I looked at Josh, I realized I had found family and I had also found myself. All those years I was really looking for my own reflection and I finally had found my own identity. I belonged.

"It's wonderful to have a little sister," Josh said with a grin, tightly squishing me in a bear hug. We spent the rest of the time camping, sightseeing, and meeting the aunts and uncles and anyone else that may have been missed. I loved every moment of my visit with Josh, Kelsey, and Mario. In the end, when the car was reloaded, I dreaded the goodbyes, but I knew he would be back. It was much harder for Mom to let go. She knew it would be a long time before she saw him again.

We held a family reunion in August 2004 and over 200 family members attended, including Josh. Kelsey and Mario were great supports, driving from Calgary to Vancouver to celebrate Josh's reunion with his family. When Christmas came, Josh sent me the 40th anniversary edition of Mary Poppins. As I watched it from beginning to end, I saw the little boy and thought of Josh and how hard it must have been for him.

My kids were growing up fast and before I knew it Lance was old enough to move out. Caitlin and Payton were pretty good buds in their teens. At times they teamed up against me when they didn't like my overbearing motherliness. They got cheeky and threatened to go live in a foster home. It was the last thing I would ever want to happen to my babies and that was the whole reason I was so obsessed over them. I knew they were trying to ruffle my feathers and see if I would take the bait. Those years were tough and sometimes I had to call Mom and she would remind me that it was all kid stuff. It would pass and they would grow up to be wonderful adults. And you know what? She was right!

Today, I hold those moments like a treasured picture… something so dear to my heart that gave me such joy. I visit my brother every chance that comes my way. Every day that goes by, I reminisce over the greatest elation of my life… restoring what was left, lost, and found.

In Closing

On October 11, 2005, our family spent Thanksgiving weekend at Mom's house. I made a big turkey and all the stuffing to go with it. Mom didn't eat with her family but she was there. Her bed was moved into the living room and she had her family around. She woke up for a brief moment and later that night she succumbed to her death. Six months of cancer treatments had failed to stop the deadly disease from spreading rapidly throughout her body.

She had had two and a half years to enjoy having all her babies home again. She had lavished all her energy, time, talents, and love on her children, grand-children, and great grandchildren. She loved us all and we loved her.

A year later, my sister Iona passed away from a heart attack due to heroin abuse. I miss her so much. She will shine in my heart forever. She tried so hard to get her life on track but the pain of losing her kids was too much. Heroin was her comfort, no matter how much we tried to intervene.

On October 24, 2013, Chloe's son died of an overdose at the age of thirty-three.

I dedicate this book to my loved ones who have passed on to a better place and to the three generations before me. Rest in peace.

I thank my best friends Nadia, Annette, and Chris for their friendship. You are truly the most fabulous BFFs and you kept me hanging in there.

And last but not least, my compassionate and undying love for all my loved ones who are living. Howie and Gabriella, you continually give me eternal love. I also dedicate this book to thank Holly, Lance, Caitlin, and Payton for their constant enthusiasm and their encouragement to write this story for the teens of today and for my future grandchildren. I would also like to thank my won-derful spouse Jack for his contagious humour no matter how long it took me to write this story. I know it wasn't easy to put up with the silent treatment and be ignored through all the hours of typing.

Thank you for loving me no matter what.

Author Biography

Eugenea Couture is a mother of four and a native of Vancouver, B.C., Canada. At the age of four, she was forced into Southern Alberta's foster care system. As an adult, she settled on the West Coast, raising her children and reuniting with her biological family so they could mend their broken relationships. Terrified by the possibility of history repeating itself, Eugenea became a stay-at-home mother so she could focus on her children's upbringing. It has been her life-long passion to share her remarkable journey and help others find their families as well.

To contact Eugenea Couture please visit:

Facebook: www.facebook.com/EugeneaCouture

Twitter: @EugeneaCouture

If you want to get on the path to be a published author with Life Journey
Publishing (a division of Influence Publishing), please go to
www.InfluencePublishing.com/InspireABook

Inspiring books that influence change

More information on our other titles and how to submit your own proposal
can be found at
www.InfluencePublishing.com

CPSIA information can be obtained at www.ICGtesting.com
Printed in the USA
LVOW13s0112140314

377315LV00003B/15/P